Chasing
the Hawk

Chasing
the Hawk

∞

Looking for My Father,
Finding Myself

ANDREW SHEEHAN

Delacorte Press

Published by
DELACORTE PRESS
Random House, Inc.
1540 Broadway
New York, New York 10036

Copyright © 2001 by Andrew Sheehan

Quotations from *Personal Best* by George Sheehan
used with the permission of Rodale Press

LIBRARY OF CONGRESS CATALOGING IN PUBLICATION DATA
Sheehan, Andrew.
    Chasing the hawk : looking for my father, finding myself /
Andrew Sheehan.
        p. cm.
    ISBN 0-385-33561-X
    1. Sheehan, Andrew. 2. Runners—United States—Biography.
3. Fathers and sons. I. Title.

GV1061.15.S467 A3 2001
796.42'092—dc21
[B]   2001017327

Book design by Virginia Norey

Manufactured in the United States of America
Published simultaneously in Canada
September 2001

BVG   10 9 8 7 6 5 4 3 2 1

To my brothers and sisters,
and to the memory of our parents

the end precedes the beginning,
And the end and the beginning were always there
Before the beginning and after the end.
And all is always now.

—T. S. Eliot

Chasing
the Hawk

CHAPTER ONE

W HEN I THINK OF HIM NOW, I see him at dawn, driven
from his bed by the sun and headed down to the ocean for a
swim. He used to call it his "morning dip." But having never actually
witnessed it, I find it odd that of all the images I hold of him in my
head, this is the one that returns most often. By the time it had become part of his daily routine, I no longer lived at home, and when I
visited, I was never up at that hour. Still, it makes a certain kind of
sense that this particular ritual should come to mind. Swimming in
the morning was something my father did alone, for the specific purpose of being by himself, and I always think of him that way—alone
and apart. He was away a good deal of the time, and even when he
was among us, he was a solitary man.

In my mind I see him on this morning a few years before his
death. He has pulled on his running shorts, grabbed a towel from the
bathroom, and, without showering or shaving, is ambling barefoot
down the stairs to the front door. Exiting onto the porch, he pauses
for a moment. His bony hand rests on his hip as he stares off at the
ocean horizon and loses himself in the arrhythmic clank of the rope

and clasp against the town flagpole, still flagless at this hour of the morning. The scavenger gulls screech at one another as they hover and descend over the boardwalk, fighting over a loose scrap of garbage. A few other gulls loiter nearby, taking furtive steps, staring sidelong and gangsterish.

The house fronts Ocean Avenue, which as the name implies runs parallel to the beach, and from the porch you can see across the road to the boardwalk, the beach, and the ocean beyond. It's late September, the official best time of year in my family. The crowds are gone, and the air is cooler, cleaner now. The light has a special clarity that seems to intensify all colors: the blues of sky and ocean, the green of the small patch of grass in front of the house, the yellow sandstone road. This makes for a disarmingly pretty scene, even as the town itself shows the creeping signs of disrepair. The boardwalk, gray now, has begun to warp along the edges. The pier seems to dip in midspan, and at the far end, an old fisherman's shack lists leftward, threatening to topple into the water. The beach itself has begun shrinking at an alarming pace, the ocean's advance now within a hundred feet of the boardwalk.

Like many shore towns, its best days now seem consigned to the past. Still, you sense that an infusion of yuppie cash and sweat could make it into a postcard scene once again, a scene not far removed from the one depicted in the hand-tinted photo from the 1920s that my mother has framed and hung in a bathroom upstairs—minus, of course, the parasol-carrying ladies in full-skirted neck-to-toe dresses. The lower right-hand corner of this bit of tourist memorabilia bears the caption: "The Seashore at Ocean Grove, New Jersey."

I never lived in Ocean Grove—I was on my own before my parents moved there—and when I visited, I would generally have gone to bed only hours before my father's sunrise swim, most likely to sleep off another late night of drinking. And yet I see him in my mind's eye as clearly as if watching from a bedroom window—his spidery frame treading lightly across Ocean Avenue, mindful of bits of glass, treading lightly across the boardwalk, mindful of splinters, and down that small flight of wooden steps to the beach. He has a peculiar, almost feminine waddle to his walk, and in the sand it's even more pronounced: chest out, shoulders back, arms and hands dangling loosely behind him. With the sun still barely free of the ocean, he saunters to the edge of the wet sand, and for a moment he ponders the ocean's chaos of blue and gray, his great unending theater.

He has never been conventionally good-looking, but even early on, he had a kind of Bogie–like handsomeness. His teeth have always been crooked, and he has an overbite, so when his lips purse, he looks a bit odd, like a fish. The weak chin is countered by the great hawklike nose which juts from his face like the blade of a hatchet. When he was younger it sat squarely in the middle of a soft, pudgy face, but as he has aged, his face has grown strikingly angular around it. His face has wizened. The lines have deepened, accentuating his blue-gray eyes. A certain Irishness has broken through, and his look has grown kindly.

As he walks into the shallow white water, it's as though I am walking alongside. Instantly, I feel the cold with him: the shock of it repels and invites at the same time. I can see him grimace, all teeth and squinty eyes, as he wades in waist-deep, and I hear as he hears the repeating crash and withdrawing snore of the waves. Raising his arms above his head, he strides into the deeper water, then plunges under the first wave available. As he invariably did, he lets out a yell of frigid shock upon his reemergence. "WooooooHoooooo." The faint echo of it bounces off the Victorian guesthouses along Ocean Avenue, and the row of facades stares impassively back. The morning silence returns except for the sounds of gulls and waves. He dives deep, and then deeper still, searching for that even-colder water that rushes blood to his head and every limb.

To know him at all is to know that he loves the water—loves the feel of it and loves the smell. Even here. Even though there is something distinctly Jersey about it. The tar, perhaps, or maybe some hint of gas or petroleum. Even at its most pungent, it doesn't bother him, because he knows it keeps others away. And it puts him in mind of what Emerson meant in his one-sentence assault on perfectionism: "Everything God made has a crack." One of his favorite, and oft-repeated, quotes.

He is a quoter of dead philosophers, an intrepid searcher of usable quotes. He scours books for them like a prospector panning for gold, and when something quotable gleams back from a page of black and white, he plucks it out and stashes it with the rest. They pepper his articles and talks, and even in conversation he drops a half dozen within the first five minutes. He has a particular fondness for a quote he attributes to William James. It went underground for a few years but has resurfaced at the time of this scene I have conjured so vividly. "The strenuous life tastes best." It describes this morning and many mornings like it. There must be challenge, and if there is none, challenge will have to be created.

He has found the strenuous life in running, and more specifically in running marathons, an activity that's about as strenuous as it could be without being downright masochistic. Having run more than fifty marathons and written about each one, he has become the recipient of improbable fame, imploring others to live strenuously and to taste of life rather than endure its passing. Even now, on this morning. Even though he can run no more marathons, he won't give up running, and he won't give up these early swims. His body, so re-

cently asleep, is now completely alive. The smells, the screeching
gulls, the salt water around his lips—on an empty stomach, he's
tempted to drink it. Afterward, he'll swear he could taste it. "Fantastic," he'll report.

It's not that he's ever been any kind of swimmer. He is not. In fact,
he's never been able to swim more than a few laps in a pool without
swallowing water. Despite his great love of the ocean, he is forever
drawn back to the land, keeping his forays within fifty yards of shore.
He's never been a fisherman, and, ex-navy man that he is, his brief fantasy of buying a boat sank quickly, scuttled by his fear of machinery,
seasickness, and nautical incompetence. He excels, however, at the
one water sport of bodysurfing, the art of riding waves without a surf-
board. And although he has never taught me, or anyone else in my
family, how to do much of anything, we all learned how to do that by
watching him. From the beach, we'd watch him—just as I seem to
watch him now—as he swam out just past the breaking waves and
treaded water, craning his neck to scan the horizon for the next large
swell. As it mounted, he'd swivel and begin swimming shoreward.

It's all about timing, bodysurfing. If you can get inside the swell of
the wave just before it breaks, it will lift you and throw you out in
front, hurtling you toward the beach. Once you catch the wave, your
work is suddenly over. The wave simply takes you. The sensation is
one of gliding; you glide on top of the flat water stretched out before
you, rocketing headlong toward the beach. Weekenders never seem
to get it. Even those who manage tend to ride the incoming waves
with their arms thrust out in front, like Superman. My father, by
contrast, cuts the water like the figurehead of an old ship, always riding his waves with his arms at his sides. He dips his head into the flat
water before him, and, shaking it off with a quick flick, he yells,
"WaaaaaaHoooooo." For him, it's play: the highest of all human

pursuits. Play needs no justification. It is the thing itself. The laboratory of all creativity. The chance for greatness.

The ocean kicks up in September. The waves, often big and well formed, offer long rides, even thrilling ones. On this day, however, two rides are enough, and at the end of the second he stands up in the shallows and trudges up the sandbar to his towel. He falters as he leans into the slight slope of the dry sand. His legs, thinner now and spindly, shimmy under his own weight. As he falls to one knee, he braces himself with an outstretched arm. He has lived a strenuous life, and he is determined to live the rest of it as strenuously as possible. But now he has cancer, and it is making new rules. It's spreading through his bones and coursing through his blood, curtailing his movements and shortening his hours. There can be no telling when the end will be, only that it will come too soon. "Carpe diem," he says of late. And I wonder if that's what he's thinking as he stands there. "Seize the day." For a moment, as he looks down at the drops of ocean water falling from his trunks onto the sand, it's as though I too am looking down, staring at his knobby feet as if they are my own. Together, it seems, we look up at the waves.

Along with a talent for bodysurfing, my father somehow passed to me his susceptibility to the ocean and its hypnotic snare. Now I watch as his eyes fix on the ocean, following the ebb and flow of the waves in infinite permutation. Never twice the same. Trying to scan it all, he's held in a kind of trance. There was a time when he might have looked out over the breaking waves, thinking himself master and owner of this particular piece of beachfront. One of the rewards, perhaps, of success, fame, and money. No more. He looks at the ocean now, and he is humbled by it, and he is happy to be humbled. "The proper response to life is applause," he often says, quoting William Carlos Williams. And it seems that in his morning swims he found that purest, most natural form of celebration. A realization that all days should start with a kind of ovation for creation.

Wrapped in his towel and dripping into the sand is where I picture him last, stuck on the sun and water, frozen in place, reluctant to turn and walk back inside. He is reluctant to say goodbye, because he has a hard time imagining that any kind of afterlife could measure up. In the years before he died, he would say goodbye to everything he loved—the ocean and the morning, his friends and family. Still, the more he said goodbye, the less he wanted to go. I see him standing there, so distant and yet so close, and I seem to be able to think his thoughts and to feel his longing.

I can hear him asking himself the questions: Why all the anger and the angst? Why all the hurt people? Why did it take so long for him to find his right place, his right size? And why now, when he seemed to find these things, would they all be so fleeting? I see him standing there, and I realize he is no longer there. He is as he has always been—distant and yet close. I seem to inhabit his body as he sometimes seems to inhabit mine. I feel his questions, and I feel their ache. I know his questions are mine. I know his struggle is my own.

∞

OUTSIDE OF MY FAMILY, my father wasn't at all known for his body-surfing. He was known instead for his running. In defining himself, he would always start with that word: "Runner." Perhaps tellingly, it always preceded other words like husband, father, or doctor. He was, after all, George Sheehan, also known as the Runner's Guru, the Running Doc, the Runner's Runner. The running sage of hundreds of thousands of runners. The running everyman.

The act of running had transformed him as a human being, and its attendant fame and money had recast his life. So forever after, in most of his waking hours—in conversation, interviews, and his writing—he performed a kind of obeisance to the sport, praising its every virtue. Once, he facetiously defined life as "those annoying spaces of time in between races."

In the late 1980s—the same period he was taking those morning swims—he stopped running marathons, because of his cancer's quickening advance. He would still run the shorter races, albeit less frequently, and when training he trained at a slower pace. Still, when I went out running with him, he wasn't so slow that I didn't have to struggle to stay abreast of him while holding up my end of one of his long, wandering conversations. So it was on a clear and blustery March day, during a long weekend home, when he and I went out for a five-mile run that stretched into nine miles.

We ran on the boardwalk into a crosswind that blew west to east, knocking back a spray from the tips of the cresting waves. The beaches were empty, the snack bars still boarded up. On the main streets of the shore towns only the occasional coffeeshop or newsstand remained open; all was quiet except for the wind, our breathing, our talking, and our thumping on the boards. We spoke in sputters, staccato between breaths: I about my newspaper job and recent articles, he about his treatments for cancer and his poor performances in recent races. I lent a sympathetic ear through Bradley Beach, Avon, and Belmar, but as the run stretched on into Spring Lake, his pace quickened, and it made me wonder how sick he could possibly be.

Always deceptively fast, he had a style of running as unconventional as the rest of him. Unlike most runners, he did most of his running out in front of himself. That is, his ass sank low while his legs churned forward, so that when viewed from the side he seemed almost to be sitting down as he ran. And yet somehow his form had its own economy, delivering, in his estimation, "maximum power and speed." Even with his cancer, he continued angling for a competitive edge. Two miles from home that March day, we let our conversation fade into the wordless breathing of harder running. A kind of unspoken excitement simmered as we began running at full stride, gliding over the boards, our feet barely touching the surface. It was so effortless, I began to feel as though we were cruising. Then, suddenly, my father faltered and slowed.

"You go on," he said. "I can't keep it up."

I slowed with him and stayed alongside.

"That's okay," I said. "We'll take it down a notch."

"No, I'd rather you go ahead," he told me. And I did.

In *A River Runs Through It,* Norman Maclean writes, "In my family, there was no distinction between fly-fishing and religion." Running played the same role in our house as fly-fishing had in his, replacing a Catholicism that came to seem as remote to us as our schoolboy stories of quick-fisted nuns. We, "the boys," had all been built for it: long and lanky and thin-shouldered. It required little or no skill, and since we were always borderline slugs and slackers, our running could make us feel virtuous in an otherwise unvirtuous existence. The rest of the time the family was together, we spent days sitting around reading papers and talking. "Talk, talk, talk," my mother would scold, but her admonishments always fell unheeded. Today, years after the death of both parents, ours remains a parlor life of Wildean sloth, our family gatherings rescued only by our daily runs. For suddenly my brothers and I are out on the boards, running a fierce slalom through the strollers and beachgoers, jetting right through them all, using them as picks on a basketball court. Pretend as we might that we are not competing, the pace dips down to six minutes a mile as we push ourselves, and then push harder, feeling the wind about our temples, the sensation of flying. Underlying it all is a bedrock principle, handed down from father to sons: we are runners—not joggers. This is not a team sport.

So when my father told me to go on ahead that day, I did so without question. I picked up the pace to where I had been before, churning down the boardwalk. But with about a half mile to go, I noticed another runner drift into the periphery of my vision. Running about thirty yards to my left on the inland road paralleling the boardwalk, he strained and struggled, and then as he gained on me I could hear the signature grunts and groans that always issued from my father at the end of his races, noises to which he credited some of his victories. Half therapy, half psych-out, they were like the trumpeting of an elephant—something he used to intimidate other runners. Hearing them, some would simply give up, suddenly unwilling to ask the same extreme effort of themselves, whereupon he would grunt and groan and blow by them at the finish, stealing some small victory. Now on this March day he was trying the same on me.

He had surprised me, using the tactics of stealth and deception, and now came the groan. While funny, it was no less a challenge, leaving me no choice but to respond. He got back on the boardwalk a few yards ahead of me, and I hustled up to rejoin him. We matched strides all the way in—all the way to the house—where he crumpled onto a patch of grass.

"Oh God. Oh God," he panted. "Oh God."

As I watched him writhe and moan on the cold ground, I thought of just how long this kind of thing had passed for normal in my family.

∞

IN THOSE LAST YEARS, my father lived with my mother in what had been a guesthouse in sleepy Ocean Grove, a seaside town on the north end of the New Jersey coastline, about a square mile in size. The streets there are lined with similar Victorian guesthouses bearing beach-themed names like Seaspray, Albatross, and Seagull. When my parents bought theirs, however, they converted it into a single-family house, taking in no paying guests, though passersby were always stopping to inquire about rooms. Four stories made it larger than most, and, primely situated on Ocean Avenue, it boasted a great and unobstructed ocean view. In fact, in its commercial days, it had been called the Oceanfront House.

For most of the century, Ocean Grove had been a religious community, settled and maintained by the Methodist Church, which sought to preserve an atmosphere of quiet reflection by the sea. It was, and is, a dry town, and lest there be any doubt about its continuing spiritual bent, "God's Square Mile" remains its slogan today.

Just before my parents moved there, however, Ocean Grove underwent a kind of forced secularization. For decades, the Methodist governing body had prohibited driving on Sundays. In reverence for the Sabbath, cars were shuttered in garages, and outside traffic was kept away by a chain stretched between the town's main portals. After an incident in the late 1970s that practice changed, by order of the state supreme court. The town police arrested the man who delivered the Sunday *New York Times* for driving through the town on Sunday. He sued the town—and won. Ocean Grove's government was declared unconstitutional for blurring the line between church and state. The Methodists lost autonomy, and the cars rolled on Sundays.

Still, the change was not so complete as to alter the basic character of the town. The guesthouses remained an attraction for the same aging Methodist vacationers, and the year-round retirees were still firmly ensconced at the time of my parents' arrival, earning it the sobriquet "Ocean Grave" within my family.

The town also housed what some residents viewed as "more than our fair share" of deinstitutionalized mental patients—an odd assortment of people who lived in hotplate boardinghouses, which were not often enough the focus of state investigations. It was because of this mix of old people and mentally ill—and the sometimes confusing overlap—that my brothers and I liked to sit on the porch and play a cynical little game we called Sane or Insane. We would drink our Molson's, rock on rockers, and watch the perplexed townspeople trudge down the sidewalk to the boardwalk. After sufficient time for evaluation, each of us would cast his vote: "sane" or "insane."

For the most part, the sane and insane lived peacefully together, even as life began to change for all. The lifting of the Sunday driving ban did, in time, send a signal to the outside world. The cars came and so did the people. In the summer, and especially on summer weekends, the town began to crowd with day-trippers, who had discovered the charms of the little beach town and passed the word on to their friends. The beaches began to swell and the boardwalk sometimes filled with visitors shoulder to shoulder.

On the shore, they are known as Bennies, the name originally given to high-rolling vacationers from New York and North Jersey, who were said to freely litter restaurant tables and bars with hundred-dollar bills—bills carrying the faceplate of Benjamin Franklin. In the forties and fifties the Bennies were sought after and welcomed, but nowadays the term is aimed disapprovingly at the nameless, faceless hordes that invade every summer. The new Bennies, though still important to the economy of the shore, are objects of scorn for year-round people.

My father shared that disdain. For him, the Bennies were just one more motivation to get up at dawn for his swim. Like most longtime residents of the shore, he patterned his day around the need to avoid the crowds. By the time they arrived on the beach, the afternoon would find him safely repaired to his bedroom (his writing room) and his manual Royal typewriter. "Too many Bennies," he would say and disappear behind the closed door.

Soon the typing would begin, and it could be heard faintly throughout the house. For years that sound meant that he had just completed a long run; it meant that he was putting down all the thoughts that had percolated during his paces. In the afterglow of his sweat, he felt a special clarity and an ease in spilling out the contents of his brain. He was fond of saying that four hours of running went into every page he wrote, and that his writing was a process of "sucking the marrow" out of those runs. Now that his running had been curtailed, his writing might follow a swim or a long walk or a bicycle ride, the kind of physical activities that did not punish his cancer-riddled legs but were vigorous enough to allow the writing to go on uninterrupted.

One summer visit, when I wandered in from the beach in the middle of the afternoon and heard that thin sound of metal spokes hitting paper, there was a brief moment when it sounded strange, oddly out of place. Then I realized that it had been years since I'd heard it, and realized too that this typing meant one thing: he was home. Not living somewhere else and visiting but, in fact, living at home. It meant that he had been back home long enough to have gotten down to a routine of writing. So hearing that sound was both comforting and disturbing, for while it meant that he was home, it also reminded me of all the times he had been away.

Years before, my father had left my mother, apparently headed for divorce. He had another woman; then he experienced a change of heart, and returned, saying that he had seen the light and vowing to stay. But that was only the beginning of a long series of separations and affairs, which went on for nearly a decade. After each such episode, my mother would take him back. It was in the middle of that turbulent period, in the early eighties, when they had reunited once again, that my parents sold the big old house I'd grown up in, in the wealthy, inland town of Rumson, and bought this old hotel in Ocean Grove. They renovated and moved in, embarking on what was supposed to be a new life together. A year later, however, my father left again—this time for four more years—leaving my mother alone, shipwrecked it seemed, in this strangely eccentric town.

While he continued to seek out his children on holidays and for an occasional dinner in a restaurant, my father essentially disappeared from our lives during those years. It was toughest on my mother, of course, but the family rallied around her, most visibly in the summer. In the summer, her children were always in Ocean Grove; they came down from the city on trains or drifted in from apartments around the shore. On summer weekends, it was hard to find a bed. The winter months were another story. My mother weathered the nights alone with only plate glass between herself and the pounding ocean wind. When you went to visit her on those cold, dark nights, it seemed unforgivable of my father to have left her this way. At times, it still does.

In the living room, none of the photographs of him were ever put away. The pictures of him running and holding trophies remained hanging on the wall the entire time he was gone—whether a testament to my mother's faith or to her powers of denial, I wouldn't venture to say. And now, he was home: home to stay; home, it appeared, to die. In his comings and goings, he had severely tested the love of his sons and daughters, but in the end, we all deferred to my mother, who took him back once again as she had so many times before. And this time, he did stay. One year turned into two, two into three, and three into four, until it became increasingly clear that he would stray no more. On my visit home that summer day, as I stood in the living room, looking at his pictures and hearing his typing, past and present were so seamlessly knit together I could almost believe he had never gone away.

The illusion had become more believable by the day as, somewhat improbably, he wrested back authority without rancor or recrimination, assuming the role of leader. Paterfamilias. And that is how things would remain, even as his cancer advanced. In time, there came the thinning of his legs, the appearance of scabs on his arms, his thin face growing puffy with cortisone. Eventually he quit running entirely as the cancer invaded his bones, and he had to struggle just to make it up the stairs. Once at the top, he sometimes disappeared into a three-hour nap in the middle of the afternoon. And still he continued orchestrating events, making the family plans. In the last years of his life, he decreed that there should be reunions: weeklong family get-togethers filled with storytelling and jokes. These reunions, he said, should not be in Ocean Grove but in places new, places special. Without resistance, we complied, and we organized. We went to Ireland in 1991, and twice we went to the Hamptons. In September 1993, as he began to fail, we had our last, hastily called, reunion. Naturally, there was an ocean nearby.

∞

IT WAS A PLACE we had never been before but one familiar all the same. It was a beach house with several (but still not enough) bedrooms. Like the house in which we grew up, it had a screened-in back porch. There were rockers and painted wicker chairs, each overlooking sand dunes that were held intact by scattered clumps of dune grass. If you walked out the back door, you found yourself walking through those dunes and discovered beneath your feet a wooden walkway sunken in the sand. The path led you to a fenced-in landing, an elevated perch above the beach, and from there you saw a pristine stretch of sand extending beyond sight in both directions.

This time it was Dewey Beach, outside of Rehoboth, Delaware, but it really could have been anywhere up and down the Atlantic. Anywhere you could leave the millions of others and lay brief claim to your own private swath of infinite blue. Summer's an endurance in cities, suffered in sweat-soaked suits and dresses. The hot blur of sound and fury makes me crave only an ocean's vista to nowhere and a few days of forgetfulness. All through August I had looked forward to this week, even though I knew it wouldn't be about forgetting.

I arrived early that Friday afternoon, earlier than the rest of the family, and at intervals in the hours that followed, I would hear the crunch of car tires on the gravel drive, then the muffled slamming of car doors. A few moments later someone would appear at the kitchen door, exclaiming over the house. "Fabulous," I would hear, or "How does Sarah find these places?" Then came the careful room-by-room inspection, as though they were planning to buy the place rather than rent it for a week. My parents arrived in the middle of the afternoon. My mother, still strong at seventy, cut a familiar figure, leaning leftward through the doorway as she lugged in a bag of groceries and ordered us out to the car for the rest of them. Once out the door, I saw him—the still-shocking sight of my father, trudging slowly behind, declining assistance.

I spoke with him a couple of times a week by phone and had tried to see him at least twice a month that summer, driving to New Jersey from my home in Pittsburgh for weekend visits. But each time, the advance of the cancer was both dramatic and alarming. To those who saw him more frequently, the progress of the cancer may have seemed slower, less perceptible. To me, the sight of him was a quick rabbit punch to the solar plexus. His legs were now pencil thin. His back was frail and bent. The prostate cancer, which had metastasized into his bones and blood, had left him barely enough body to hold his clothes. Now as he shuffled toward me through the gravel, he waved his bony hand aloft and managed a faint "yahoo." I hugged him lightly there, feeling as if I had put my arms around an empty box.

"Oh baby," he said. "Andrew baby. Great to see you, baby. Great to see you." And then I put my shoulder under his shoulder and helped him up the stairs. A man who had completed his fiftieth marathon only a few years before.

The house was a basic beach house: knotty pine walls, an unused fireplace, and the requisite large wooden table, soon to be cluttered with newspapers, books, and teacups, and circled by chairs draped with wet beach towels. Within a few hours the place would fill to twenty people, and their orientation would be brief. They would spread out to the porch, the landing, and the beach, finding places to settle as if they had lived there all their lives. Although it was a rental, we had a sense of ownership. Not just of the house but of the month. It was another September, a time of year with a special sense of possession for us. In New Jersey, it was always the time of reclaiming our turf from the Bennies. The coastline highways were clear, and the post–Labor Day silence seemed to ring in the ears. September always held the promise of clear blue skies, water still warmed by the summer heat, and the smack of chilled air on your wet body as you emerged from the surf. That, it seemed to us, was the very best of life—and a terrific cure for hangovers. But this September was different. We knew our father could die at any time.

There are a remarkable number of us Sheehans—twelve brothers and sisters—and, believing this to be the last family gathering with our father, nearly all had made the trip, either alone or with spouses. Each of us came in expectation of great drama, only to realize once we got there that everything was unscripted. And so we simply did the things that we had always done: run on the boardwalk and swim in the ocean, vainly attempt to bodysurf the unaccommodatingly small waves. We read on the sunporch in the afternoon heat and ate big dinners at night, our hunger stoked by the cool September breezes that made us feel alive, vital, even in the face of death. No one in the immediate family had ever died, and in a sense it seemed the right thing to do—to carry on as if nothing extraordinary were happening.

What passed for discussion was the ongoing but unacknowledged storytelling competition that has persisted within my family for decades. It had been a craft under private development in each of us since childhood, when we learned how to turn any common occurrence—a train ride or a trip to the store—into a story. Since there had been a limited amount of attention going around, you learned to grab it. You polished your imitations and your routines and when you saw an opening in the dinner conversation, you performed, hoping to keep the collective focus of the family.

That week seemed to be a time for opening the vault—dusting off the best of old school-day stories of senile priests and predatory nuns. I wondered at their appropriateness, but my father gave his tacit endorsement of our laughter with his own. It was he who was directing, asking for more stories, pretending all was normal, although clearly all was not. He wasn't swimming or running as he had been only a few years before. Now he could barely walk without help lest he tempt a fall. Two and three times a day, I would hear him say, "Uh-oh," and I'd turn to see him lose his balance, vainly grasping for a chair or table before hitting the floor with a dreadful thud. We would all run to help him, but he would be dismissive. Once he just lay there staring up at the ceiling and said, "I feel like the one-hoss shay."

I had no idea what he was talking about, but later in a library I looked up the phrase. It was from an old poem by Oliver Wendell Holmes, which my father must have recited as a schoolboy. It was about a deacon who built so fine a handsome carriage, or shay, that "It ran a hundred years to the day." The shay outlived the deacon and was passed on to a parson, who was riding in it on its hundredth birthday, when it suddenly disappeared beneath him. The parson found himself sitting on his ass on Main Street. "You see, of course, if you're not a dunce,/How it came to pieces all at once,/All at once, and nothing first,/Just as bubbles do when they burst."

My father was capable not just of the occasional one-liner about his falls—he even managed to turn one such incident into a story of his own, for the amusement of a group of us who had pulled our chairs close around him on the sunporch one afternoon. Recently, he recounted, he had taken a fall on a sidewalk and ended up lying alongside his car. A lady stopped and looked down at him, and then walked by without offering assistance. "She must have thought I was trying to fix the car," he said—a line that touched off a chorus of laughs from everyone, since my father had proven all his life that he was incapable of fixing anything.

As his story fed other stories and jokes, we found that our frivolity had no safety net. At one point, when the storytelling reached a great pitch of laughs and mimicry, my father, raising his thin hand in the air, abruptly silenced it, saying he needed to nap. My brother George helped him off to a room upstairs, leaving us to face one another and the unavoidable truth of his impending death. The great weight of his disease had now shackled him, perversely forcing him to give us what we had longed for—the sense that he was ours, committed and un-equivocally. Things had never been better between my father and his family. He appeared to have made his peace with everyone, though only now that he was dying. It saddened you to realize that the resolution had been so long in coming. But no sooner did you think that than you had the even sadder realization that his impending death had probably played the biggest hand in bringing it about.

The women in the family had long dealt with strong emotion by means of the closed-door caucus: secret meetings held mostly in various bedrooms, where, in the company of a few sympathetic others, they would say all the things they couldn't bear to tell the person for whom they were truly meant. For years, such caucusing had focused on my father's dalliances, but here in Rehoboth I stumbled into a bedroom, only to find three of my sisters talking about our mother. In hushed voices, they worried about what would happen to her afterward, after his death. Tears were wiped off in front of bathroom mirrors, and the caucusers returned to the group, all smiles.

Underneath the constant laughter, a strong tide of emotion was forever rising and falling. And still, the seemingly misplaced juvenilia of laughs and storytelling was not as inappropriate as it might have seemed. In our peculiar way, we were still celebrating his return, even as we were keenly aware that he had returned late. It seemed that just as the party was starting, he was leaving for a more pressing engagement. Time was sweeping by quickly now, and you could do little but wonder at the swiftness of its passing. Yet we were still capable of joking about death, mocking its imminent arrival. At one point, my father lay down on a wicker couch beside a candelabra stand that held votive candles, much like the ones you see in Catholic churches, which can be lit to accompany prayers of special intention. Someone laughed. When we looked over at my father, the reason was clear. With his arms folded across his chest, he was unwittingly giving us a preview of himself stretched out in a coffin. We turned and looked at one another and laughed that forbidden church-pew laugh from when we were kids.

That week, he mostly sat on the back porch, wrapped in a towel, writing or reading, and then looking out at the dunes. I stole long looks at him there to record his face: his washed-out blue eyes peeking out from amid the wrinkles, his eyes darting from side to side as though his mind and spirit were unwilling captives of his dying body. Seven years before, he had come back, returning to my mother and family with the news that he had inoperable prostate cancer. He was penitent and remorseful then, but like most of the others, I had a hard time taking his repentance on face value. I figured he was scared, that he didn't want to die alone. In the years leading up to that return, he had pursued women, he had pursued fame, and all of that time he had forsaken his family. Now that he was dying, he wanted us back; now, it was only family that mattered.

Although his explanations did not add up, he had been welcomed back just the same. The shock of his illness and the sympathy it engendered made any expression of anger and hurt seem inappropriate. Recriminations were few and hard feelings went unaired. I was amazed at times by the hubris. How he had somehow made himself so invulnerable to prosecution. But now as we gathered at Rehoboth, the time had long passed since his right to assume his old place in the family would be questioned. We no longer seemed inclined to question even his right to pretend that he had never been away.

But the truth was that, even before he left my mother for the first time, he had been slipping in and out of our lives at will. He would do his doctoring, his running, his writing, and then sort of present himself in our midst, taking what he wanted of our company and then taking his leave. The pattern continued after he was officially gone from the house, since my mother allowed him unrestricted access to his family, granted him the right to drop in from time to time to celebrate the holidays and eat the dinners and hear the stories. If it was late, she would sometimes make a solo bed for him.

It was not in my family's nature to completely reject my father. In some deep way, perhaps a clinging to safety in numbers, we don't go in for expulsion of our members. The matter has come up a few times when a drug counselor has suggested that we ostracize someone with an addiction. No one had the stomach for it. And so it was a nonnegotiable, unimpeachable fact of our existence that there would always be a place for my father, an opportunity to choose again what he had spurned. Still, it was an uneasy arrangement. Resentments festered underneath. On rare occasions he got more than he had bargained for, usually from one of my sisters who could no longer stand the pretense. My mother, however, would intervene and not allow it. She always seemed to believe that someday he would resolve things and come back for good, and deep down, we were at least hopeful of the same thing. When he finally did come back, it was as though everyone wanted him to succeed, and, wanting it so much, tacitly agreed not to do or say anything that would threaten the peace.

As I sat on the stairwell toward the end of our week in Rehoboth, I watched him, squirreled away at a corner table in the living room, hunched over a yellow legal pad, writing. He often said no one should write about anything unless he was a participant, and so now he was writing again. Not about running but about dying. To him, dying was another kind of sport, one pitting him against death. It was a blood sport like a bullfight, only in this contest the matador, dodging and dancing in his suit of light for as long as he could, knew that in the end he would lose. Until then, there would be a great savoring of life, a graceful acceptance, and a final peace. This became the topic of his last book, *Going the Distance*. How best to die.

"It's going to be a great book," he liked to quip. "It's the sequel that's going to be a problem."

There was no typing on the Royal that week, because he had left it at home. Yet he had found this corner table in the living room, and for hours you could see him hunched over it, putting his almost illegible scrawl onto the legal pad. He was writing, as he so often did, in plain sight of people around him as they talked among themselves. Though once I would have resented this separateness, oddly enough I felt no such resentment now. Instead, I felt a comfort just to be in the same room.

∞

DURING THE TEN YEARS leading up to his death, I had rebelled against the family pattern of appeasement by having it out with my father—not just once or twice but time and again. In those years, I had told him exactly how I felt about his leaving, about his coming back, about a whole battery of filial grievances. I had forced myself to tell him, not because I wanted him out of my life but because I was trying desperately to keep him in it. I had always tried to stay close because of the simple fact that I loved him. He was my father and I probably would have loved him no matter what kind of man he was. I loved him in spite of his faults, and in many ways because of them. But more than that, I had always felt that if I were to judge him, I would come perilously close to judging myself. Life and time had shown me that I was more like my father than I liked to admit. There were moments when I seemed not to know where I ended and my father began. Many of my physical habits were borrowed, consciously or otherwise, from him—my afternoon runs, my habit of doing the *Times* crossword in front of the television, my tendency to grind the gears when I downshift. As I've grown older, I've seen how his features—his eyes, his lines, his nose—seem to be supplanting my own. In odd, transfixing moments before the mirror, it sometimes feels as though it is my father who inhabits my body, not myself.

And the resemblance goes far beyond the surface. I, too, spent years feeling alienated from other people, was often ill-at-ease in groups, could be just as intemperate and just as quick to anger. So I always tried to stay close to my father, or at least to keep him in sight, even when he distanced himself from us. I pursued him, partly because I knew that I was not only similar to him but that if I chose not to understand him, I would repeat his mistakes. Unfortunately, I made the same mistakes anyway, and a lot more of my own. I had the same wandering eye as my father, engaged in the same sort of dalliance, but in my case it was my wife who left. At the time of the week in Rehoboth, I was recently divorced, and in the midst of a period of desperate inner strife.

As I was working my way through that storm, my father was finding peace. The disease had humbled him, and it had sweetened him, too, leaving him vulnerable to sudden swings in emotion and quick to tears. There was a new gentleness about him, a new playfulness as well. As his body seemed to fade away, his spirit calmed, so it was peaceful to be in his presence. Where once he had been frenetic, he was now serene. Where once he had been distracted, he was now focused not on himself but on other people, including me. He had become a real father to me, an adviser valued in crisis because he had weathered similar crises in his own past. Perhaps he would be the healer after all.

∽

THE WAVES AT REHOBOTH were too small for bodysurfing. Toward the end of the week, I went for a swim and ended up treading water offshore about fifty yards out. From there, I swiveled about and scanned the ocean's horizon and the endless shoreline, feeling minuscule and alone. Then I saw them, massing on top of that wooden landing before moving slowly down the stairs. I made out two of my brothers, Tim and John, both tall and dark, holding up the withered frame of my father, walking toward me on the beach. I saw my sisters behind them, their striped beach towels flapping in the wind like banners in a motley procession of royalty. I saw my father leading, or being led, hobbling lightly on his bony legs. There was a towel covering his thin shoulders like a cape, and as he approached the high-tide mark in the sand, I saw him smiling in anticipation of his final swim.

They took the towel from his shoulders, exposing his sunken rib cage. The chilled air hit him, and he shook from the cold. His flesh-draped bones reminded me of some saint painted by El Greco, determinedly peaceful, preparing for a final ritual. I could see on his face the anticipation, the fear, and yet the resolve as he walked toward the ocean.

I swam back in to join them, and Tim, John, and I encircled him, escorting him into the ocean step by slow step. First the foamy edge, then the shallows. The small waves that had been a disappointment that week were a blessing now as we walked him in waist-deep. Small as they were, they threatened to knock him over, and I stood in front of them as they rolled in, trying to shield him. In a tiny moment of fear, I realized that I couldn't block the water. A wave broke on me and jolted him. "Easy, easy now," and, "Ugh, oh," and then, "Okay, okay, nice and easy now. Nice and easy." A wave approached him about shoulder-high, and he let himself fall into the crest of it. For a second or two he was gone, but as the wave rolled past, his gray head popped out of the water and his eyelids sprang open, revealing blue eyes full of surprise. After extending his thin arms in a few tentative strokes, he pronounced himself done with his swim.

We put our hands underneath his arms and shoulders and supported him, my sisters hooting and applauding as we walked to the high-tide mark. Like paparazzi, a few of them clicked cameras. Tim, John, and I strutted upright, and my father smiled with great self-satisfaction. He had run his fifty marathons, but he had never done anything this courageous. He was laughing now, and I could feel only his joy at having done it. In bittersweet September, he had come back to the ocean, and there, surrounded by his children, the struggles of a lifetime seemed to crumble and resolve themselves on the warm, wet sand. He had completed his lifelong odyssey. At long last, at this moment, he had become the man he was meant to be.

This is my last great memory of him. In less than two months, he would be dead. Now as I look back to that day at Rehoboth Beach, I write not so much to explain but to understand all that led us there. His life and my own. I had always chased my father, chased after his love, chased him through his many changes. I chased him even when I thought I was running in the other direction. Today, even though he is gone, I chase him still. I know he is the key to my freedom.

CHAPTER TWO

WHEN MY FATHER WAS FIVE, his father bought a rambling mansion on the ocean's edge in Long Branch, New Jersey, where the children spent their summers with their mother. The house is gone now, but when I was a boy it was still standing. And though it was no longer in his family, my father knew the people who lived there, and he once drove me there for a swim. We had been driving along the ocean in his phlegmatic Volkswagen Beetle when without explanation he took a sudden detour off Ocean Avenue. The car coughed and sputtered up a yellow stone driveway to the front of the magnificent house, where he mercifully cut the engine. It was a big, billowing, brown-shingled palace with a flat deck over the garage, where we found the present inhabitants sunning themselves. "Mind if we take a dip?" my father shouted up to them as we walked by. "Sure, George, help yourself," came the reply, but my father was already headed toward the beach below.

Giving me one of the very few glimpses into his past that he would ever offer, he stopped for a moment and pointed up at the deck, then told me how his mother—my grandmother—would sit there with her book in the afternoon and oversee her fourteen children as they played in the ocean waves and sand dunes. "We'd draw up sides for baseball right here," he said, pointing then to the flat grass in front of the dunes. His siblings—a group large enough for a seven-on-seven game of baseball—tried to get in nine innings before dinner every night, and when his mother finally called them, each would wash before sitting down to a white-table-clothed meal of roast beef or turkey. When summer ended and it was time to return to Brooklyn and school, he told me, they cried inconsolably all day long.

As a boy following my father through the dune grass that day, such a way of life seemed hard to fathom. Though I knew virtually nothing of wealth and class, I knew enough to understand that living in a summer house with your own private stretch of ocean was luxury of unimaginable standing. And I was puzzled by this, for I never thought of my father as coming from a rich family. But then again, there was really so little I knew about him, or his past. His brothers and sisters all lived nearby, but we hardly ever saw them. He himself was so determinedly remote that even in those rare moments when I was alone with him, I wouldn't have dreamed of asking questions. I just watched him closely and wondered.

The ocean was rough that day, so I played in the white water and watched him bodysurf. I could tell the waves here were different from the shorebreakers at our beach club. They crested and broke farther out, and when they broke, they broke more gently, ensuring a longer ride. I watched him glide unconcerned through the black pilings of some wave-battered bulkhead that jutted up through the water. He eased through the pilings, and at the end of a ride he stood up in the shallows and said, "Great water." Then he swam out again.

Today when I think of him gliding across that water, it seems there was very little he wanted to recapture from his childhood—except perhaps for those waves, that beach, and a late summer afternoon baseball game, long ago.

∞

IN TIME, I LEARNED that the rest of the year, my father's family lived in an elegant brownstone in the Park Slope section of Brooklyn. A five-story affair with eight bedrooms, it still stands at 109 Eighth Avenue, in the middle of the block between President and Carroll Streets, towering above the sidewalk like a cathedral in a vise, sandwiched between two others of its kind. If you go there today and tune out the traffic and the noise, you can picture a very different Brooklyn, in a more gracious time, when people strolled slowly past the rows of brownstones that descend gently off Prospect Park, and stopped to admire the little gardens beside each stoop. The neighborhood was an urban wonder, and yet so pastoral that it was hardly urban at all. At the center was the park, with its dogwoods and maples, its lakes and gardens, and in its depths, bowers that could transport you to the middle of the Maine woods without much imagination at all.

Throughout the fall and winter, the Sheehan children would roam the park each day after school, and at nightfall, tromp, heavy-footed and famished, back down the slope, home for dinner. The front windows of the brownstones revealed living rooms of rich mahogany, glowing invitingly from fires in fireplaces of carved marble. It was not the Fifth Avenue of the Astors, Morgans, and Rockefellers, but it was the place where the newly affluent Irish displayed the lace-curtain elegance that was their answer to the gilded age, the place they raised their large broods of a dozen or more children, my father's family among them.

I imagine it to be almost a dream world, one buffered from the shocks and vagaries of the city, where parents need not fear for their children, and their children need not fear at all. But as a boy, my father was an uneasy child, frail and bookish, prone to daydreaming and afternoons spent by himself, according to his brothers and sisters. He lived in a world all his own, and at times he appeared overmatched even by the mostly genteel world outside.

One day, the story goes, he appeared in his mother's kitchen asking her for a dollar.

"A dollar?" she asked. "For what?"

"So I can buy back my bicycle from the boy who stole it," he said.

When I was growing up, my father most often cut a solitary figure, sitting in the corner of a sofa, reading or writing, oblivious to the comings and goings of the rest of us. So, when I think about him in his boyhood home, it's easy to conjure a very similar image: that of a young man nestled in the same pose, reading a book on a couch in Brooklyn, as his brothers and sisters run and play all around him. He has tuned them out and they break his trance at their peril. He seems unaware of them until he is jostled. He glowers, and for a second everything stops. Then he goes back to his book and the noise resumes.

"In a room full of people," his sister Ann once told me, "he could be by himself."

In the mayhem of a large family, my father quickly developed a profound need for solitude, and a prickly defense to protect what little he had of it. His ferocity is well documented by his brothers and sisters, who still remember the time he held his little sister Margy upside down by the ankles over the banister until she promised never to interrupt his studies again. When I read his book *Running & Being,* I knew he was telling the truth when he described his childhood this way: "I was a born loner. I came into this world with an instinct for privacy, a desire for solitude and an aversion to loud noises, to slamming doors and my fellow man. I was born with the dread that someone would punch me in the nose, or even worse, put his arm around me."

Being the firstborn, my father was given the name George Augustine Sheehan, his father's name. And from the beginning it was clear that he was to be his father's son. Throughout his childhood, my father had a special place beside his father, and from that close vantage my father was expected to learn and emulate. Though one of fourteen children, he was in many ways raised as an only child.

With no small amount of envy or wonder, even decades later, his brothers and sisters recalled that my father was the only child to eat lunch with their parents. His mother would dress him up, Lord Fauntleroy–style, and have him join them at the exclusive table. From the parlor door, the other children would see him there, a little adult, presumably talking of the events of the day. Their ears burned to hear their mother fawn and dote. "My George," she would call him, saying time and again to whomever would listen: "My George is such a pleasure."

My father's room was at the top of the five-story brownstone, and he got up the earliest to attend classes. His mother had rigged up a bell with a cord descending to the kitchen. She would pull the cord to wake him, unaware that my father had stuffed his socks inside it to muffle the clang. "Don't let the darkness deceive you, dear. It's time to get up," she would call sweetly. "Let me hear your footfalls, dear." Though he appears to have been coddled, there was a message behind the nurturing: he was expected to get up and succeed. It was an unwritten contract, not negotiated or signed, but binding just the same. The tenderness bestowed was always pregnant with great expectations.

Like his father, he was intelligent, intense, and driven, and he would parlay these qualities into a successful medical career. Like his father, he became a cardiologist. ("A heart doctor," we would say as kids.) And, like his father, he would marry and have a very large family. Years later, my father would question whether he had ever lived a life of his own choosing, lamenting that everything had seemed predetermined.

"I never had a choice in anything," he told me once. "I feel as though everything in my life was decided for me."

My father told me this on the occasion of his leaving my mother for the second time. It infuriated me at the time, seemed a pitiful dodge of responsibility, a rejection of all that he had made in life, myself included. Yet, from what I've learned since about his childhood, it appears to have been so—at least in his youth. His family's hopes were vested in him from the start, and that left him limited choices. My father would have to take the path clearly laid out by his father, lest he disappoint.

∞

AS LITTLE AS MY FATHER talked about his childhood or his brothers and sisters, he spoke even less of his father, who died two years before I was born. As a child I never heard my grandfather mentioned—not until I was seven or eight and asked my mother about some framed photographs displayed on a table in our living room.

"Who is that man?" I asked.

"That's your other grandfather," she said, to differentiate him from her father, who was still living. "He was Daddy's daddy. He's not here anymore, but he was a very kind and good man."

After that, I often stared at those photographs, wondering what he had been like and trying to see my father in his face. To this day, it's hard to see any resemblance between them. In those pictures, my grandfather looks like a full-faced Irish politician of the day. He beams, an outgoing man exuding goodwill, grinning and grabbing hands in firm fellowship. In stories gleaned from my mother and later from my aunts and uncles, I discovered that he had been a doctor of some renown, which extended beyond Park Slope throughout the city. He treated the wealthy, Mayor Bill O'Dwyer's wife among them, and his children still remember taking day trips to Gracie Mansion, where the mayor's wife would spoil them with cookies and lemonade.

My grandfather attended many wealthy patients, but he was also a doctor to the poor and a man of social conscience. A loyal son of the Catholic Church, he treated scores of nuns and priests gratis, a service eventually recognized by the Vatican with a proclamation signed by the Pope himself. When his patients could not pay, he'd forgive their bill. Often he would even leave them money—money they could use to buy the medicine he had prescribed—which the patient's family would find on the night table after he left. His benevolence to the poor didn't result in much belt-tightening on his part. While he possessed no love of money, he lived as an aristocrat, employing both a chauffeur and a cook.

The day my father showed me their old beach house in Long Branch, I had an inkling of something I would come to understand later on: my father always felt himself to be an impostor around wealth. Though he had lived near rich people from childhood on and was thought to be a rich man himself, he always viewed wealth with suspicion, no matter how much money he made. He never wore expensive clothes, never drove expensive cars, never even took a vacation. His wallet rarely held more than ten dollars, and he was forever fumbling in restaurants when the check came. The one time I asked him for investment advice, his response was: "Don't ask me. The

Sheehans have never been any good with money." He never acted the rich man because he never believed himself to be one. He believed wealth was the thinnest of illusions—a conclusion he came to honestly by watching his parents.

Throughout childhood, his parents' opulence always threatened to outstrip their means. Money was not as bountiful as appearances indicated, and its scarcity was a constant worry to his mother. From without, his family appeared to be typical New York lace-curtain Irish, but the inside revealed a different story. As his brothers and sisters remember it, they lived like "ruined royalty" in their towering brownstone, where the lights didn't work, the clothes were often threadbare, and it was a challenge to scrounge up enough change to go to the movies. My grandmother screamed at waste, yelling at the children in exasperation, "We're one step from the poorhouse."

Until it was close upon him, my grandfather remained oblivious to his brushes with insolvency, counting himself privileged to be a doctor and exceedingly lucky to have dodged the bullet of manual labor. Even though he had been born on a farm, he was said to have no aptitude for chores or repairs. "He barely knew which end of a nail to hit," says one uncle, attesting to my grandfather's profound distaste for physical work.

My grandfather's own grandfather had emigrated from Ireland during the potato famine and settled as a tenant farmer near the town of Red Hook, New York, about one hundred miles up the Hudson Valley and just north of Poughkeepsie. When my grandfather's father married and started a family, he tired quickly of that hardscrabble existence and moved his growing family to Brooklyn. There, my grandfather finished high school, and then floundered in a series of menial jobs. He was unsure of direction, but in those days you could go to medical school without first going to college, and that's what he did.

Although he had no money then, he met and married Loretta Ennis, the youngest daughter of a plucky Irish immigrant who had made a great success of things in his short time in America. Her father, James Ennis, had been a policeman in Dublin. He played the cornet and once toured Canada with a police-department band called The Queen's Own. During the tour, he bolted Canada for Brooklyn, where he soon became the owner of several bars, and later the vice president of a brewery. My father's mother, Loretta, was the youngest of James Ennis's eleven children and had all the advantages of wealth and education.

When my grandparents married, my grandfather took on the life and manners of New York's Irish aristocracy. The ways of gentility seemed almost second nature to him, his transition from immigrant son to landed gentry was that swift. At the beginning of the marriage at least, money poured in steadily both from the practice and from my grandmother's dowry. My grandfather took to wearing Chesterfield coats and shirts with French cuffs. Each day at noon he would climb the stairs from the office he had set up in the basement of the brownstone to the dining room on the first floor, and there my grandmother would serve him a double-loined lamb chop, broiled rare. Every morning, she served him breakfast in bed.

Times were so good, he even bought that big house by the ocean in Long Branch, so his wife and kids could escape the city each summer. My grandfather would joke about the expense of children, telling people, "I invested in livestock and lost all my money," but as more babies arrived and the older ones started heading to college, the jokes ceased to be funny. When he finally woke up to the grim fiscal reality of the situation, it further exposed what had always been his not-so-hidden dark side: his volcanic temper.

In my family, it was referred to as an Irish temper, as if it were part of an ethnic as well as a familial legacy. My mother used to say of my father's temper, "He got it from his father," for she had heard the stories about my grandfather and his Vesuvian eruptions. They occurred infrequently. Less than once a year. But on those days when the pressures got to be too much for him, he would rage and yell and throw things, and the children would scatter to all four corners of the house. Expensive vases, finely finished chairs, no object was safe. But he struggled hard against that inner tempest, as my father once recounted. Sometimes in the middle of the afternoon, the family would hear his muffled yells, and then he would mount the stairs from his office, his face flushed red and eyes full of rage, headed for the bathroom two floors up, where he'd hurl a large bar of soap against the wall, over and over. Downstairs, the family would hear the thump of the soap hitting the walls at irregular intervals, the frequency gradually decreasing, until finally, after ten minutes or so, he would descend the stairs, still breathing hard but considerably more composed.

When I was in high school, just before my father left my mother the first time, he, too, began erupting. One of the things most likely to set him off was our entrenched resistance to his efforts to wake us. Every morning the hallways of our house were filled with the sounds of his shouting and banging on doors. But in a family of inveterate sleepers, my brother Peter was champion. One morning when he was unable to rouse him by yelling, my father threw a boot at Peter, which hit him on the shoulder. From the door of my bedroom, I saw Peter lift his head from his pillow after the moment of impact, only to drop it back down in deep repose. A few minutes later my father returned in full fury, grabbed Peter's desk chair, and hurled it at his bedroom window. By this time I had fled downstairs to the kitchen, where I winced when I heard the tremendous crash and tumble of broken glass. A few seconds later my father appeared before me, redfaced and panting. For a moment I thought he might come at me, but he turned and walked quickly out the door. I heard him floor the accelerator, sending the car shooting down the driveway, kicking up stones in its wake.

For both my father and my grandfather, anger seems to have stemmed from a deep inner frustration, a feeling that they were not living the life they were meant for. My grandfather's crisis was precipitated by his belated realization that although he had gone to medical school straight out of high school, he had a much deeper aptitude for medicine than most of the doctors around him, and that he wanted to make a greater dent than he could in private practice, perhaps by going into medical research. Unfortunately, by the time he realized this, his medical practice was so entrenched a part of the community that his loyalty to his patients prevented him from realizing his dream. His ambitions would have to be suppressed, although it now appears that they were merely transferred to his oldest son, George.

"Young George," as he would be known, showed promise early on and did not disappoint. He excelled so much in school that he won a full scholarship to Brooklyn Prep, a Jesuit high school for boys, where he graduated at the top of his class. He then got a free ride to Manhattan College, followed by another scholarship to Long Island College of Medicine, where he received his medical degree. He worked seriously and alone. Although never spoken, the message was clear from father to son: the son must succeed where the father fell short. My father assented without a word. The burden was passed from father to son. And so, too, it seems to me, were the hidden resentments and the anger.

〰

IN THE LAST YEARS OF HIS LIFE, few days went by when my father wasn't wearing his royal blue Brooklyn Prep sweatshirt, a gift given him along with a plaque from the school's alumni. The sweatshirt bore the school insignia and its Latinate name, "Schola Preparatoria Bruklyneisis." For him, the school had been an Academy of Athens in Flatbush, the place where the Jesuits versed him in Latin and Greek, and in their version of the wisdom of the ages: a sound mind in a sound body. Brooklyn Prep was where he first became a runner.

He won a scholarship to the school after finishing in the top three of a competitive exam given citywide, and once in, he strove to be the best. He had an uncompromising need to win. A loss in a chess match might end in his toppling the board. In baseball, he had to be the catcher, since the catcher ran the team. At the summer house in Long Branch, he even turned bodysurfing into a competition, drawing up competitive teams, inventing a point system that gave favor to the team whose rides lasted the longest.

The will to win prompted his decision to become a runner, or, perhaps more accurately, it explains how he defaulted into it. Wispy thin and possessing no great athletic skills, he was nonetheless determined to excel in some sport. Football was out of the question, and basketball practically a foreign sport, but he had his heart set on becoming a baseball player. In the summer, with his brothers and sisters, he played stoopball, boxball, and everyone's favorite, stickball. The family would square up sides and play in the middle of an Eighth Avenue empty but for the occasional car. They kept score with chalk, inning by inning, right on the street alongside home plate. "In stickball," my father would later write, "no matter what your ability there was the occasional miracle when broom met 'Spaldeen' and the ball would go high and far up the block for an unbelievable distance. It would be a memory never quite erased by past or subsequent failures."

On the mornings of Dodger games, he and his brothers moved the game in front of the home of the Widow McKeever, whose late husband had been an owner of the team. She would come down her front steps in the late morning, cooing at the darling boys playing in front of her house. It was a clever ploy, of course, because she would always give them free tickets to the day's game. Ducats in hand, they would walk through the park to Ebbets Field, where inside that cloistered world of dirt and grass, my father would spend the afternoon rising and falling on the pitches thrown to Dodger batters. He longed to emulate them, but he just wasn't good enough to distinguish himself. Although he was okay in the field, he didn't have the power to hit anything much greater than a Texas Leaguer. On a whim then, he went out for the cross-country team at Brooklyn Prep, and it was as though he had fallen in love. This was what he was truly meant for.

It was certainly not one of the glory sports. Actually, it wanted for any spectators at all, except for the few old men who appeared near the starting line of each race. Its very name, "cross country," with its evocation of pastoral runs through the English countryside, made it seem out of place in an urban environment. But running seemed specially tailored for my father. After school, the team of knobby-kneed, narrow-shouldered boys would range freely over the fields and through the wooded recesses of Prospect Park. In the fall, as darkness fell earlier and earlier, they ran on into the night, guided only by the dim glow of the occasional light stanchion. To my father, it felt like freedom: freedom from the classroom, from his books, and for a time at least, from other people's expectations. He and his teammates ran as a team, but clearly it was not a team sport. And this held another kind of appeal for my father. He was free to veer off from the others and cut his own trails through the woods, leaves and branches crunching underfoot and the chill wind whistling by his ears.

My father was fast. Not so exceptionally fast that he could make it

as a sprinter, but fast for a distance runner. The other qualities required, endurance and perseverance, were merely a matter of will, of
which he had an abundance. Since he had a great need to succeed,
there was little question that he would. It would be entirely up to
him, however, since in running, unlike other areas of his life, there
was no one breathing down his neck. His coach at Brooklyn Prep was
Bob Giegengack, a classics scholar who also taught Latin. In both en-
deavors, Giegengack was inclined toward the Socratic method, not so
much pushing his boys as getting them to see the worth in pushing
themselves. "Gieggie," as the boys called him, got the best from his
boys and never took the fun away. Forever after, my father would
bristle when he saw high school track coaches berating their runners
who performed poorly. "That guy should be coaching football, not
cross-country," he would say. It seemed to my father that these kinds
of coaches poisoned the waters, turning running into a chore when it
should be play.

By his senior year, my father had become one of the best schoolboy runners in the city, and Giegengack took him up to Manhattan
College in the Bronx to meet the track coach. The three of them
walked over to Van Cortlandt Park, a vast expanse of grass and trees
in Riverdale, where the Manhattan coach had my father run over the
flats. When my father came back around, the coach offered him an
athletic scholarship. Later that year, my father finished second in his
class at Brooklyn Prep, and would probably have gone to an Ivy
League school if money hadn't been an issue. He took the scholarship
to Manhattan College instead, and years later remained quite proud
of the fact that it was an athletic scholarship rather than an academic
one—even though he now excelled in both worlds.

Throughout their childhood years, his brothers and sisters tried to
stay out of his way. To them, he seemed to inhabit a world they en-

tered only at their own risk. His stony stare seemed unequivocal: he didn't need them, let alone their approval. And yet, toward the end of his life, he complained at how little praise or support he had gotten in his youth. "I don't know," he told an interviewer before he died. "Maybe the immigrant experience, Irish Catholic upbringing, siege mentality. My family never complimented me." And because of that, my father went on, he began to overcompensate in his every pursuit. "In just about everything I did—college, medical school, running, writing—I felt that I was a cut below where I wanted to be. So I had to do everything I could to be the best."

As far as he was concerned, his brothers and sisters should have known he was carrying the hopes of the family, and that beneath that burden he felt insecure and in many ways inadequate. But to them he was always a chilly, unapproachable figure. As a result, relations with his siblings were strained and would remain so for most of his life. It was only in his running that he could shake off the anger and alienation he felt within his family. On those fall afternoons in Prospect Park, he shed the burdens that weighed so heavily on him the rest of the time. The ground churning underfoot, the trees sliding by, the rhythm of his breath like a mantra—the act of running made him feel at one with himself and the world; it made him feel free, strong, capable, vital. In running, he began to believe in himself.

Throughout his high school and college years, my father knew he could always find freedom by slipping on his track shoes and heading out the door. Running was his safety hatch, his pressure valve. After college, he gave up running, choosing to live like the rest. Twenty-five years later, as pressures and constraints pushed in from every side, he remembered how running had made him feel free. He looked to running to save himself again.

CHAPTER THREE

THE SPECTACLE OF THE DRUNKEN SON—so often played out by me and any number of my brothers—was rarely seen in my father's family. His mother saw to that. Since drinking had been a problem in her parents' household, she did what she could to encourage sobriety in her own. At the end of the day, she would pour her husband a solitary rye and put a teaspoon of rye into a very large glass of ginger ale for herself. Even when their children were in college, they would not be invited to join this ritual. So it was with considerable amazement that my father heard his younger brother, Jim, announce to their parents one night that he was going to the neighbor's house for drinks.

"But, Jim," his mother said, "we're going to have drinks here."

"Yes," Jim replied, "but they put liquor in theirs."

My father could never be so openly defiant of his adoring mother or of his demanding father. But only parents as naive as his could have believed that he wouldn't eventually stray. Their path was too narrow, their expectations too high. So it came to pass, on the day he graduated from medical school, that my father turned in a drinking performance that, to his parents, came as a stunning surprise.

Before the graduation ceremony that evening, he and a few fellow med students spent the afternoon drinking at the swank Hotel Bossart in Brooklyn Heights, where my father became so liberated by drink that he climbed a tree on the sidewalk outside. When his friends finally coaxed him down, they hailed a cab and delivered him to 109 Eighth Avenue. After carrying him up the stoop, they propped him against the front door, rang the bell, and fled. When my grandparents opened the door, my father collapsed into the foyer ("like a wet rag," my uncle remembers), and the jaws of my grandparents dropped in static horror.

Since it was vital that he recover himself, because he was to deliver some remarks at the commencement, my grandparents doused him in a cold shower—clothes and all—until he was lucid again. He somehow made his speech and, quite remarkably, managed not to embarrass himself. What was equally remarkable was that my grandmother's belief in her son's perfection never wavered. She continued to dote, believing him—despite this one alarming indiscretion—as constant as the Northern Star. "My George could be put into a den of thieves, but he'll never change," she said. The incident would be stricken from memory.

Even in temperate Irish households, alcohol is always a presence, a specter from the past. Like some fearsome beast locked away in the cellar, alcohol is hidden, ignored, kept at bay, in the hope that if no one acknowledges it, the beast will just someday roll over and die. The very fact that it's been banished, however, makes it so irresistibly alluring that, one day or another, the children will need to go down and have a look for themselves.

For my father, alcohol had other attractions as well. Tightly wrapped and ill at ease around other people, he secretly longed for the sociability that seemed to come so easily to other young men. He wanted a good time, he wanted romance, and both seemed completely unattainable without the loosening, freeing effects of alcohol.

Just as he had with running, my father looked to alcohol for its transformative powers. The introverted George and the prickly George now became the affable and social George. Alcohol somehow removed that towering barrier between himself and everyone else. It gave him the ease to say what he felt and the abandon to do as he pleased. By downing a few swift drinks before approaching a woman, he could sometimes summon the cocktail courage he needed to overcome his paralyzing fear. Or if he had no luck with women, at least he could now hang with the boys—though at times even his mates found him a little too gregarious and lively. As his tree climbing outside the Hotel Bossart foretold, my father became a drinker of the lampshade-dancing variety.

If he was developing too keen a fondness for alcohol, however, his mother would be the last to see or admit it. And this is the interesting thing about that beast in the cellar. Once it comes out in the open, the silence about the beast continues. In fact, the beast is protected. If after medical school her son George began to stumble in half drunk at night, it was because he was "blowing off steam." If her other children began drinking nightly, it was because they were contending with pressures of their own. One of her own brothers, who had been a heavy drinker, died in his early thirties.

"Of consumption," she would say grimly.

Today, her surviving children more accurately surmise that his death resulted from the overconsumption of whiskey. Even when some of her adult children became problem drinkers, she could not see it, let alone bring herself to say the word *alcoholic.* After her husband died, she herself began drinking in earnest and drank nightly until her death.

My father drank after medical school; he drank after the war; and he drank steadily into his marriage, though I knew nothing of it. By the time I came around and was old enough to have much awareness, he had pretty much quit drinking. When a close friend told him he was "one drink away" from becoming an alcoholic, the words seemed to hit their mark—though not before my father's drunken tree climbing had become something of a regular event at parties in our suburban town. Growing up, I rarely saw him drink, and I saw my mother with a glass of wine only at the Thanksgiving or the Christmas Eve dinner table.

From what I observed, they were close to being teetotalers, and they expected the same of their children—that part of the message was clear. But they never directly warned us about alcohol abuse, never lectured us about the potential dangers, and certainly never informed us that alcoholism seemed to run in the family. And when the beast finally reared its head among their children, it was met with the time-honored response of silence. When my older brothers started coming home drunk, they were rarely admonished. When it came my turn, the silence continued. My mother was also fond of the "blowing off steam" explanation for drinking, even when we were "blowing off steam" every night. In fact, my chronic drunkenness never bothered her nearly as much as my sobriety. The possibility that I or any other of her children might be alcoholic was unacceptable.

"Stop this nonsense," she told me once after I'd put together a few sober months. "Go have a beer with the others."

Once I quit drinking, I felt more alone than ever in my family, and the feeling put me in mind of the father of my youth, who would have just quit drinking at about the time of my first memories of him. His was a kind of mirthless sobriety, and I remember him being extremely uncomfortable around drinkers. Once at a party at our house—which he was putatively co-hosting with my mother—I found him sitting alone in a room reading a book, waiting for the evening to come to an end and for all the loud guests to go home. I would think about that scene during the early days of my sobriety when I tried to go to parties with my drinking friends. Without alcohol, I too felt completely disarmed. Unable to tell jokes or stories, unable to mix it up with the drinkers, I would slink out the door and go home early. I felt sorry for myself, and looking back, I feel sorry for my father. Both of us were going through a time when the loneliness of our youth, which alcohol had banished, was upon us once again.

Until it stopped working, alcohol gave me great social powers. When I discovered alcohol, I, like my father, found it knocked down the wall of separation between myself and everyone else. Suddenly, like him, I felt in tune with the world instead of disjointedly out of step with it. With confidence and ease, I drank and smoked, told stories and jokes, and felt that there was no other life. Every time I drank, fears would vanish, inhibitions would fade, and I would become my truer, unfettered self.

Perhaps I had always felt the lure of that release. I remember one Thanksgiving, when I was a boy, I saw my mother at the dinner table with a glass of red wine before her. I asked her for a sip, and on a lark she handed me the glass. When I took it to my lips, the shock of its dry, brackish taste repelled me. At the same time, I felt a strange tickle in my brain. It was as though some quick and painless electric charge had shot through my head and then dissipated just as quickly. I took another sip so I could feel it again.

"Hey, Andrew," my mother said in surprise, "that's enough."

After I quit drinking, I'd think back to those first sips of alcohol and how strangely exciting they felt. But mostly I think about the look on my mother's face. I still remember how her eyes widened in that sudden flash of alarm, and how they stayed on me several seconds too long. She took the glass away, put it back on the table, and looked at me again. Perhaps it's a leap to say that she saw my father in me at that moment, but thinking back, I can't help but feel she was looking back, across the generations.

∞

THE SUMMER MY FATHER GRADUATED medical school, there were plenty of reasons to drink. For one, he had quit running. In those days, young men simply quit playing sports after they graduated college. To do otherwise was prolonging adolescence. Without the release of running, he looked to drinking as a more socially acceptable outlet for his frustrations, one that might ease him through the terrifying ordeal of looking for a wife. He drank with impunity in those days after medical school. And if he was drinking more than other young men, who would have noticed? Who would have cared? That was in 1943, and people had other things to worry about. And besides, there was a lot of drinking going on.

That summer, unbeknownst to his father or anyone else in his family, my father enlisted in the navy; he was scheduled to go to officer's training school in anticipation of an assignment as a ship's physician. Meanwhile, his father was busy making his own plans for him. With some pulling of strings, he had arranged for him to get a fellowship at Harvard, and one night with great satisfaction he announced this to my father at the family dinner table. That's when the truth came out.

This was the only time anyone can remember my father standing up to his father, and it would provoke a scene as well remembered for its violence as for its uniqueness. Not only was my father choosing the navy over Harvard, as he announced to the astounded group in the dining room, but he was going to be married, to a woman he had met only months before. The old man stared at his son for a few moments, then flew into an ungovernable rage. The family scattered in panic as their father hurled each and every dining-room chair into the living room, all the while raining down invective on the bowed head of his eldest son.

"That's the most irresponsible thing I've ever heard," the old man boomed. How could he? How could he say no to Harvard? How could he marry a woman he had known only for months? How could he risk leaving her a widow?

"How could you put a young woman in that position, George?" my grandfather thundered.

"That's my decision," my father replied.

∞

THEY MET AT THE BEACH CLUB. It was a private beach club of insouciant elegance, a wealthy Irish Catholic enclave called the Monmouth Beach Bath and Tennis Club. There were tennis courts and cabanas for the more prominent families, and a great, rambling, white-shingled pavilion with a larger than Olympic-size saltwater swimming pool. Along the length of the beach ran a boardwalk perched above a seawall and overlooking the ocean. Immigrant Irish girls worked as waitresses in its tearoom and served the matrons who congregated each noon around its tables on the sundeck. Membership signified the attainment of particularly elevated status among Irish families with money, and the club was known locally as the Irish Riviera.

My parents' courtship is a very real and immediate thing to me. As children, we went to that same beach club, and occasionally when I'm back on the Jersey Shore I stop by to see a sister who is still a member there. It remains a timeless kind of place, frozen in the 1940s, or perhaps some even earlier era. It's the kind of place that puts you in mind of Scott Fitzgerald, walking poolside with some Princeton boys in baggy pants, searching for his Zelda. And it's very easy to imagine that day in June 1943 when my father was also looking for a woman. But since he hadn't the slightest clue of how to go about it, it was she who would have to find him.

All day long, under the blue sky, tanned bodies in bathing suits circulated from beach to ocean, ocean to pool, pool to lunch, and lunch to beach again. Not my father, however. When my mother first spotted him, solitary and apart, he was sitting on a bench, wearing a seersucker jacket. His foot was propped up on the bench, his elbow resting on his knee, his chin cupped in his hand. As she watched him stare off at the ocean, the sight of him struck her, and she knew she had to find a way to be introduced to him. My father had come with a group of friends from Brooklyn, nonmembers who would regularly crash the club in search of Irish pulchritude. Since my mother knew one of his friends, the way was paved for her.

Her name was Mary Jane Fleming, and she was a raven-haired beauty who looked like Ava Gardner in a bathing suit. She too was the product of strict Irish Catholic parents, but while she was forever mindful of the limits they put on her, she was freer than my father to flirt with the edges. Somehow my father managed to catch her, although it was really she who caught him; she only made it appear that he had done the seducing. Presenting herself to him surreptitiously, effortlessly sidling up to him, she ignored the ham-handedness of his advances and made it all feel easy.

Even during that week in Rehoboth, we were still asking her to tell the story one more time: how she was already going out with a friend of my father's who had gone to Brooklyn Prep. How that young man—tall, muscular, blond, and handsome—was everything my father was not. And how even when my father began pursuing my mother in the weeks that followed, the boyfriend never saw him as a threat. Before the boyfriend shipped out with the navy, he asked my father one parting favor. And as she got to that part of the story we had our mother repeat the famous line: "Look after her for me, George," he had said.

At Rehoboth, we all fell out laughing yet again. "How could you do it, Mom?" we asked, as we had done so many times before, revelling in the story of our very proper mother's faithlessness and deceit. "How about you, Dad?" we asked of the snake himself, who sat there smirking sheepishly.

∞

MY MOTHER WAS BORN IN CHICAGO but her family moved when she was a young girl. They came to the Jersey Shore, to the little town of Atlantic Highlands, which sits on a bluff overlooking the ocean and the mouth of New York Harbor. In the late 1930s and early '40s, she went to Manhattanville College, a Catholic girls' school in Harlem, run by the Sisters of the Sacred Heart. In the summers she would return to the shore, where, under the watchful eyes of her parents, she had her pick of boys. She was a beauty of local legend—a legend still being discussed years later, when I started going to bars. On occasion, an older man would come up to the barstool next to mine and tell me just how beautiful my mother had been in her time. Sometimes, even then, the comments had an inappropriately lascivious ring to them.

How odd, then, that she would fall hard for my father, who was not the beneficiary of good looks and whose appeal was hidden to most. But to her, there was something familiar about him, perhaps even familial. There was something intriguing about him, too. She saw in him something more, something unusual, something that set him apart from those good-looking achievers who were courting her. "He had terrific eyes," she told me once. "They were very deep. Very kind. You could tell there was something going on in there."

Theirs was a romance similar to others being played out all across America in those days—quick romances hastened and intensified by the war. Driving down Ocean Avenue in my father's roadster by the light of the moon, the air tangy with the smell of the ocean and fraught with the imminence of their inevitable separation, they must have found their nights together almost unbearably exciting. Not that they were hellbent on flouting their upbringing. On their first date, my father took his future wife to the house of his favorite aunt, who cooked them dinner and then served tea. But the war could imbue even a quiet stroll on the beach with drama. World events seemed to breathe on their every hour together, making it seem as though each one might be their last. They were sure what they felt was more than infatuation, and they trusted what they felt. They exchanged vows in a local Catholic church on Easter Sunday the next spring. When he shipped out in May of 1944, she was pregnant.

My mother returned to her parents' home, and she wrote daily to my father's ship out in the Pacific. One day she wrote to him about the arrival of twins—George and Mary Jane—born on Christmas Eve 1944. But a follow-up letter reached my father before the original announcement, so that the first words he read on the subject were, "The twins are doing fine." He read on to find out about his new son and daughter.

A shipmate next to him at mail call elbowed my father in the ribs in excitement, yelling, "My wife had a baby."

My father stared down at my mother's letter.

"Only one?" he deadpanned.

My mother spent the rest of the war at her parents' house with her older sister, Margaret, who had a husband in Europe and a newborn of her own. Together, they washed their babies in the kitchen sink, revisiting in their minds the scenes of their short romances. In only a short while, my father would have been away from my mother for longer than the entire time they had been together. She would look deep into the eyes of her babies, searching for his eyes, fighting to keep intact his ever-vanishing image. On Sundays the two sisters would walk down the road to the church and pray they would see their husbands' faces again.

WHEN WE WERE KIDS, my brothers and I ran around the backyard playing Army. Aiming our makeshift carbines and tommy guns at each other while making our ack-ack burping noises to simulate gunfire, we'd jump from behind trees and shout, "You're dead," whereupon our intended victim would obligingly pantomime a groan, swoon, and roll. Our favorite TV show was *Combat,* with Vic Morrow, but my mother couldn't stand it when our war games were enacted indoors. "You got Kirby. You dirty Kraut," we'd yell, tearing around the house until she kicked us out.

We longed to ask our father about the war, but Mom assured us that he didn't want to talk about it. So we had to be content with a leather-bound book about his ship that we found up in the attic. Inside was a picture of him flanked by two others with a caption that read: "Doc Sheehan and assistants." It showed our father standing on deck with the wind blowing in his face, looking a little like Montgomery Clift—narrow faced and hollow cheeked with a big tuft of black hair. The picture held us rapt. When we did cajole a few words out of him, he said only that life on the ship was deadly dull. Under more persistent questions, he once allowed that the ship had been in battle. Excited by this, we pressed him for stories of hara-kiri pilots, U-boat torpedoes, descriptions of great plumes of flame on deck.

"What was it like?" we asked.

"I have no idea," he replied. "I hid under my bunk until it was over."

My entire life, I imagined that the USS *Daly* had roamed the Pacific in search of something to do. Similarly, I pictured my father attending to a peacetime sick bay of dysentery and summer bronchitis. Recently, I discovered that wasn't the case. With just some cursory research, I learned that the *Daly* had been in nearly every major Pacific engagement, including the massive naval battle at Leyte Gulf, where it torpedoed and helped sink the Japanese battleship *Yamashiro* in the Surigao Strait. The *Daly* was at Iwo Jima, rescuing survivors of the carrier USS *Bismarck Sea,* and at Okinawa, where a kamikaze pilot crashed into the side of the ship, causing numerous injuries and deaths.

As ship's doctor, my father must have had his hands full the entire war—to a nightmarish extent. He was not a surgeon and never felt comfortable at the sight of blood, let alone gaping wounds or severed limbs. When the attacks came, he would have been grossly unprepared for what he was to encounter. He also had the kind of personality that is badly out of sync with the camaraderie of navy life, the towel snapping and short sheeting that men on warships resort to as an escape from the alternating waves of fear and boredom. Never wanting to be a "tin can sailor" like the rest, he would have found no relief from such antics. All that roughhouse jocularity would only have made my father feel even more alone.

Worst of all, surely, was Nagasaki. The *Daly* sailed there after the

A-bomb leveled the city. My father never told me about Nagasaki until late in his life. When I asked him how it had affected him, he said,
"I don't think it had any emotional impact on me whatever at the
time. I remember it just looked like a blueprint to me—a blueprint
of a city." It wasn't until a year later, he said, when he was back sitting
at his desk in Brooklyn, that it hit him. "Oh my God," he whispered
to himself. "All of those people." Seventy-four thousand people had
been killed, another seventy-five thousand wounded.

The war had shaken him in ways he didn't comprehend and later
was unwilling to explore. Once he finally got it out of his mind, he
didn't want to look back. Never wanted to speak of it again. He built
a wall around it, and it seemed to have made him even less able than
before to trust anyone with the knowledge of his vulnerability.

When the *Daly* returned to Charleston, South Carolina, my
mother took the train down south to meet her husband. Although
she was ready for him, she was prepared for the eventuality that he
was not ready for her—not ready for marriage and not ready for fatherhood. I imagine that for him, meeting her again that day, the
prospect of their reunion would have seemed as terrifying as the war
itself. He was returning to a wife he barely knew and two children
he'd never seen. And he knew nothing of married life. While other
couples were locked in French kisses, my parents merely held each
other's hand and walked tepidly along the dock.

My father had nothing to fear, however, for my mother took it
upon herself to do all the work of easing him into his new life. He
gladly delegated the job of raising children to her, and the rest was a
matter of imitating what he had known in the past. Family, career,
marriage—all fell quickly into place, apparently without effort. Initially they moved back to Park Slope, where they rented a brownstone, and he parked his roadster on the street. He set up shop as a

physician, working rounds just as his father had done before him at nearby King's County Hospital. My mother organized everything, leaving my father to his doctoring. In short order, there were two more children—a boy, Tim, and then a girl, Ann. They were on their way to becoming a family of almost Irish proportions.

Until close to the end of his life, I always knew my father to be reluctantly Irish. When my maternal grandfather would regale us with nostalgic anecdotes about the Irish in Chicago or the Irish back in Ireland, my father would sometimes shoot him a daggerlike look over his half-moon reading glasses before returning his eyes to his book. I sensed that he was secretly shamed by the American Irish, people who clung to old-world identities, who were at best provincial, at worst xenophobic. For his part, my father wouldn't tolerate ethnic slurs, and once smacked my brother for using the word *nigger*. When I asked him years later where he had gotten such conviction, he told me that when he was a kid, his parents would send him out for the paper, with directions to buy it from a newsstand owned by an Irishman eight blocks away, rather than from one of the Jewish-owned stands in the immediate neighborhood.

"I knew that was nuts," he told me. "Even then."

For his part, he thought of himself as an American. He had, after all, fought a war for America (a war Ireland had sat out), and when the war was over he had American longings. As the money arrived, he wanted the big house with the lawn and the trees. He wanted to drive his roadster along the ocean again. ("That wasn't a car," he told me once, "that was a way of life.") Most of all, he wanted to be free of the Brooklyn of his family—free to make his own decisions, free to create his own life.

His ever-growing family with its insatiable demand for space gave him all the excuse he needed to leave Park Slope. But while most everyone else in Brooklyn headed out to Long Island, my father envisioned one monumental traffic jam of people trying to get back and forth from the city. Declaring the island "a two-lane highway," he opted for New Jersey. The Jersey Shore. The place he had summered in his youth, and the place where my mother had grown up. My sister Nora, the fifth child, was born in Red Bank, New Jersey, where my parents had bought a serene white-shingled house with a lawn and a large oak tree. And still it was not safe harbor. Upward mobility frightened my father to no end, leaving him ever fearful he wouldn't be able to sustain that climb.

With the memory of his parents' precarious finances permanently engraved in his psyche, he could not shake the specter of financial ruin. In New Jersey, he traded in his gas-burning roadster for a Volkswagen and began working at his practice all hours. "He was gone from seven o'clock in the morning until nine at night," recalled my mother, who was left to run the house entirely by herself. Within a few years, she discovered to her surprise that he had not only paid off the mortgage but put away $10,000 in the bank. All the while she had been living on $450 a month with five children. Forever after, my father was known as the cheapskate he really was. He once told me that he had been a smoker in medical school but had quit, not because of the health risk but because he was too cheap to buy cigarettes.

As a doctor, my father was fated to balance his financial insecurity against his standards of integrity. Like his own father, he charged only five dollars a visit and saw poorer patients for free. But the patience and gentleness he was known for in his practice would sometimes fray as the pressures of providing for his large and growing family mounted. An elderly Russian lady, who had become a regular, caught an unexpected dose of his temper when she began to recite her usual litany of complaints. "Why do you come here?" he interrupted, midsentence. "I have not helped you and never will. You have the same complaints as the first day I saw you."

She looked at him in shock.

"Where is my Dr. Sheehan?" she said. "You are not my Dr. Sheehan. Where is my Dr. Sheehan?"

My father believed that what she was seeing *was* the real Dr. Sheehan, the one he'd been trying to keep under wraps.

With the arrival of two more children, Sarah and Peter, the demands became even greater. Big as it was, the house in Red Bank had become too small. And soon an eighth child would be born—me. So, reluctantly and with great fear, my father made the ultimate move—he bought a house in Rumson, New Jersey.

In the early postwar years, Rumson was a very affluent, predominantly Protestant and Republican town with mansions to rival those of Connecticut suburbs like Westport and Greenwich. The town had its own country day school, a tennis club that looked like Wimbledon, and a country club that excluded blacks and Jews. The house my father bought there was gray shingled, covered with ivy, and encircled by a plaster band of garlands and Greek friezes. It was said to have been designed by Stanford White himself, and it did look like some of the shingle-style Victorians White had built around the turn of the century on the shore, but we were never able to uncover any proof of that provenance. By the early fifties, those huge old houses had fallen from favor. People wanted new construction. My father, however, saw a deal and took it. "I got it for the price of a barn," he would later brag, but at that time, the price—$27,000—left him sleepless. Although it was indeed a bargain, the old dowager who sold it to him was glad to see it go. "I finally got rid of my white elephant," she told a friend.

Drafty, dust laden, and in need of repair, the house nonetheless evoked a long-ago era of opulence and splendor. With its carved staircase, half-dozen marble fireplaces, and nine bedrooms, it would have been fit for the family of any rich industrialist, and there were nights when we thought we heard their ghosts creaking up the stairs and slamming the window shutters. In very little time, however, my parents filled it with real bodies. There would eventually be twelve children in all, arriving at intervals of roughly a year and a half. The family grew so exponentially that we became a cause of wonder in the town, provoking unsolicited questions on the playground. Once, a kid asked me why my parents didn't use birth control—one thing among many about which I had no clue.

I didn't understand that the size of our family marked us as Catholics in a town where there were few. My parents, however, were keenly aware of their minority status, and my mother, at least, was determined not to stick out. She fought hard to keep up appearances. "You're not leaving this house dressed like that," was one of her oft-repeated phrases, regarding any kind of slovenly or unconventional dress. "You're not going to call attention to yourself."

In this she was a true product of her upbringing. Her father, Peter Fleming, had grown up near the stockyards of Chicago but had worked his way through school, becoming a successful businessman, full of Horatio Alger–like admonitions about how best to live. Her mother, Anna, was an exceedingly proper Irish woman who would not tolerate any public lapses in character in either herself or her children. She knew too well what was said about her people—how they drank, how they stole and fought, how they refused to assimilate, and how they had virtually ruined the cities they had descended upon in such droves. As she and her husband took their place among the ascendant Irish of Chicago, gaining grudging acceptance among the city's elite, she saw to it that her family of six children—my mother was the third—gave no occasion for criticism.

"She demanded that we always be well dressed and well mannered," my mother told me. "She didn't want to give them any room to talk."

"Who?" I asked. "Give who room to talk?"

"The WASPs," my mother said.

The social anxiety stuck with her, and it would stick with us. In Rumson, whether the stigma was real or imagined, we thought our ethnicity marked us as outsiders. Still and undeniably, the Sheehans had taken their place on that mandala of wealth and prestige that was Rumson Road, a winding drive with a hundred magnificent homes recessed from the roadway, and separated from each other by the winding gravel driveways that snaked between five-acre lawns. Each of the houses was unique, each tasteful and stately, each signaling wealth with all the subtlety of a lion's roar. My father fought his fears of maintenance bills, property taxes, and college educations, and all the while tried to belong, to fit in. It was important to him not so much to assimilate as an Irisher but to get beyond being Irish. A clean break. He did not want the fatalism or the old songs in his house.

As much as he wanted to create his own life, however, what he created would have an eerie similarity to what had gone before. With the inevitability of a photograph coming into focus in a pan of chemicals, it seemed it couldn't have been any other way. The house itself would take on the feel of 109 Eighth Avenue—the fallen plaster, the leaky faucets, the lights that didn't work. By his own admission, my father was "too close with a buck" to call in the repairman except in the most dire of circumstances. And he had also inherited his father's ineptitude in the face of anything broken. I remember once he tired of his sweater catching on an exposed nail in the kitchen. So he secured a hammer and tapped it in. Exceedingly pleased with himself, he turned and addressed the dinner table: "Anything else need fixing around here?" The question set us howling. But a quick inventory of our own talents would have proved just as funny. The entire family was powerless to fix anything, let alone this broken-down palace. We had become the ruined royalty of Rumson Road.

The imprint of the past would be everywhere. Looking at those pictures of my grandfather, so decorously displayed on that table in the living room, I could never have imagined that it was really he who dominated our lives. He died of cancer, two years before I was born, at the age of sixty-three. But, even though I never knew him, I was in many ways the product of a code of conduct he had left behind, for without reflection and by rote, my father simply followed his father's way of fathering.

First and foremost, the father was to be the boss, his authority never challenged—a rule passed on from father to son along with the temper to back it up. There were other rules. The father was involved in weighty pursuits, involving the lives and deaths of other people, and the family must resign itself to playing a supporting role. The needs of others would come before their own. Further, children should not look to the father as a chum. "Children want a father, not a friend," my father would say, though by the time I came around, he'd begun to seem more like an enforcer than either friend or father.

As a boy, I looked often at those pictures of my grandfather in the living room, having no idea that this man I'd never met or spoken to was shaping my life. But that man made my father in his own image, and somehow, without even trying, my father did the same to me.

Chapter Four

I F IT COULD BE REFINED OF its sharp edges and dark corners, the big Irish Catholic family might be the best of all places to grow up. It feels a privilege to be enveloped by its warmth and humor, and in the best times, there is a profound sense of belonging, of being surrounded by a familiar circle of like faces, mirroring your own. You think: if only we didn't have a weakness for judgment and ridicule. If only we could be consistent in our support of each other. If only our communication could be more direct, our nature less withholding.

Without these defects, you believe, the Irish family would be the best of places, but then you think again. You believe that if it was stripped of these faults, the whole institution might also be robbed of its essence. We'd no longer have the belly laughs, the deep sobs, the flights of lyricism. You ask yourself: Is there something in the alchemy of darkness and light that gives the family its uniqueness, its power? Or is that just one more rationalization? Rationalizing, of course, being the thing we appear to do best.

There is something in the Irish family that cries out for protection.

Something that guards its very weaknesses as a kind of treasure. I cherish my family because I see its time slipping away. Perhaps I cherish it because its time has already passed—gone with the Baltimore Catechism and old-school Catholicism. I want to protect the family from the criticisms of outsiders. I guard even the words and phrases we used in childhood, not wanting to trade them in for the current vernacular. I still call a refrigerator an icebox. We never had an icebox in my life, but my parents called the refrigerator an icebox, and so I hang on to the word. It speaks of a time lost and a way of life that will not survive.

But are the family and its ways really that fragile? Not long ago, I sat with a group of my father's brothers and sisters on a windy summer day on the Jersey Shore. We had sandwiches and iced tea on the screened sunporch of my aunt's house, and we talked about their growing up. These particular aunts and uncles were the younger children in the family, and as a group they have a special ease around one another. They seem to enjoy their own company above that of all others, a trait, I think, of brothers and sisters who have essentially raised themselves.

We talked about their family, but all the while it seemed to me that they were talking about my own—that their family and mine were one and the same. The traits, the rules, the unspoken contract that bound them—exactly the same. As in my family, I found that theirs was two families—the older family and a younger one. When I talk to people in my father's family, it's interesting to me that the older and the younger members tend to differ in their views of their father. The older children seem to regard him more fondly than do the younger ones, remembering him in much warmer tones. As in my own family, the younger ones tend to feel slighted. Deep down, there is a feeling that the father continued to have children long after he was interested in raising them.

My father's family and my own family have suffered similar problems and have dealt with those problems in similar fashion. When I speak with my father's surviving brothers and sisters, I see that my family has played the same parts, traced the same steps. How humor, wit, and laughter did battle with anger, alcohol, and depression. I have walked in these steps with the eerie feeling that I was merely playing out a part or fulfilling a contract—predetermined and predestined. My father's family holds up a mirror to my own. I feel the weight of the last generation on the present, and I believe I feel its imprint just waiting to be passed on to the future. I want to break the cycle, and I know that breaking it is no parlor game for the ages. It is a question of survival.

∞

BEING ONLY FIVE OR SIX at the time, I remember the words and the conversation only as sounds in the wind. Yet I can still see us all at the beach, sitting around my mother and the large wicker basket she toted everywhere when we were kids. It is a summer day at the beach club, where my parents first met nearly two decades before. With my arrival there were eight children, and since then two more, so there is a crowd of us, sitting on the blanket she has spread just beyond the high-water mark in the sand, within earshot of the crashing waves. Calmly and serenely, my mother reaches into the basket and hands us each a sandwich wrapped in wax paper, telling us each to mind the sand. After distributing all the sandwiches, she begins to eat the last one herself. As a breeze blows off the ocean, she leans back on her forearm, closes her eyes, and lets it comb through her short black hair. My father is at the office or the hospital, but later in the day I hear my mother say, "There's Dad," and I turn and see him in his street clothes, waving from atop the seawall. A short while later, he has changed into his trunks and is swimming in the ocean. He then comes running up the sandbar to our blanket and falls onto it like a big, wet, frisky dog.

I remember those days as very happy, unencumbered by worry and tension. But I also remember the happiness of those days as fleeting—at least for me. My memories soon give way to a time when my father's distance from the family began to feel painful, hurtful. As a doctor with a busy practice, he left early in the morning and returned home late. Most days, I would barely steal a glimpse of him before being sent off to bed. I came to view him as a forbidding presence hovering at the edge of my life, in contrast to that earlier image of him when he seemed so different, so amazingly free of rough edges. Recently, I asked my older sister Nora if she remembered that time the same way, and she told me she did.

"It was the last time that everything made sense," she said.

Our older brothers and sisters recall a more lighthearted, more playful dad—an organizer of baseball games and trips to the beach throughout their childhood. I'm amazed when I hear them recount their memories of a blizzard that occurred shortly after the move to Rumson, a day when my mother and father engaged each other in an improbable backyard snowball fight, their yells and laughter muted by the falling snow. Those first years in Rumson would always be remembered as a special era in their lives. That such a time existed at all seems almost mythic to me. But they describe a period of fun, even glamour. My mother had a flair for throwing parties and was said to be able to host dinners of twenty or more guests without apparent effort, while my father's intelligence and sharp wit made him a sought-after guest at other people's parties. My parents lived in a seemingly charmed time in a charmed house. Or my mother did, anyway. It would soon become clear that my father did not share her vision of paradise.

Perhaps there were just too many kids. By the time I was born, there were already seven children—George, Mary Jane, Tim, Ann, Nora, Sarah, and Peter. After me, four more would follow—John, Stephen, Monica, and Michael. Then there were always the friends, who came and went though the unlocked doors of our house like characters in a British farce. After creating a family in the size and image of that of his boyhood, my father also tried to reproduce the isolation he had found refuge in as a child, carving out a separate space for himself. While I vaguely remember him having dinner with the family when I was very small, early in my childhood he began preferring to have dinner alone. The swinging door to the kitchen was always wedged open during the day to accommodate the constant flow of human traffic. But after my father returned at night, it would be closed. I remember peeking through that door and seeing my mother serve my father dinner at the kitchen table.

I don't know if I understood his distance, though I seemed to have the same need to be alone, having already developed an aversion to noise and commotion. During the day, our house was always noisy, low rumbles rising to great crescendos of wailing children. The cries followed a predictable sequence: moments of wild excitement and shouting as each new cycle of play began, soon to be punctuated by the thud of someone falling or being hit. Then, the brief silence that preceded the bellowing shrieks of the injured. "I told you children before," my mother would yell, completing the pattern. "Take this outside." We would scatter, but sometimes I would stand frozen in the crosshairs of her glare before dutifully following the others out the door. The truth is that I was much more of an observer in those days. Prone to injury and intolerant of pain, I preferred the privacy of my room or some other place that I had staked out to be alone. But the option was rarely mine. I was part of the pack, and obliged to go where they went.

Cross-eyed at birth, I had to wear glasses before I got to kindergarten, and I was so fragile that I broke the same arm not once but twice, before the end of grade school. I longed to be good at sports, but each attempt resulted in one more in a series of pathetic and unabating mortifications. At the start of each pick-up baseball game, I had to suffer the indignity of squaring up sides, when my no hit–no glove status was always publicly exposed. ("Why do I have to take Andrew again?") Each backyard football game seemed to end with my hobbling off field into the house with some sort of injury. When I had the temerity to try out for Pop Warner League, they made me the waterboy, and in Little League, when I stepped into the batter's box, my coaches leaned on the backstop and yelled, "Okay, Andy, a walk's as good as a hit."

Baseball was the ultimate disappointment. The coaches stuck me out in left field where no one our age could pull the ball. So I was relegated to standing out there all alone, all afternoon, lost in fantasies about making spectacular plays: I would catch balls on the run, spin and fire the ball homeward, nailing the runner at the plate. Once, when I was deep into this very fantasy, the spell was broken by my coaches and teammates, yelling and pointing at me. I looked down to see a ball dribbling past me, a few feet to my right. I chased it deep into the outfield, but by the time I reached it the batter was rounding second with others in front of him, heading home. A single had suddenly turned into a three-run homer. As always I withdrew into another space, an internal world all my own.

"Snap out of it," my mother used to yell whenever her voice failed to pierce my fog.

"He's a dreamer," she always said of me. "He lives in a dream."

But if my insularity mirrored my father's in his own childhood, he showed no awareness of it, and no concern. He seemed not to notice that when the others left for the beach, I often stayed home to spend the hot summer afternoon in front of our black-and-white television, listening to Red Barber and Mel Allen do the play-by-play of the New York Yankees, my boyhood idols. My mother, however, would beg me to go outside and play, thinking it unhealthy for a child to spend so much time alone. Once, in the middle of an afternoon game, I was startled by the arrival of my father, who presented himself in the doorway.

"Your mother thinks you and I should do something together," he said.

It was a stunning offer, and I was shocked, even a little frightened to see him standing there. But I heard the sense of obligation in his voice, the utter lack of any idea of what we might do together, and I sensed his hope that I might let him off the hook.

"That's all right, Dad," I obligingly told him.

"Okay, then," he said and left.

The Yankees were something of a forbidden pleasure for me, since it had been drummed into everyone that we were a "National League" family, loyal and true. My father, of course, was a lifelong Brooklyn Dodgers fan, who detested the Yankees. Even after the Dodgers moved to Los Angeles, he and my older brothers continued to pine after them like unrequited lovers. The Yankees remained objects of scorn, but not to me. I saw them as gods; my idolatry of Mickey Mantle knew no bounds. Before I reached second grade I knew the batting averages of even the most minor players. Once, my older brothers taunted me, telling me that John Blanchard, the Yankees' backup catcher, had been killed in a car crash, which prompted me to burst into tears. The story wasn't true, but they used it to punish me for being a Yankee fan.

One time when I was cocooned in front of an afternoon game, I heard my mother talking to my father in the other room. "George," she said, "someone has got to take him to a Yankee game." In the weeks that followed, I waited, but no offer came. When I asked my mother why, she explained that, being a Dodger fan of long standing, my father just couldn't bring himself to take me to a Yankee game. So when the day finally came that I found myself riding up the New Jersey Turnpike and over the George Washington Bridge to the Bronx, it was my mother who was behind the wheel.

For her efforts she had to endure a decidedly one-sided conversation, as I prattled on about Mantle, Maris, Richardson, and Tresh, my monologue reaching great peaks of passion as we parked the car and approached the stadium on foot. After we slipped through the turnstiles, I ran ahead through the portals, and suddenly my black-and-white image of the field was blown apart by an incredible burst of colors. The green of the stadium grass, the red dirt of the infield, and the cream-colored facade against the deep blue New York sky. Then, of course, there were the Yankees themselves in their white uniforms with blue pinstripes. I couldn't believe that on this day and at this hour, I inhabited the same physical space.

They would win, of course. Something like 9 to 1. In the late innings, my mother asked an usher if I could go down to the rail next to first base. There, I stood only fifteen yards from the rookie Joe Pepitone, thinking I might pass out from the thrill. After the game they let us walk around the field by way of the warning track, and my mother and I walked hand in hand around the great stadium, past the dugout where the great men sat, staring up at all the empty seats. It was the greatest day I had spent on earth. It was a day I owed to her—not to him.

∞A

MY MOTHER WAS BOTH BEAUTIFUL and tough—a duality she inherited from her mother. We called her mother Nana, and I remember her only as a sweetly gentle and angelic-looking old woman, who would run her fingers through my hair while asking me about school. By reputation, however, she was a hard-as-nails disciplinarian of her own children. And her ferocious concern with proper comportment was passed down to my mother, whose standards were so high that they gave us the sense we were different from other people in our town. We felt that we were "in" Rumson but not "of" it, and this outsider stance had ramifications in every area of our lives.

Although we were well off, as just about everyone around us was, my mother never let us think or act that way. The other children had color televisions, and they went on trips, skiing at places called Sugarbush and Vail. Sometimes they came back with tans in the middle of winter from places called St. Thomas and Aruba. We never went anywhere, made do (unhappily) with our black-and-white TV, shared bedrooms, and wore hand-me-down clothes. She was a Democrat in a Republican stronghold, after all; she didn't want us to identify with the privileged.

"But, Mom," we often complained, "they have their own phone." Or, "Mom, they have a trampoline."

"*They* are not *you*," she always answered.

Actually, we kind of liked thinking of ourselves as different from other people. From the beginning, I remember that being a member of my family conferred a sense not just of difference but of vague superiority. It started, I think, with Catholicism, the way it was drummed into us.

Our school, Holy Cross Grammar School, was less than a half mile down the road, and each morning my mother dressed us boys in gray slacks and blue blazers, the girls in dress uniforms of blue serge. On cold winter mornings, we crowded onto the cold radiator in the kitchen, waiting for the heat to kick on. When we were running late, she licked a handkerchief and, stretching the skin of our faces taut, wiped the smudges off with such vigor that we glowed red. Then she sent us walking up the road to another day of chalkboards, wooden desks, and catechism.

We were taught by nuns, of course, who in the pre–Vatican II euphoria of the early 1960s seemed to be on an unchecked ego trip about being Catholic. As junior members of the one true faith, we were swept up in our feeling of specialness, thinking ourselves the envy of others. It had nothing to do with wealth; rather, for me, it had more to do with my perceived lack of it. Wanting badly a spiritual trial, I prayed for the strength to endure our home's lack of hot water and paucity of working appliances. The fact that the house could quite actually be described as a mansion was lost on me.

As that young Catholic boy, I was apt to clutch the tribulations of my life to my chest, "offering them up" to help free the trapped souls of purgatory. As we watched television, my brothers, sisters, and I searched for fellow Catholics. We knew Danny Thomas and Perry Como were "good Catholics," and we identified as many celebrities as we could in that column, just as I would count the number of Yankee players on the American League All-Star team. We had Fulton Sheen. We had the Singing Nun. We had the avuncular Pope John XXIII, but most important, we had the president of the United States, John Fitzgerald Kennedy.

As the nuns never tired of telling us, Kennedy was the first Catholic president, and they revered him as much as any saint. My mother loved him, too, and she always stopped her ironing or cooking and turned on the TV whenever he held an afternoon press conference. As she sat on the edge of the couch, drying her hands in her apron, her face lightened and grew wide in a smile, as she watched him playfully handle the questions of the reporters. I couldn't follow the banter, but my mother laughed at Kennedy's quips, and later, at dinner, she relived the whole event, quoting this answer and that joke.

As kids, we got caught up in it, too. My brothers and I would mimic Kennedy's Boston Brahmin accent, assuming for some strange reason that we would talk the same way when we grew up. Secretly, we imagined a kind of kinship with the Kennedys. When we saw those scenes from Hyannis, we saw ourselves: a great lot of Irish playing touch football or running on the beach. They even looked like us—so much so that we began to feel like our town's own version of the Kennedys, an association that fueled yet another kind of ego trip. The Kennedy identification and Catholicism dovetailed into a powerful force, making us feel we were part of something large and important. To me, it was all somehow wrapped up in the person of my mother, who was beautiful just like Mrs. Kennedy.

Lacking any sense of closeness with my father, I lived to please my mother. She was devout in her religion and I emulated her, making a project out of piety. Early in school, I became a star at catechism, and though I could barely read, my mother gave me an illustrated copy of *The Lives of the Saints.* At night in bed, I studied their otherworldly portraits, becoming strangely captivated by the martyrs: Saint Sebastian, riddled with arrows, looking forlornly to heaven; and Saint Stephen with his bleeding head, holding his killer's stone in supplication. I had fantasies of dying and being canonized as the youngest saint. Secretly, I was already in possession of a title of my own making: "The World's Holiest Boy."

In church, I stood next to my mother, waist-high, in the pew every Sunday. The figures of the saints in the stained glass windows held me rapt the entire mass. A single ray of colored light, shining through an inlay of colored glass, absorbed my entire focus, illuminating the dust that floated in that amber light and seemed never to land on the heads of the parishioners. Above them on a pillar beside the altar, there was a statue of Jesus, revealing His sacred heart. Sometimes, if I stared long enough and hard enough, everything around that statue blended into one color, and He seemed to fly. After mass, the spell broken, I stayed close to my mother's skirt as she talked with other parish women outside.

"He'll be the priest of your bunch," a woman remarked to my mother one day, looking down at me, and I was sure that this was so. For everywhere there were signs—signs calling me to the priesthood, signs of God's assent that I was worthy. When I heard rustlings in the bushes, that was a sign. When I peed white instead of yellow into the bowl, that was a sign, too. I told anyone who would listen that I planned to become a priest. To aspire to a religious vocation was something that set me apart from my brothers and sisters, since my siblings wanted no part of it. Today it's not hard to see that it gave me the attention we all craved. It must also have seemed a guarantee of that which I held most precious—the love of my mother.

No doubt my religious calling served also to keep my father at bay, even if it didn't necessarily endear me to him. Since we younger children had little contact with him unless we had transgressed, my father had begun to take on a grim reality for me—that of a frightening disciplinarian. Some nights when he walked wordlessly through the house, I could feel his anger as a palpable, if suppressed, presence. Forever vigilant not to trigger it, I probably resorted to piety as much out of fear of his temper as anything else.

"Wait till your father gets home," my mother would say on particularly bad afternoons, mostly to my brothers. He duly meted out the spankings my mother prescribed, but only once was I on the receiving end. I can't remember now what I had done, but he grabbed me by the arm and (keeping to his practice of hitting only below the waist) gave me three crisp spanks on my bottom, which glowed hot in a way it hadn't before and hasn't since. Another time, having been told by my mother to "wait till your father gets home," I spent a long afternoon in an agony of apprehension. When my father arrived home, he took me by the arm and walked me into the living room, where he sat down on the couch.

"Okay, where do you want it?" he asked.

When I burst into tears, my terror-riddled face must have been too much for him. He got up and left the room without raising a hand to me.

∞

I KNOW NOW THAT DURING those years—and even some of the years remembered by my brothers and sisters as being such happy times— my father was becoming a caldron of discontent. He had attained all that seemed attainable and still it underwhelmed. "Life always disappointed him," my mother told me once. "The dreams just never measured up when they came true."

From without, he did seem to have it all. He had built a thriving medical practice and had a well-earned reputation as one of the best doctors on the shore. Friends, family, membership in an exclusive beach club—he had everything most people aspire to. But in time, as he would make clear in his writings, the practice became a burden, the friends a bore, and the family an ever-tightening noose. His frustration mounted and his temper flared. Boiling ever closer to the surface was his fear of being trapped—the feeling that his accomplishments had become the very things that enslaved him. It was as though in building this envied life, he woke up one day and discovered that he had built a prison instead, however grand and golden it may have appeared. And he had no idea how to find a way out. Nor could he think of anyone among his friends who was equipped to counsel him. Everyone else, it seemed, was happy and content. By instinct then, he took his problem to the familiar place. He turned to his religion, to Catholicism and the mass.

On Sunday mornings he was even less tolerant than usual of lateness. Outside the station wagon he stood, counting each one of us as we tumbled in until the car filled up and my mother drove off. The last stragglers were hustled into his Volkswagen. Once in church, determined to maintain order, he stood in the church aisle, ushering each of us into one of the two pews we occupied. I remember sitting behind him in the summer and watching the sweat begin to seep through the back of his khaki jacket. I wondered at the grimness of his face and the deep lines carved across his forehead. "Worry lines," we called them. When he prayed, he buried his face deep in his hands, pushing those lines to the edge of his hairline. I wondered why he was always worried, and I wondered whether worry was making him old.

After mass we drove over the bridge to Sea Bright and to the German baker for our order of crumb and cinnamon buns. Back home, we all tore into them, tasting the sweet reward of our piety. But while all seemed right for us on those Sunday mornings, it was not so for my father. The fiery sermons of the intolerant old Irish priest didn't sit well with him, and he hungered for something more than rules and rote. Seemingly out of the blue, he shocked everyone by renting a small storefront in Red Bank, where he created the St. Thomas More Reading Room, filling it with reading materials on Catholic theology. It had the old tracts of Aquinas and Augustine along with the freshest copies of *Commonweal.* On occasion, my father would pop in to see if there was anyone about, but it remained empty except for the occasional bum. He waited for the discussion to start, and he waited in vain. Eventually, he just shut the place down.

Still, he was deeply Catholic, and he hadn't stopped admiring the Jesuits who had taught him at Brooklyn Prep or the Christian Brothers who had taught him at Manhattan College. They had taught him how to think, and he wished that same education for his sons. So, along with my mother's father and a local Catholic Wall-Streeter, he began holding meetings in our living room, where they planned a fund-raising drive to create a Catholic boys' high school. Within two years they raised $400,000, and in 1960 they bought one hundred forty acres of farmland in nearby Lincroft, founding the Christian Brothers Academy. My father was enamored of the land itself, an old horse farm with a decaying stable and an enclosed oval for training standardbreds in the winter. But if in walking the grounds and planning the buildings he was looking for some kind of spiritual awakening, he did not find it, nor did he find it in his talks with the Christian Brothers who would eventually teach there. He would, however, brush up against it when George and Tim enrolled there and joined the cross-country team.

Early in the school year, the Brothers made all freshmen—fat or thin, athletic or bookish—run a mile around the campus. Although George and Tim would have preferred basketball, the Brothers quickly recognized their potential as runners and recruited them for the cross-country team. When they raced on late-fall afternoons, my father packed up early from the hospital or his office and drove out to Lincroft to watch the meet. My brother George remembers him appearing at various junctures of the race, and instead of exhorting him to catch someone out in front, my father surprised him, repeating only one word. "Relax," he yelled, "relax," reflecting an old belief that you need to be loose to run well.

As he watched the skinny boys, their long legs loping over the rutted fields, he remembered his own competitive days. And at the sight of their pained expressions, the sounds of their pants and groans, he felt oddly envious. Not that he even considered joining them. It would be an inappropriate, unsightly thing for a man of forty-four years. Besides, like his friends and relations, my father had another, more acceptable, means of release.

∞

I DON'T REMEMBER HIM DRINKING in the house, but now I know he did. I know he drank heavily on weekends and sometimes made scenes at people's parties. My parents went out to parties, and occasionally threw one of their own. Not just elegant dinner parties, but big drinking parties with all their family and friends. It was a time to break out for them, and a cause of great excitement for us children as we each claimed a seat on the stairway to watch it all unfold.

My uncles arrived in their buttoned-down white shirts and thin black ties knotted up to their throats. After a few drinks, they loosened those ties and rolled up their sleeves, their shirttails sneaking out of their pants. They loved to drink beer and smoke cigarettes, and we loved to watch. We ventured among them, trying to get close so we could smell the smoke and their beery breath. They bent down and put their faces to ours, asking, "What grade now?" and, "How're the nuns treating ya?"

My mother shuffled us away.

"Andrew, get your uncle Mike a beer," she would say, and I would run to fish a cold can out of the barrel of ice she kept in the kitchen. Then I would return to our stairway perch so I could watch some more. My uncles and their friends laughed great loud laughs, and at times they argued even louder, pointing at one another, shouting at close distance, making us wonder whether there would be a fight. But then they would put their arms around one another's shoulders and laugh some more. At only one party do I remember my father with them. With a beer in his hand, his mouth open and his crooked teeth showing, he threw his head back in a high-pitched laugh.

It didn't register as anything important at the time, but at a subsequent party I found my father reading alone in a corner of that same room, waiting for my uncles to leave. Sometime in the preceding year, he had become more and more bored at these parties, with the result that he began getting ever more outrageously drunk. Sometimes argumentative, sometimes playfully inappropriate. He once told me about a friend confronting him, warning, "George, you're one drink away from becoming an alcoholic." It stung but did not stop him, and at another party he climbed a tree on the host's front lawn, refusing to come down despite the repeated pleas from below. His behavior was so dependably outrageous in those days that his brother-in-law took to filming him in Super 8. When the films were shown at a string of future parties, my father watched in red-faced shame.

"If you want to be cured of drinking, that will do it," he would say later. And that pretty much ended his drinking days.

But his abstinence made for even more tension. Then came one of those 3:00 A.M. calls that doctors used to answer themselves. It was the husband of a patient. Could he come over to see his wife? She had chest pains and was having trouble breathing. Could he come over now? My father got up, dressed, and then punched the wall, loading the punch with all his frustration and anger. When it landed, he shattered his hand. That was the spring of 1963, and to hear him tell it years later, it was the defining moment of change: a cataclysmic event after which nothing would be the same. His nadir. No longer could his unhappiness be hidden, at least from himself—it had exploded into an act of violence against himself and now stared back at him in the form of a plaster shell around his right hand. Unable to swat even the occasional tennis ball with his cast-covered hand for months thereafter, he followed the lead of his sons and the other skinny boys at Christian Brothers. He began to run.

It was with no small amount of wonder that I stood on the back porch one day that summer and watched my father running the perimeter of our backyard. The backyard covered two acres, and I watched as he ran the length of the house, trotted down a small slope, turned right at the neighbor's fence. After cornering again, he ran the far straightaway and up to the back porch and then around again. Before his running days, when he was really mad, my father would say three words in succession: "shit, piss, and corruption," and everyone knew to scatter. Now, as he ran past me, he said only two of them each time he exhaled.

"Shit-piss." Inhale. "Shit-piss." Inhale. "Shit-piss."

After more than twenty-five years of inactivity, he was running again, and every stride was painful. Years later, though, he would describe the undertaking as a kind of conversion experience. Looking back, he said he ended one life and immediately began a new one. To those close to him, however, the change appeared more subtle, more nuanced. Initially, he took pains to hide the fact that he was running at all. Running in public would have been viewed as subversive in a town such as ours—perhaps in any town. In the early 1960s, there was no such thing as a middle-aged man jogging on the street. Thus, he began his running in the privacy of our backyard.

He would circle the yard eight times to a mile; in time he wore a slender dirt path through the grass, as one mile grew to two. We would all stand on the porch and watch. Sometimes I ran behind him. But when I faltered after a lap or two, my father kept going. His workouts became even longer, until, predictably, the backyard track grew monotonous. Not to be contained any longer, he took to the streets, despite the honking of horns and the sounds of laughter from the cars that passed him. By then, he didn't care. Feeling the blood pumping through his body, the air filling his chest, and his deadened senses coming alive as the trees and hedges slid by, the scent of honeysuckle and fresh-cut grass wafting up at him, he sensed an awakening of his whole being. It signaled a complete change in his existence, a rejection of what had gone before. Years later, he would pen a kind of manifesto of running. In it, he said that running had made him realize that he had, in effect, been living someone else's life, not his own:

"At the age of reason, I was placed on a train, the shades drawn, my life's course and destination already determined. At the age of 45, I pulled the emergency cord and got off the train and ran into the world. It was a decision that meant no less than a new life, a new course, a new destination. I was born again in my 45th year.

"The previous me was not me. It was a self-image I had thrust upon me. It was the person I had accepted myself to be, but I had been playing a role."

It wasn't until years after I first read those words that I considered their implication: namely, that prior to running my father felt he had been living a lie. At the time, I suppose I passed this off as poetic license, seeing it as a metaphorically vivid description of psychic change and not a disavowal of fatherhood and of my own existence. So I never thought to wonder: if he was getting off the train, were my mother and the rest of our family still on it? Later, the depths of his discontent became clear—as did his resolve to put his entire life on a new path. Still, even back then, in the eyes of the town at least, my father was breaking out, making a bold statement, albeit of unclear intent. "Why does your father run around town in his underwear?" we children were asked. I recall being unable to answer, recall too a touch of embarrassment. My father, however, began to revel in the outrage his running provoked, and, in my mother's mind, he began to court it.

"George, you're not going outside dressed like that," she said one winter afternoon when he appeared in the kitchen wearing thermal long johns under his gym shorts. But it was to become his standard winter dress—and by no means the worst of his outfits. At Christmastime one year he tied angel's wings onto his back and went running down the road. He came upon a couple standing outside a moving truck, watching the movers unload furniture into their new house.

"Go back," he yelled. "They're all nuts."

"You better believe it," intoned one of the movers.

❧

IN TIME, MY FATHER ASSIGNED a whole host of astonishing personal transformations to running: it made him stop drinking, freed him from anger, got him in touch with himself, and made him a creative being. (These things were all true to some extent. But the degree to which he fell short of his self-description would always be a source of private jokes among his children.) As a boy of eight or nine, I noticed only that he grew a little kinder, a little less threatening. Then I became aware of something even more astonishing. For the first time in my life, he seemed to notice me. Perhaps one day during a backyard run he turned around and noticed me running after him. Or maybe he saw himself in the lonely way I skulked around the house. Whatever the reason, he started to spend time with me, taking me for long rides in his Volkswagen to races all throughout the region. In those early days of running there were almost always races on the weekends, but you had to be willing to travel far to find them.

On Saturday mornings before sunrise we climbed into his little metal shell of a car and waited for the reluctant engine, wheezing and moaning at the first turns of the ignition, to cough and turn over. Then we headed out through the dark suburban streets onto the parkway and the turnpike. We drove mainly in silence, each of us lost to his own thoughts, but the silence was always comfortable, companionable. I remember one morning when the bright orange ball of the sun rose through the tangle of power lines and over the refineries of North Jersey, and I watched him—his chiseled profile outlined in the orange glow. He looked like an Indian brave to me, and seeing him that way made me feel as though we were on some kind of mission or quest.

He had a distinctive way of driving, a style that for some reason has now become my own. Although his legs were long, he pulled the seat up so close to the steering wheel that he almost enveloped it in his chest. With his head crouched over the wheel, his great hawk nose was always threatening to touch the windshield. He insisted on driving a stick shift, although I learned later that he never really mastered it. He rode the clutch hard and slipped from fourth to neutral, braking without downshifting.

The car itself had a smell that my sisters found repulsively akin to the odor of a hamster cage, an olfactory hybrid made up of coffee cups, sweat-soaked shirts, and long-forgotten food wrappers, all stored in the backseat for future cleaning. For me it was the smell of those special outings, and I didn't mind. On the radio, he searched the dial for any kind of talk, preferring that to music, but those were the days before the all-news stations and the call-in shows. Once, when we were driving along the coastline, he tuned in a static-clouded station where men were talking about moving at so many "knots" and being that many miles "starboard." "That's the ship-to-shore transmissions," he said. "I used to listen to that in the navy." We listened to those distant voices out on the ocean as we traveled over the still-dark roads. We listened until ship-to-shore faded away, and my father captained us on into dawn.

One chilly fall morning we drove to Warinanco Park, a large expanse of fields and trees on the outskirts of working-class Elizabeth, New Jersey. Under a stadium grandstand was a locker room, smelling strongly of body odor and even more strongly of wintergreen liniment, and alive with the excitement of a dozen or so men getting ready for the race. My father joined them, happy to be part of the pre-race camaraderie, raising his voice as loudly as the rest. Then, they all filed outside to the cinder track, where they began running in place, trying to loosen up and stay warm. My father wore a shirt emblazoned with the words "Pioneer Track Club," which was more prophetic than any of them knew, for he and his friends were, in fact, pioneers of a practice that would in the future attract millions. On this late autumn morning, however, it was only their small group: a dozen pairs of cold legs on the starting line.

I ran too, my father entrusting me to a very tall and congenial black man who in earlier times had been a race walker. When the race started, the men lit out—once around the track before fanning out into the green grass of the park that lay beyond. I tried to stay as close as I could to the heels of the race walker but after a little while I began lagging. He stopped and waited, and then, seeing that I was tired, pointed me back to the stadium, where I waited for the men to return. As they came running back onto the stadium track, they all strained toward the finish line, my father grunting and groaning the loudest. Once over it, he panted and hobbled around with the rest of them in exhaustion; the men stumbled toward one another, laughing and slapping one another on the back. They smelled of sweat and wiped their runny noses on their forearms and spat great gobs into the dirt. I stayed close to my father and felt a tremendous jolt of pride when he began introducing me to his fellow runners. "This is my son Andrew," he said.

Once, on a hot Labor Day weekend, we drove all the way to Westport, Connecticut, and after the race we saw a photographer taking pictures. My father asked him to take a picture of us there on the courthouse steps. It's a picture I have today. In it, my father, dressed in running shorts and a tank top, is proud of his new athletic figure, showing it off in three-quarter profile. I'm wearing shorts but looking very awkward with dress shoes and black socks, shoulders squared to the camera. I look so serious as I squint into the sun. Sometimes, when I look at that photograph, the two of us seem so apart in the universes we were occupying that I want to jump into the photo and mediate. I want us to lighten up, to relax, and to enjoy each other. But mostly, I'm content to appreciate those weekend days for what they were: two people reaching out in loneliness as far as they possibly could.

CHAPTER FIVE

O NE DAY I FOUND a big wooden 1940s-vintage radio in a closet of our house, and I commandeered it for my own. I brought it up to my room and placed it on my desk at the head of my bed. It was open in the back, exposing its guts of wires and circuits and several long tubes, which glowed yellow-amber when I turned it on. Since I was afraid of the dark then, my mother would give me a choice at bedtime: I could either listen to the radio or keep the light on. I always chose the radio, and when she left the room, I would turn the radio around and listen to the tunes in the glow of the tubes. I listened to songs like "Be My Baby," by the Ronettes, and "Walk Like a Man," by the Four Seasons, at the lowest volume possible, and I fought off sleep to hear my other favorites late into the night.

When they started playing the Beatles in the winter of 1964, I waited to hear "She Loves You" and "I Want to Hold Your Hand." As I lay there alone at night, I actually believed they were performing live at WMCA radio station. In my mind, I pictured the four of them, standing in line, waiting to play, over and over again. The Sunday night they played for real on Ed Sullivan we all crowded around the television in anticipation, and when Ed swung his stiff arm in introduction, there was a great charge of excitement in the room. The camera doted on each one as they played, and we all engaged in rapid commentary. "That's Paul," said my sister Sarah, already an expert. "He's the cutest one." And, "That's George. He's the youngest." My mother, staring at the TV in apparent shock, said only three words, slowly and distinctly.

"Go, Rome, go."

It was more than their girlish hair and androgynous looks. It was as if in the screams of the young girls in the audience she could hear the floodgates opening. In the months that followed, as her own home became festooned with posters and other Beatle regalia, and my brothers and I grew bangs down to our eyebrows, she tried to turn back the tide. "Get that hair off of your forehead, once and for all," she demanded. She found boys with long hair, especially her sons, repellent. "What's the attraction?" she queried in frustration. "Why in the world would you want to look like a girl?"

If sexual ambiguity was what was bothering her, she never said so—not directly anyway. In a Catholic household, there was no more-uncomfortable a subject than sex. Only once do I remember an adult talking about it in our house, and tellingly that wasn't either my mother or my father. It was my grandfather. For a lark, my sister Ann asked him if he had married my grandmother out of passion.

"PASSION!?" he thundered. "Let me tell you something. The human body is the ugliest thing to look at in the world. Passion. It's gone in ten minutes."

Whether or not my mother shared this view, I would never know, and don't much care to know, possessed as I am of any child's ambivalence about the sexuality of his parents. What I did know was that she was rarely physically affectionate with her children, and that she often seemed disconnected from her own physicality.

My mother, though beautiful, was in many ways strangely at war with her good looks. At the same time that she had the vanity of a model—always well coiffed and neatly dressed, ever stealing glimpses of herself in the mirror—she distrusted her beauty, believing it had brought her unwarranted attention. She believed in substance and was disillusioned to discover that beauty opened doors too quickly. When she was younger she told people she couldn't wait to be forty, so people would stop doting on her looks.

With the boys, she never broached the subject of sexuality, though sex, or the fear of sex, always loomed large in the background. With the girls, there were early skirmishes over clothes that foretold future battles. When their school uniforms arrived each year, she produced a ruler to measure the inches from knee to hemline. If they wore something the least bit frilly, she derided it as "too kittenish" and told them to take it off.

"Men can't control themselves," she warned. "It's your responsibility not to encourage them."

When confronted with changing fashion, my mother tried to hold the line in her own house. In the mid-1960s, she fought things like Beatle haircuts and short hemlines—often unsuccessfully. Unfortunately for her, she would soon be fighting changes that posed much graver threats to her way of life.

∞

WITH HIS RUNNING, my father had become even more of a phantom than before. Sadly for me, he stopped inviting me along to his races and grew distant once again. It wasn't a cold distance—it was more benign than that—but he was distant just the same, if only because he was never around. During the week he was working, and on weekends he was traveling far for a race or running some incredibly long workout in preparation for a marathon. Only a year after he'd begun running again, my father ran his first Boston Marathon, a feat that thoroughly confounded us when he returned with the details of the long road from Hopkington to Boston, and the terrible Heartbreak Hill. It was twenty-six miles, an incredibly long distance; so incomprehensibly long that on our next long car trip we asked him to show us. "Okay," my father said as we drove. "We'll start here." At that point, we had just gotten onto the Garden State Parkway, and by the time he said, "All right, that's twenty-six miles," we were on the turnpike and more than halfway to New York City. We looked at one another in slack-jawed amazement.

After running in Boston he had driven all night to get home, and he hobbled stiff-legged around the house during the entire week that followed. A few months later he ran a marathon in Atlantic City, and when he got home that afternoon, he appeared in the doorway with a face of alabaster white. After he trudged slowly up the stairs to bed, his steps those of an old man, we heard him moaning from behind the closed door. My mother shook her head in bewilderment, but then attended to him uncomplainingly, bringing him tea and hot towels. It wasn't the running that disturbed her but the changes caused by running, which, for my father, ran deep.

Before running, there was no questioning Catholicism in our house. After running, my father remained a Catholic in name only. It wasn't something that happened overnight, but almost from the onset of those running forays into town, he began drifting away from the church. Within a year or two, he stopped going to mass completely. In those days he liked to tell the story of the runner who was reproached one Sunday morning as he ran by the church.

"You should be inside," the churchgoer told the runner.

"I've seen more of God in the last hour than you'll ever see in that church," the runner replied.

It might seem unremarkable now, but my father's rejection of Catholicism was a shocker at the time. Even now, leaving the church is not as easy as it may appear, not just because of the social stigma but the internal rumblings: the hooks are set very deep. Yet, if my father felt any ambivalence, he didn't show it. He merely stopped going to church and went running instead.

My mother, however, suffered terribly. For her it was both a private and a public hurt. She worried about his soul, and since his absence from the pew beside her could not be hidden, she worried about appearances, too. Perhaps even more painfully, she worried about the effect on us. And she made it clear that my father's defection was not an opportunity for discussion or debate. As we were being herded into the station wagon for Sunday mass one morning, my laggard brother Peter made the mistake of trying to opt out of the trip, saying, "Dad doesn't even go anymore." One hard glare from her ended such talk for good.

∞

MY MOTHER STILL ENJOYED throwing dinner parties then, especially the smaller, more intimate dinners with their closest friends. She used to feed us spaghetti in the kitchen while cooking a standing rib roast or a leg of lamb for her guests. Under the chandelier in the dining room, the table would already be set, with a fine white linen tablecloth and napkins setting off well-polished silver and long tapered candles. One of their best friends was a New York ad executive named Schuyler, a tall Dutch aristocrat who, no matter where he was, had the air of a man strolling a country-club patio. His tennis skills were legendary in our set, and one particularly daring and decisive act of athletic skill had put him into the pantheon in the eyes of us kids: called to the rescue one day when a bat was discovered flying through our house, Schuyler took his racquet and swatted it dead in one quick stroke as if returning a serve.

Schuyler wrote ads of a certain literary flair for Abercrombie & Fitch, which appeared in the *Times* and *The New Yorker*. Often he worked in references to my father, employing him as a kind of regular character in his copy: "As my running doctor friend in Rumson says . . ." Schuyler would write in the ads. He was a rare friend for my father, an intellectual peer. He had a loud booming voice and a great laugh to match it. Whenever he came over for a dinner party, I hung around the dining-room doorway to listen.

One night over dessert, coffee, and brandy, the conversation somehow turned to the subject of my father's absence from mass. Challenged by Schuyler, my father begin to take shots at legalistic Catholicism. To my mother's horror, he began scoffing at the infallibility of the Pope and the notion of mortal sin. "Where did they come up with all this stuff?" he chided.

My mother folded her arms in resignation and looked down as her beautifully planned dinner party began disintegrating. But Schuyler was captivated. Loving a good argument and having too good a time to stop, he egged my father on.

"So what are you going to do, Georgie boy?" he laughed. "What are you going to replace it with? All of your running around?"

"Why not?" my father returned. "I'm discovering my body," he said, and he began telling that table of Catholics that he had rejected the dualism of St. Paul—the notion that we must choose the spirit over the body. Rather, he said, he was "listening" to his body, remaking his body, and had found that by running every day, whole new worlds were opening up for him: emotional, intellectual, and spiritual. Further, he refused to see the body as an object of shame. While this may not have touched directly on the verboten topic of sex, my father was perilously close.

"The body is perfection," he said. "Even my body."

At this Schuyler threw back his head and let go a table-shaking laugh. "Oh, George baby, you're too much," he laughed. "You're really too much."

For the rest of the night my father glowered and seethed in silence. He had no tolerance for being ridiculed. After that night, the dinner parties came to a virtual end. My mother was left to balance two worlds: the world of her husband and the world they had once inhabited together. Even if he no longer wanted them, she would remain faithful to her friends and her faith. But while she kept at least one foot planted in that world, my father was rushing headlong into a new one of his own creation, and not looking back.

At the family dinner table, he now talked incessantly about running and the body. Every night, it seemed, we heard about the body and its majesty and potential. Every night, my mother endured his remarks in jaw-tightening silence. While we children didn't talk about it, I had become aware of the tension between them, and I sided with her. The nuns who taught us had put us squarely in the "body is bad" camp, and for me, all my father's talk had an alarmingly pagan cast. I was still the holy boy, still taking my place next to my mother in our church pew.

It would be wrong to say that my mother resisted all social change; she was, in fact, a liberal Democrat and something of a civil rights activist. One afternoon when I was a boy, I remember her moving the ironing board into the television room so she could watch the civil rights march on Washington. I sat down and watched with her, listening to the speakers on the steps of the Lincoln Memorial and marveling at the great masses of people flanking the reflecting pool of the Washington Monument.

"What are all those colored people doing, Mommy?" I asked.

"They've gone to Washington to ask President Kennedy for their freedom," she told me.

"Will he give it to them?" I asked.

"He'll try, dear," she said.

One summer a few years later, she invited five black kids down from Newark to spend the week with us. Whether or not she was aware of the trouble it would cause I don't know, but she brought them as guests to the beach club one morning. Before the end of the day, a number of club members had gone to the management to complain. When the managers asked her not to bring the black children back, my mother didn't argue. She simply took us all to the public beach for the rest of the week. She wasn't a radical, but she had her beliefs and she would not be deterred.

In Red Bank, where they had lived before moving to Rumson, the railroad tracks sliced through the town, separating blacks from whites; the blacks lived on the West Side, the "wrong" side of the tracks. Most of the women in Rumson had never set foot there. But my mother, who still had ties to Red Bank, had become something of a fixture in the black community, involving herself in many of its organizations. She made her biggest mark with the idea of turning an old school into a community center. When funds became the problem, she invited a hundred or so well-off friends to the house, fed them an elegant buffet, then sat them all down and hit them up for money.

The long and obstacle-riddled task culminated in a renovated building with community rooms and a basketball court, and I can remember going there on opening night, walking close to her through the dimly lit streets to the hall. Inside, I was startled to find that she was known by virtually everyone there—not only by the adults but by the little children as well, who addressed her deferentially as "Miz Shan." My mother moved easily and without a hint of awkwardness or fear, seemingly unaware of the respect she engendered—a beautiful, graceful woman, with more than a touch of street in her. That night, I felt intensely proud of her, but I also felt suddenly small to be next to a person of such substance. While I walked with her, I wished she had put a little more street in me.

∞

MY FATHER APPROVED of her work in the community but had no interest in participating in it. He was charting his own course, which seemed to have little to do with her—or any of us.

Although physically in our midst, he continued to occupy a separate mental space, which was becoming increasingly remote from ours. Each night, he sat in front of the television, surrounded by a pile of books—old books, dog-eared and frayed. He looked down at them through a pair of half-moon glasses, underlining the passages that struck him. There could have been a glass dome around him, so effectively did he filter out voices and conversation. But when something interested him—somebody on television, for example—he tuned back in. He'd look up over his specs for a minute or two, then return his gaze to the book in front of him.

In the afternoons, he haunted used-book stores for titles and authors long since discarded, convinced of the somewhat ecclesiastical notion that everything worth saying had been said before, probably better. "Don't read anyone unless they're dead," he told us. The first dead guys were the old Catholic standbys, Augustine and Aquinas, and then William James, Santayana, Ortega y Gasset. He didn't talk to us much except at dinner, where he'd use our conversations as opportunities to hold forth on his current dead philosopher of favor. "You know what [William James, Santayana, Ortega] would say about that," he would interject into whatever we were discussing, and then he would proffer this or that quotation. I couldn't help noticing that those philosophers seemed to claim a bigger share of his attention than we did. He was becoming an autodidact, hungrily amassing information from every source. There was no such thing as useless knowledge; every kind of knowledge produced ideas. Out on the roads, his workouts began getting longer and more frequent as he chased ever more eagerly after new ideas, for it was during his daily runs that they came to him. When he relayed them to us, I never really felt he was talking to us; he seemed to be using us as the most convenient sounding boards.

What seemed to bother my mother most about these intellectual forays was what she considered their frivolousness. My father had begun espousing the theory of a philosopher named Johan Huizinga, who proffered a new theory of the nature of man. Namely, that the race, known as "Homo sapiens" in recognition of its brain capacity, was just as much defined by its capacity for play and therefore should also be known as "Homo luden"—man the player. The concept proved a revelation. Homo luden. The phrase seemed to pop up in nearly every conversation. Running and the pursuit of knowledge became play, and play was the key that unlocked all doors. In play, there was a sense of wonder, he said, as he recounted the glory days of playing stickball as a schoolboy in Park Slope, when the world came alive through color, smell, and touch. We couldn't help but laugh when he told us, "I aspire to become a fifth-grader again," but our mother was not amused. "Be serious, George," she often pleaded.

But in his rejoining glare, I could see that he was as serious as a heart attack.

An uneasy silence developed between them, and she even grew impatient and quick-tempered with us, suddenly overwhelmed by the burdens of motherhood. "Oh, what is it now?" she would say whenever I bothered her with this concern or that. Where she had always been the accessible one, now she was as distant as our father was. It was as if she had another child with whom to contend—my father—and he was one child too many.

Like her children, my father was heading off in directions she couldn't, or wouldn't, follow. Also like her children, he would soon plant himself firmly at the center of the culture wars that had begun raging at the time. My father had too much of a tin ear to care about the Beatles, but he cared mightily about the Vietnam War, positioning himself in direct opposition to her.

In our house, as in houses across the country, the Vietnam debate had begun to rage. Never before had an international event taken on such immediate, personal significance. At the center of this were my older brothers George and Tim, who by the late 1960s were at my father's alma mater, Manhattan College, and both of draft age. Early and quickly, my father had made up his mind: he didn't want them to go. Perhaps it was the horror of his own war experience, but for him, any rationale for the Vietnam War paled when compared with its cost. It couldn't possibly be worth the lives of so many young men, let alone those of his own sons. He framed his opposition with a typically unique argument.

"Everyone has a piece of the truth in the world," he said. "Nobody possesses the whole truth."

It became his way of explaining that no religion, no government, no person had the big picture. Rather, he said, we all had just a piece of it, and that if we could respect each other's "piece of the truth," we wouldn't have war. "Who are we to force our piece of the truth on the Vietcong or anyone else?" he said.

On Sundays, our priest defended the war from the pulpit, chastising the dissidents, saying, "Theirs is not to reason why. Theirs is but to do and die." My father of course wasn't around to hear it, for he had stopped going to mass. And now the same willingness to question authority that had led him to question the priests and the Pope was causing him to criticize Lyndon Johnson and Dean Rusk and Robert McNamara. He called them liars. My mother believed this close to heretical, and, still hanging on to her belief that people in power told the truth, she dug in against him.

"These are our leaders, George," my mother said. "They know more about this than you do."

∞

WHAT EFFECT MY FATHER'S religious apostasy and his antiestablishment politics had on me is hard to pinpoint. I do know that in fifth grade, I gave up the idea of becoming a priest and changed from a brown-noser of nuns to a nun-baiter. In our town, there were rich boys who pretended to be gangsters, and I began to tag along. We rode our high-handled Stingray bikes like choppers through the tony suburban streets. I watched them steal *Playboys* and cigarettes from the local dime store and put cherry bombs in people's mailboxes. Soon, I was joining them in their exploits. Once, we stole the nuns' keys and made duplicates. At night we broke into the school and stole a few cases of soda. There was a shack in the woods behind the school, and after school we hung out there drinking the stolen hooch like we worked for Al Capone.

Our nuns were the Sisters of Mercy—old and old-school. The

school itself was attached to a retirement convent, and the nuns who taught us were getting their last whacks at spoiled little rich boys with annoyingly long hair. In seventh grade, the boys had a competition to see who could get whacked the most. We kept a tally, and I finished third, with something like nine slapping incidents.

They hit swiftly, the nuns, and from the belt. There would be a flash of white, and then the crisp smack of bony nun hand against my cheek. It would sting, turn tingly hot, and seem to hang there like a warm patch. I always felt like crying, but I didn't. Instead, I wore my reddened cheek like a badge of honor. I was relegated to the back of the room with the bad boys—a kind of murderers' row of bad boys—and from there we whispered comments when the nun turned her back: little matadors baiting the bull to charge. There was an older nun I used to taunt in this way. She hit me once, but then began to ignore me, acting as though she didn't hear my back-of-the-room remarks. She told everyone else to ignore me, too.

"Just pretend you don't hear him," she said. "He only wants attention."

She was right, of course, and deep down I knew it. Stuck in the attention-starved middle of my family, I was always lost in the shuffle, virtually ignored by both of my increasingly preoccupied parents. One night when I was in fifth grade, my mother and I were watching television, and I was surprised when she stroked my head and tousled my hair. It felt comforting and warm. When I asked her to do it again the following night, however, she snapped, "What's wrong with you that you need so much attention?" With the demands of twelve children, my mother often had trouble responding to each individual's needs, but I felt ashamed and weak for having asked.

Around this time there was a priest, a friend of the family, who would come to stay for long weekends. I think now that he must have known I lacked for attention, because he doted on me, asking me what I liked to read, what kind of music I liked, what I thought about things. One night, he told me to come up to his room to talk some more.

"You look cold," he told me when I got there. "Why don't you get in the bed."

"I'm not really cold," I told him.

"Get in the bed," he said.

And so I did, and when I did, his pants fell to the floor and he climbed into the bed with me. He put his hand down my underpants and pushed my hand onto his penis. Time seemed to stand still. We lay there in silence. The room we were in belonged to my brother John, and as if by rote, I began talking about the covers of *Sports Illustrated* John had pasted on the walls around us. "That's Carl Yazstremski of the Red Sox," I remember saying, as if anything I said could have made sense of what was going on. Then I told him I had to go to my room.

"Stay," he said.

"Father," I said, "I need to go to my room."

I sensed that he was angry.

"Oh all right, get out of here!" he said.

As I walked toward the door, he hissed, "Don't tell anyone about this."

When I walked down the hallway, I felt strange. Not hurt physically, but numb and strangely distanced from what had happened. I remember feeling as if I were outside myself, observing my body walking down the hall.

The following night I told my brother Peter what had happened, and we resolved to tell no one else. We decided only to have nothing more to do with the priest, and that's the way it was settled. From then on, I just kept the incident to myself as if it had never happened. In the weeks that followed, I looked back on that night, and I felt as though the experience had had no effect on me, no impact. I could only remember that strange numbness I'd felt just after it happened. That numbness returned whenever I thought of the incident—numbness and a strangeness that became more and more unpleasant. I began to build a shell around it, told myself not to think of it anymore. The shell grew thicker and thicker.

But I was changing, and the shell seemed to serve my changes well. No longer my mother's boy, I had begun looking to my father as a model. In the great Vietnam debate of 1967, though I secretly agreed with my mother, I was far more attracted to my father's side. My older brothers agreed with him, and so did my older sisters. As a sixth-grader, I put my questions aside and began parroting my father's politics as my own. I became precociously political, and in a gesture that rankled the nuns, I started wearing a peace button on my blue Catholic-school blazer.

"What is that thing?" one sister demanded to know.

"It's a peace button," I said.

"Do your parents know you wear that?" she asked.

"Yes, they do," I said smugly, throwing up what I knew to be a shield against confiscation.

The old rules were in flux, and even the nuns knew it. Our family was changing, too. When Christmas came around that year, my brother Peter suddenly poked his head into the room where we were all sitting in front of the television and shouted, "Timmy's a hippie!" With that he disappeared, and we all followed him into the kitchen, where my brother Tim stood with a suitcase, having just come back from his fall semester at college. He had, in fact, turned into a hippie. As he stood there, we stared incredulously at his long hair and mustache, his ripped jeans and tire-tread sandals. My mother walked in and gasped, putting her hand to her mouth. "Oh, Timmy," she said, her voice cracking, barely choking back tears. We kids followed him around the house—at a slight distance—as if he were a just-landed spaceman. We craned our necks around the doorway to the living room, just to see him sitting alone and cross-legged, listening to *Sgt. Pepper*. Then we looked at one another and shook our heads.

Unlike everyone else, my father was delighted by the change in his son—and the change in Tim's friends, as well, who were similarly hirsute, their faces suddenly concealed in bushes of hair and mustaches. My father not only welcomed them, he was completely enchanted. It was as if he had been waiting for years for them to show up. In contrast to his own hidebound friends, it seemed, these were people with whom he could hold a serious conversation, people not so invested in the status quo.

They talked on into the night, their discussions long and free-ranging. My father paced around and around the kitchen, engaging them in debates about politics, sex, and religion. As I saw him in the middle of this long-haired scrum, his head leaning forward, his eyes lit up, I felt his excitement. His mouth seemed always open, poised for interjection, anticipating the direction and flow of the discussion. I longed to be part of it, to be able to engage my father in this way. I envied my brother and his hippie friends. I wanted to be a hippie, too.

That winter, my father became a supporter of Eugene McCarthy, the gray-haired, poetry-writing senator from Minnesota, in whom he sensed a kindred spirit. On my school blazer, I began wearing a pin with the McCarthy campaign's multicolored dove. In the spring, my father ran as a McCarthy delegate in the New Jersey primary, with a campaign that consisted of one mailing. And although I can't remember my father ever making a speech or even knocking on a single door, I thought of how that flyer was showing up in mailboxes throughout our town, flaunting my father's "subversive" politics for all to see.

Even when my father lost the election, his effort seemed no less heroic to me. I wanted to be his ally, his fellow dissident. I scanned the newspapers and listened to underground radio, struggling to be able to stay on his level in talking about the politics of the day. There were even times when I seemed to be able to impress him with my knowledge. So I was crestfallen when my father's involvement with politics ended as quickly as it had begun. After the primary, he just lost interest. Martin Luther King had already been assassinated, and Johnson had announced he would not run. A month later, Robert Kennedy was shot and killed, and the country seemed to be coming apart. But even before the riots in Chicago and the election of Nixon, my father's focus on his burgeoning theories of fitness and sport had sent him hurtling in another direction. The year 1968 would prove to be a watershed not just for the country but for him. For in addition to everything else that happened that year, it was the year of the Mexico City Olympics. His experience there would change his life.

Except for his yearly trip to Boston, my father hadn't been outside of the New York, New Jersey, and Connecticut tri-state area since the end of World War II, more than twenty years before. And then came the opportunity to go to the Olympics. It came to him by way of a friend, a newspaper writer who was going to Mexico to cover the games. The local newspaper—*The Red Bank Register*—offered my father a chance to tag along. While they couldn't afford to pay him, they would be happy with any missives he could throw together on the games, they told him. He didn't hesitate to say yes, for it seemed a spectacular opportunity to see the games and to publish his first articles in a newspaper. But as the day of his departure grew near, doubt consumed him. The night before, he paced the kitchen floor, his hands deep in his pockets and his shoulders hunched.

"I don't want to go," he said. "I really don't want to go."

"George," my mother pleaded, "you can't back out now. It's already paid for."

"I know, but maybe I should just cancel."

The next day, he dragged himself reluctantly out the front door, a sad and lonely figure who folded himself up into his friend's car and was driven away. Within a few days his stories began appearing in the *Register,* and two weeks later he returned ebullient and smiling. The same kitchen where he had paced in fear could now barely contain his excitement. He told us of being uplifted by the spectacle of the parade of nations in the Estadio Olympico, of being caught up in the wild exuberance of the Mexicans with their flag waving and cheering.

Mexico was the living embodiment of everything he had been talking about in theory, his ideas of sport and human potential made flesh. He'd been privileged to circulate through the Olympic Village itself, which seemed a kind of utopia, a community of people of many different nationalities all chasing greatness, all bound together by their common pursuit. In the morning, he ran with world-class steeplechasers Gaston Roelants and George Young, his own credentials never questioned. The spirit of community in the Olympic Village was inclusive enough to make him feel a part of it. Curiously, the Olympics caused him to think beyond winning and losing. As he said in one of his articles, it was a "competition distinguished as much by camaraderie as by performance." When he went to see the weight lifters, he stood with his friend outside the staging areas when they finished.

"How did you do?" his friend asked the weight lifter.

"Eighth," the lifter said dejectedly.

"Eighth in the world," my father's friend said.

And the weight lifter suddenly lightened and smiled in newfound self-satisfaction. And so that became their standard chat with the athletes.

"How did you do?"

"I got twelfth."

"Twelfth in the world," they would say.

Each competitor had lived up to his or her potential, and to my father, that became the important thing—not necessarily the winning. America's great miler Jim Ryun struggled in the heat and high altitude while Kip Keino beat him handily in the 1,500 meters. But Ryun, my father would write, had run a great race, one of the best in his career, the best race he possibly could have run. My father gloried in having seen Bob Beamon shatter the long jump world record and at seeing Beamon sob so hard at his own achievement that he couldn't stand up. The whole experience stunned my father. So great the sense of honor, so great his sense of privilege to witness it all that he couldn't help but become angered when politics interceded, even though he shared the protesters' views.

When American sprinters Tommie Smith and John Carlos went to the awards stand, they threw their black-leather-gloved fists in the air and looked down when the National Anthem was played. My father struggled with his feelings.

"The Mexicans couldn't understand it," he said. "For them to do that was just bad—really bad."

He wrote a piece in the paper that seemed almost to endorse the medal-stand protest, in its condemnation of ABC's nationalist Olympic coverage, which insisted on tallying the number of U.S.

medals and ranking them against other nations. In truth, however, the Smith-Carlos protest bothered him deeply. He couldn't get beyond the feeling that it was a distasteful and grossly impolite act of radical politics.

Mexico had given him a new vision. On his return, he was jubilant—even triumphant—at having witnessed an event of such extraordinary power. It was a wonder to see him at the head of our very long kitchen table, a once stony presence now transformed, suddenly unable to stop talking. Gone was his reserve as he gestured wildly with his arms, describing this jump or that race. He continued unabated until he noticed my mother eyeing him from the other end of the table.

"Well, did you miss me?" he asked expectantly.

He didn't get the answer he wanted.

"No," she said curtly. "You weren't gone long enough."

She continued eating her dinner as my father's chin dropped to his chest, his mood suddenly deflated.

Even though I was still young and they were still together, it was clear to me that my parents had become badly out of tune. When they spoke to each other in their tense, labored way, it was impossible not to hear the errant bow sliding off the cello strings. I believe my mother must have felt my father slipping away, and his search beyond his family, his medical practice, and his church must have frightened her. And still her actions could surprise you. After Mexico, when the *Register* asked my father to become a regular sports columnist, it was my father who balked, and my mother who encouraged him.

"You have something to say," she told him. "You should say it."

In his writing, she would support him as she always had. Long ago, she had fallen in love with his integrity, his deep intelligence. In honoring that, she had provided a framework in which he could function, had managed the details of his daily life. Now, he seemed to be asking for something more. And she was either disinclined or unable to provide it.

He did at last agree to write a weekly column about running and fitness for the paper. This column, which my mother had encouraged him to write, seems to have been the first of its kind in the entire country, and it launched him on a new career. In prodding him forward, she had inadvertently pushed him toward a whole new life—one that would eventually exclude her.

In the summer of 1969, Tim, the hippie, went to Woodstock, and in the fall he found out that his girlfriend was pregnant. Even though Maureen wasn't yet showing, my mother quickly discerned the situation; she confronted Tim and then ordered him upstairs to tell my father. Tim dutifully dragged himself upstairs and found my father in his bedroom, lying on the bed, reading a book and watching the Jets on his little black-and-white television. Tim sat down on the bed beside him, but before he could muster the courage to break the news, my mother came in.

"Well, did you tell him?" she said.

Unable to stall any longer, Tim finally got the words out: "Maureen's pregnant. We're going to get married and have the baby."

"Well, that's a good start," my father said.

My mother got angry.

"George, don't make a joke out of this," she flared.

"Don't tell me how to react," my father snapped back.

My mother left the room, and Tim and my father went back to watching the football game.

"You'll be fine," my father said. "I'm not sure about your mother and me."

As the decade closed, my mother, like my father, disappeared from the house. Most nights after feeding us, she would rise from the table and announce that she was off to one meeting or another, pursuing this social cause or that. On the nights when he was not at the paper typing his column, my father sat on the floor before the television surrounded by his fortress of books and papers, reading and writing. If I attempted to interrupt his mental juggling act it was at my own peril, for he was loath to stop his activities for questions or comments from his children. If on occasion I dared anyway, he generally stared straight ahead while I spoke, only to mutter something curt in response. I began to realize that I stood in the way of him and whatever he was focused on. I had become a bother, an obligation, an obstacle.

CHAPTER SIX

I SEE MYSELF QUITE OFTEN these days. He's a latter-day version of the teenager I was twenty-five years ago—hair down to his shoulders and parted in the middle, hands sunk deep into the pockets of a pair of torn jeans. Sometimes when I'm running in the park, I pass him, walking alone, looking up at the trees or staring blankly at his shuffling feet. Other times when I'm driving I catch a glimpse of him walking on the sidewalk, deep in thought, oblivious to the roar of the passing cars. Startled for a second, I have to force myself to refocus before continuing on.

Sometimes I see him sitting on a playground swing, hanging with a few of his friends, sneaking a joint between cupped hands, a scene so reminiscent of my youth that I shudder. I remember what it was like to feel the gradual onset of the pot, subtly changing the whole nature of the swings, the seesaw, the sandy soil, remember fixating on the rusted bolts as if they could tell me something I needed to know. But I knew only that I was frozen in time, stuck somewhere between childhood and adulthood. When I thought of the future, I felt paralyzed. As I sat there stoned on the swing, I didn't tell the others, but I was scared to death.

It stayed with me for years, that feeling of being caught in between times, waiting for things to change. It's as though I was forever consigned to the backseat, stuck back there with the second half of my family, always observing the others in front. There were seven others up there—Peter, Sarah, Nora, Ann, Tim, George, and Mary Jane— plenty of people to emulate, plenty of mistakes from which to learn, although I was always adept at inventing new ones of my own.

Frightened as I was, I grew up after the really scary times. I was too young to be drafted in Vietnam—too young to be a bona-fide hippie. Real hippies called kids like me "mini-freaks"—the junior version, not quite official. I was fourteen years old in 1970, and spent the summer before high school hitchhiking around the county with some other mini-freaks, hanging out in the parks where the real hippies hung out. We grew our hair long and began smoking pot just like them. I listened to Dylan and the Beatles, read Salinger and Kerouac. I knew I was on to something, and it felt like something very big. But I was right to be afraid. I was heading for some serious trouble.

Today, when I see that teenage boy, I feel far more kindly toward him than I did to myself at the time. I was embarrassed by the pettiness of my own little drama when I was living it, contemptuous of the inconsequential nature of my despair. Today, I know that even rich boys get the blues—and I know how serious they can be.

∞

FROM THE OUTSIDE it might have appeared that I had begun coming into my own. Once I ceased laying claim to early sainthood and became combative with the priests and nuns, as I did starting in fifth grade, I found that combativeness made me cool. No longer the outsider, I suddenly had new standing in our class, a popularity with the most popular boys. Even with my peace button stuck on my blazer and my newly shaggy hair, I was considered cool enough that the kids in my class accepted my difference.

Basketball was another social bond. The Knicks were everything to me and my friends in those days—Clyde, Jazzy Cazzie, Dollar Bill, and later the Pearl. Every day after school, I joined the others on the blacktop behind the school, each of us choreographing elaborate fantasies of greatness as we threw up rainbows of basketballs at the aluminum backboard and listened for the elusively satisfying *swish* of the ball sinking unimpeded through the net. Day after day, we refined and honed our game.

I made the team, and in eighth grade I landed the prettiest cheerleader, whom I kissed for the first time in the back of the bus returning from a tournament one night in North Jersey. Our wet lips slid against each other's until she slipped her tongue into my mouth, showing me how. My heart raced for days, and I wanted nothing but to be with her and to kiss her again. After school, I found excuses to leave the basketball court so I could meet her in secret places we had designated in advance. One rainy afternoon, we went to the shack behind the school. There were shards of broken glass on the wooden floor, and an ancient mattress where we lay down. We kissed there for hours but dared go no further. In her arms in that musty shed with drops of rain falling through the leaky roof, I felt at home.

"I love you," she said.

"I love you, too," I said.

It was true. I did love her, but as the year went on, I found it difficult to be with her. When she told me she loved me, her feelings didn't match the way I felt about myself, and the result was that I began to distrust her. Perhaps she didn't really love me. Or if she loved me, she had been duped, I reasoned, and I reasoned further that her love must therefore not be worth anything. I began feeling that my popularity in school was fake as well. If the other kids wanted to be my friends, their friendship was based on something equally counter-feit. I began to believe that it would be easier to be alone. Playing my rebel role to the hilt, as though determined to make an outcast of myself, I refused to cut my hair for graduation, and the nuns forbade me to attend the ceremony. After that, I broke up with the girl, stopped playing basketball, stopped seeing those friends.

∞

WHEN I REACHED HIGH SCHOOL, I was a stoner. I drifted through the hallways high, trying to be invisible, trying to blend into the institutional green of the lockers. I had virtually no friends except for other stoneheads—vacant-eyed, long-haired boys of stammering speech who cultivated an image of serious drug use. Most were being brought up by single parents, either widowed or divorced, and most of those parents were working or otherwise occupied in the afternoons, so we had our pick of houses at which to meet after school. We holed up in the attics of those houses, smoking pot and listening to bluesy British rock. And we were moving on to other drugs, more dangerous drugs, as they became available.

I had decided not to go to Christian Brothers—the Catholic boys' school that my father had founded—and opted instead for the local public high school. I'm sure it hurt my father, but he didn't say much about it. Since he was now espousing a "do your own thing" philosophy, what could he say? For my part, I knew I didn't want to be in a school of all Irish and Italian boys; I wanted to blaze my own trail. When I got to high school, however, I just merged with the anonymous heap of freshmen and felt terribly alone. I missed my old girlfriend; I missed my old friends. But in a very short time I found the dopers. At least with them I didn't have to put on a show.

After school, we cleaned the stems and seeds of the pot on the covers of old Cream records and listened to Clapton's guitar breaks on "White Room" and "Crossroads" over and over again. For fun, we'd listen to the Mothers of Invention, hooting as Frank Zappa sang "I'm losing status at the high school . . . I used to think that it was my school," which invariably provoked us into outbursts of derision against the football players and the cheerleaders and all the others we viewed as social climbers. Among us wayward boys there was no real communication—just a tacit understanding that we were all damaged goods. Simply by virtue of knowing this, we had minted a kind of pact: we were living on the edge, but at least we were all on it together. That's what passed for community, and it was about as much community as any of us could stand.

Each of us was trying to find an escape from family and school, from futility and boredom. On Friday nights we went out driving in the ever-vanishing countryside of Central Jersey, listening to loud rock music and getting high. It was aimless, destinationless driving, but it helped to pass the hours. I liked to sit near the open window, feel the wind and watch the dark fields fly past. Sometimes we drove the restricted military roads, straight-shot roads with no traffic, where we tried to tip eighty miles an hour.

And still I was different—even from them. I was leading something of a double life. I had a sport and that made me a jock. In high school, I ran both track and cross-country, reserving a special affinity for cross-country. And here I fell in with another group of misfits—science geeks mostly, who had joined the team simply because no other sport would have them. Each autumn afternoon, our nerdy band ran out of Rumson and over the Navesink River Bridge into the wooded and leafy enclave of Locust, a town of old farms and wealthy country estates. Roller-coaster trails snaked through the woods there, and I loved running through the amber, red, and purple-leaved trees with the dappled sunlight falling on our bony shoulders. I, of course, was the hippie of the group. Always wearing a red bandanna around my head to keep the long hair out of my face, I thought of myself as an Indian warrior on some kind of spiritual quest. For my father, running was about expanding the boundaries of human potential; for me, it was a search for transcendence, and there were times when I felt I'd achieved it, when there was a freedom and happiness that came flooding through me as I ran.

Bob Dylan was another sort of high, another form of transcendence. His music became like a place to me—a dark, dreamy world into which I could always flee. He had come into our house via the folksingers who preceded him. My father was partial to the Weavers and Pete Seeger, and my brother George bought albums by the Kingston Trio and Peter, Paul and Mary. In and around that time, a copy of Bob Dylan's *Freewheelin'* found its way onto the living-room turntable, causing a minor uproar.

"Who is that whiner?" my mother complained.

Forever after, she hated the sound of his voice, though for years she heard little else drifting from the living room as I stacked his albums on the spindle. To Dylan I applied the same diligence I once had to Yankee batting averages, committing every lyric to memory, grappling with his circus of desultory images, trying to divine the hidden messages. At night, I surreptitiously smoked dope outside, then came back in to listen to "Queen Jane Approximately" and float on top of this poetry of futility. In a highly charged, highly romanticized way, Dylan's lyrics defined and framed my own wayward life, and I began to see myself in their words and images. "Mr. Tambourine Man" lent poignancy to my druggie forays into the night. "Positively 4th Street" fueled my anger against people I thought of as enemies. Listening to Dylan made it feel good to be all banged up and wounded. He made it all seem vaguely heroic.

So I listened on into the nights, fantasizing about becoming a kind of mystic poet myself. When I failed in my attempts to write like Dylan, I found it easy just to pretend that I *was* Dylan—a great poet, only in waiting. I bought a leather jacket, smoked cigarettes, and walked the beach at night, swinging back and forth between feelings of uselessness and some narcissistic notion of future greatness. Confronted with failure, I could always seek cover in that grandiose image of myself.

My mother saw me drifting away before her eyes. When my friends came to pick me up on Friday nights, she was horrified, assuming that these scruffy, long-haired misfits were the cause of my drifting. "It ain't their fault, Ma," I would say to myself in mock Dylanese. "I'm a lost boy, too." One night as I was walking out the door, she grabbed me by my arm and swung me around. "Be careful," she said, and her voice quivered and broke as she said it. Our eyes locked, and I saw the alarm and fear in her eyes, sensed her despair. But she could never really give voice to her fears, couldn't bring herself to be any more direct.

Minutes later, I was riding around with my friends, smoking a joint and staring out the window. But the encounter had shaken me. I felt guilty for causing her to worry. At the same time, I couldn't begin to explain to her what was wrong. How could I tell her about a pain I couldn't name?

∞

MY FATHER AND I HAD BEGUN living in completely separate worlds. Even though we lived in the same house, we were two planets spinning in separate orbits, I drifting in from my pot-smoking afternoons and he moving from one pile to another of his books and papers. We circled each other in avoidance, each fearful of being intruded upon, each reluctant to enter the other's world. If I was in trouble, he seemed not to notice. What was worse, he seemed not to care. Mainly, he seemed not to want to know, the better to be able to focus single-mindedly on what was now his primary pursuit—his new career of writing and philosophizing.

Though he was still practicing medicine in those days, his interests clearly lay elsewhere. His weekly column consumed him—the great newspaper beast ever demanding to be fed. He rampaged through his books and magazines in constant search of new ideas, any scraps he could throw its way. But after a time the beast could not be sated. My father would need a steadier, more substantive source of ideas. He needed a philosophy—a cogent system of thought, a wellspring from which he could continually draw. And that's what he was in the process of developing in those days.

"Life is an experiment of one," he liked to say, and he became that experiment in progress, converting our house into his laboratory. In short order, his nascent philosophy of running and sport began to expand, not only in its intellectual scope but in its demand for physical space. When his papers and books could no longer be confined to his bedroom, he staked out more and more of the house for his obsessions. The living room and the hallways became an obstacle course of paper mounds. Great leaning towers of manila folders teetered at the edges of the dining-room table. Oblivious to anyone else's needs or priorities, he moved the piles from place to place, ever adding to their girth with new clippings and correspondence. Though he was close enough to touch, he was now a citizen of another world. Oddly enough, however, I knew that as separate as our worlds were, they were also somehow parallel. I concluded, from what he said at the dinner table and from what I read in his newspaper columns, that my father was a hippie—just like me.

Although he never grew his hair long, the philosophy that would someday make him famous seemed to me to be a direct outgrowth of hippiedom. In the simple act of running—of putting one foot in front of the other—he had found something that was more than the sum of its parts, something that would eventually coalesce into a philosophy so idealistic that it seemed another outgrowth of the counterculture. I saw him construct it, piece by piece, as his dinner-table spoutings found their way into his newspaper columns. "Less is more" and "Do your own thing" were the underpinnings of what he wrote. In his running, my father had found a new, stripped-down freedom, and the hippie in me couldn't help but admire the Thoreau–like austerity.

After all, he liked to say, running cost you virtually nothing. All anyone needed was an old pair of Hush Puppies and perhaps an old sweatshirt. "The ideal warm-up suit is a grey non-descript Salvation Army cast off," he would write. "Anything more would be a burden, and it has advantages. No one would bother to steal it." Like the hippies, he abandoned the constraints of conventional fashion. Having never cared much about the way he dressed, he now seemed not to care at all. Where he had rarely worn ties before, he now forswore them forever.

"I will never buy another suit, a shirt and tie or a pair of dress shoes," he wrote. "For the runner, less is better. The life that is his work of art is understated. His needs are little, his wants are few: one friend, few clothes, a meal now and then, some change in his pockets, and for enjoyment his thoughts and the elements."

When I read these things, I thought how strange it was to have a hippie for a dad. Even if he was a distant father, he had left me little to rebel against. Rebelling against him would have meant putting on a Brooks Brothers suit and applying to Wharton. And even though he had abandoned politics while I remained an activist, he was tilting at the same windmills, taking dead aim at his entire generation.

We may call them the great generation now, but even though they had defeated Hitler and built a new America, my father seemed unwilling to give the people of his own generation their due. Instead he wrote searing criticisms, perhaps even more venomous than those of the young people throwing stones. He was contemptuous of his generation not so much for making war in Vietnam but for making a waste of everything else—a waste of their bodies and a waste of their lives. It was his opinion that his peers had very little to show for their single-minded pursuit of money and security except for conspicuous wealth and even more conspicuous potbellies. He railed against "Flabius Americanus"—the fat American.

If that seemed harsh even to me, I couldn't help but admire his courage when, long before others, he took on the American medical establishment. It wasn't a fight I particularly cared about at the time, but the sheer rebelliousness of it was appealing just the same. Sinking his teeth into the soft, plump hand that had fed him throughout his life, he wrote: "The United States is the best place in the world to be sick—but the last place in the world you want to remain well." As we heard time and again over dinner, he believed that the physician's mission should be wellness—not just the treatment of sickness and disease. One of the first voices for preventive medicine, he went beyond that to suggest that the medical establishment was actually discouraging people from living healthy lives, since doctors routinely cautioned against "stressful activities" involving intense physical exertion. "If the aim of the medical profession is to stop the average

American from exercising," he wrote, "it couldn't have done a better job."

In assailing the ethos of Western medicine, he even touted alternatives such as acupuncture. And in a column that would have made any hippie proud, he praised fourteenth-century Tibetan physicians who had given up surgery and relied instead on trying to turn bad karma into good. Karma, it seems, was a more worthwhile barometer of health than electrocardiograms. "Mostly one's health is dependent on having good karma—a combination of a good lifestyle and the expression of real self in the sum total of thoughts, words and deeds. A bad karma causes illness."

When I heard it and read it, I found his argument compelling. The medical establishment had things ass-backwards: our culture invited us prematurely to death's door, where we would be miraculously saved by billion-dollar technology. Wouldn't it be better, he argued, if we could avoid illness in the first place? Wouldn't it be better to live a healthy life?

My father believed that the best way to deal with sickness was to stay well, and the best way to stay well was to exercise. It was not a new idea. It had been advanced quite thoroughly by a cardiologist who was a friend of my father's, Dr. Kenneth Cooper, of Houston. Years before, in his book *Aerobics,* Cooper had described the health benefits of exercise that worked the cardiovascular system, citing data in support of the idea that sustained exercise in general, and jogging in particular, could help people lose weight, lower cholesterol, and prevent heart attacks. Dr. Cooper and his book had, in fact, spurred a short-lived fad for running back in the late sixties. Unfortunately, it didn't catch on, and people settled back into their sedentary routines. Now, my father aimed to become a better salesman.

In addition to the column he wrote in our local paper, he started one in *Runner's World*, a small but nationally distributed magazine published out of California. Quoting Chesterton, who said that one should never do anything "just because it is good for you," he began selling fitness not as castor oil—something unpleasant but good for you—but as a source of fun. His pitch was the idea of play.

"Play is the key," he wrote. "We all love to play. We only like the jobs that have a play element for us. Anything as practical as physical education is not going to get to first base with most of us." If play was the thing, then we should all try to "discover our play." Although my father's play was obviously running, he didn't want to be prescriptive. People should bike, swim, cross-country ski—whatever they liked. "Do your own thing," he said, always adding the proviso: "as long as it raises your heart level to more than 120 beats a minute for a half hour—four times a week."

From my seat at the dinner table, I had heard about play for years, and, following his prescribed example, I had become a loyal "Homo luden" myself. I already knew that in my father's universe, play wasn't just a way to get in shape: it was life altering. And mind altering, too. Here my father took a rare foray into psychology, or more specifically into the work of one psychologist, Abraham Maslow, who wrote of so-called peak experiences, describing them as those moments "when a person's powers are at their absolute heights, and he becomes a spontaneous, coordinated, efficient organism functioning in the great flow of power that is so peculiarly effortless that it may become like play—masterful, virtuoso-like." A life of play would yield many such moments, and I was on board for these peak experiences, ready to join my father in pursuit of them. The purpose of play, it seemed to me, was to remain a hippie. Running would be my way of achieving a natural high, which, unlike a drug high, would be sustainable and healthy. Even through my worst times, even when my father and I weren't talking at all, I still ran.

Then in the summer after my freshman year, the chilly silence between us seemed to thaw. There were no bad report cards, no school controversies to fill the house with tension, and every Monday night there was a race. It was our favorite race of all, five kilometers around a seaside lake called Lake Takanassee, in the fading coastal town of Long Branch. We would set out to drive there a few hours before sunset, and as we rattled down the road in his Volkswagen, I felt a renewed sense of closeness with him. Our meeting place was the Church of St. Michael, a large red-brick Roman Catholic church next to the ocean-fed lake, with a statue of Michael the Archangel raising his sword over the front lawn. Every Monday we found a group of a hundred or so runners gathered off to the Archangel's side, awaiting the start in the orange light of dusk. We ran four times around with an extra straightaway to make it just that more painful in the end. For my father, it was home court, and he loved its every detail, as he loved the hometown attention of the other runners.

"Hey, Doc," they called out when we arrived. "I'm gunning for you tonight, Doc."

We always ran hard into the summer sun, which would begin setting on the idyllic little lake as we circled it. Afterward, we drove to the lemon ice stand on the boardwalk, then walked down to the beach for a quick dip before the sun went down. Stepping out of the surf, toweling ourselves off, we felt alive and happy. And as we trudged up the beach with the sound of the waves breaking behind us, it was easy for me to believe that the distance between us was not very far, that we could hold on to the feeling we had at those moments.

The camaraderie of our Monday nights at Takanassee, however, proved as ephemeral as the fading sunlight shimmering on the water. Though my father espoused running as a curative for all that ailed, it was not enough to deliver or transform me. When I looked inside myself I felt a pain and I saw an ugliness. And feeling and seeing that made everything on the outside ugly, too. A dull gray miasma tainted my world and everything in it.

But I don't think I ever seriously thought about unburdening myself to my father. As close as I felt to him on those nights, I had already seen that he wasn't really looking for company on his journey. Running was not a team sport. Life, as he said, was an experiment of one. He invited everyone to pursue their play and peak experiences—but on their own, not with him. He was a loner, unable to reach out to other people—even people in trouble. It was nothing personal. He just didn't have it within himself to do otherwise. His burgeoning philosophy fortified that insularity.

∞

ONE NIGHT IN THE KITCHEN my father attempted to justify the moat he had dug around himself to keep us at bay. He was standing hunched over, his back turned to us, his family, as we sat at the dinner table. In response to something one of us said, he wheeled around with arms wide and pleading. "Look," he said. "I'm an ectomorph. What do you want from me?"

Chasing down one of his more obscure philosophical tangents, he had latched on to a theory called "constitutional psychology," put forward by a Dr. William Sheldon of Harvard, whom he had been quoting of late. Sheldon theorized that body type was destiny, in terms of one's psychological and emotional makeup. The three basic body types, which Sheldon called "somatotypes," accounted for much of what we think of as distinctive about ourselves. For example, my father, being thin and frail, was an ectomorph. This body type made people shy, retiring, and solitary by inclination. People of medium or muscular build were called mesomorphs, and fat or obese people were called endomorphs. Mesos like violent encounters and mixing it up on the football field or in life, endos enjoy a reputation for affability while ectos wish only to be left alone.

In my father's view, this theory went a long way toward explaining his own nature and proclivities. It explained why, for example, he had picked a noncontact activity like running. "Football," he explained, "is an act between consenting adults." It was a game designed for mesomorphs and endomorphs, who had a primal need to beat the crap out of each other. The body-type theory also informed his entire view of the world, and what was left of his political concerns. He recognized then-President Nixon and his secretary of defense, Melvin Laird, as mesomorphs and felt that that accounted for their having expanded the war in Vietnam. Squat, bald, and tense, Laird seemed to epitomize the world leader as aggressor, a man who repelled him at the most visceral level.

"Just to look at him," he said one night, recoiling in revulsion from the television, "is to know what kind of guy he is."

A side benefit of embracing this theory was that it absolved him from any obligation to change. Body type, after all, defined a person's emotional or psychological disposition, even his own. Being thin and fragile was all the explanation required to explain why he was the way he was. He no longer had to apologize for his asocial tendencies. In declaring himself an ectomorph, he was claiming his right to remove himself from polite society—including ours, if he so chose. "I am the person of my youth," he wrote. "The person who was hypersensitive to pain, both physical and psychic, a nominal coward. The person who did not wish his neighbor ill, but did not wish him well either. That person was me and always had been."

My father used Sheldon's theory to rationalize and justify all sorts of objectionable behaviors, often to lengths that would have seemed comical if he hadn't been so cool and distant. While no one in my family was brazen enough to challenge his adequacy as a father, we didn't hesitate to make jokes about the lack of medical attention we got when we were sick or his ability to tune us all out. His response was, "Look, I'm an ectomorph. What do you want from me?"

I was an ectomorph, too. Once, when I remarked on this fact, hoping that he'd acknowledge a common bond, my father agreed. "That's right," he said glibly. "We both had a horrible childhood, and we both like to be alone." Conversation finished. That is how things got said in my family. Only in flip asides or in displays of anger could important things be told, and he was indeed telling me something important—that the fact that I saw myself in him, and he saw himself in me, was the opposite of a bond. The very traits we had in common ensured that we would remain separate and apart. The best he seemed able to offer was benign neglect. I didn't really know what I wanted from him. I only knew that I wanted something more.

CHAPTER SEVEN

H E SEEMED TO BE A HAWK, my father.
When I was in high school, I used to watch birds. I'd roll a
joint and set off into the woods with my Peterson guide under my
arm. There, I'd search the blue swatches of sky through the branches
and scan the tree limbs, looking for anything I hadn't spotted before.
I'd go on looking for hours, crunching the brown underbrush and
fancying myself some kind of hippie naturalist or latter-day John
Muir. But in my search for warblers, vireos, thrushes, and tanagers,
those Jersey woods usually yielded nothing more than everyday
robins and jays. Sometimes when I was out walking it did occur to
me that it was a little affected, this bird-watching thing. One afternoon, wandering around stoned and alone, I felt oppressed by my
own affectations, a prisoner of my own pretense. I was about to turn
back when I heard a sudden rustle of branches. I looked up to see a
dark flash of wings—the broad, muscular wings of a large bird flapping hard against the sky. It was a hawk flying out of the trees, and
for a few seconds I watched as it rose above the highest branches be-

fore disappearing behind them. A hawk in New Jersey, no less. To me, a great victory for nature; a minor miracle.

When I saw that hawk fly out of the woods that day, it struck me that that was what my father seemed to be. He was like some great bird, strangely out of place, cast there by fate, trying to get free. I suppose it was my father himself who planted that notion. In one of his newspaper columns at the time, he had identified himself as a hawk, wanting to be self-sufficient and free, and he quoted Thoreau, who once observed such a hawk in the sky over Concord.

"It appeared to have no companion in the universe and to need none but the morning," Thoreau wrote. "It was not lonely but made all the world lonely beneath it."

The day I recognized my father in that hawk, I began to understand him. He was alone but not lonely, unfettered by convention, keeping no one's counsel but his own as he sought some higher truth. My father seemed to need no companions, for he was becoming a kind of world unto himself—increasingly hard to approach, and, like Thoreau's hawk, a source of loneliness in me. Those nights at Takanassee, he seemed to be a hawk as well. Magnificent in profile, his chest puffed out, and that great hawk nose cutting the air as he glided smoothly, economically, effortlessly over the pavement. On hotter nights, he fashioned a handkerchief into a hat. Knotted at four corners and fitted snugly atop his head, it looked like a bird's crown, and while he ran his blue-gray eyes darted beneath it, searching for the next water stop. He seemed hawklike by nature, not so much predatory but independent and searching, alone in his pursuits and happiest that way. When obligated to be social, he looked like a hawk trapped, resentful of his captors and scheming his escape. When freed, he liked to fly alone.

∞

STILL, THROUGHOUT THOSE difficult high school years, he always seemed somehow within reach. Perhaps that was because even when he showed no other interest in me, my father was always interested in my evolution as a runner.

Where he had never deigned to teach me anything before, he freely dispensed detailed instructions about running, training, and technique. "Shorten up your stride," he counseled. "Maybe try some intervals," he advised. "Breathe with your belly," he prescribed. The same thing applied to running injuries. One day I told him my running was causing me chronic knee pain and he stopped everything he was doing to attend to it, sitting me up on the dining-room table and flexing my leg up and down.

"Does it hurt now?" he asked. "Now? How about now?"

He stood back and rubbed his chin.

"I don't know," he said. "You might need the orthotics."

While it was nice to bask in that attention, I wondered: was he really concerned about me or just me the runner? Any problem that wasn't about running was met with complete indifference. Once when I complained to him about a strep throat, he didn't even look up from his book. "Take some penicillin," he said and kept on reading. In one sense, all of his children who ran were like laboratory mice to him. Since he wrote about sports medicine and the treatment of such injuries, he had a whole stable of subjects on which to try out various remedies. But it was deeper than that. My father really did believe in running. Perhaps he felt that in running everyone would find their own way, just as he had.

In the spring of my sophomore year in high school, I became very serious about my running. Early in the track season, I ran a 4:45 mile, a very respectable time that I aimed to lower into the 4:30s in the season ahead. So great was my resolve that I stopped my pot smoking and even cut off my long hair to reduce wind resistance. On the weekend before the Boston Marathon, one of my father's friends called to say he couldn't make the trip. The man offered my father his race number in case anyone wanted to run in his stead.

"Why don't you come up and run it," my father said to me.

"Boston?" I asked, stunned by the idea.

"You could do it. You're in terrific shape."

"But I've been training for the mile."

"That doesn't matter. You're in great shape."

It wasn't something I felt I could turn down. It was not only a chance to be with him, it was as if he were offering me a rite of passage. The marathon was the ultimate test of a runner, the embodiment of the semimystical experience he had been speaking and writing about. In my father's excitement over the idea, it was as though he were asking me to climb Everest or hunt down Moby Dick. This was the great event—the event after which nothing would ever be the same. How could I refuse? Why would I want to? This was my chance to share in earnest what was common to both of us.

"It's the Boston Marathon," he said. "What else is there?"

"All right," I said. "I'll do it."

My father smiled in satisfaction.

∞

AS WE DROVE UP TO BOSTON that Sunday, I couldn't shake the foreboding feeling of a neophyte paratrooper prematurely placed on a plane for battle. The doubts I had about my physical training were dwarfed by just how unprepared I felt mentally. I needed to get focused, but our first steps into the hotel lobby revealed that I would have no time for private reflection. Runners in sweatsuits recognized my father on sight and approached from all directions. The place was abuzz with the marathon, and when we walked in, it was as though the flurry had found its center. They knew my father from the magazine, and they peppered him with questions. There on that carpeted floor, beneath the chandeliers, he engaged a huddle of runners in an impromptu discourse on training, injuries, and, particularly, strategy for those running a marathon for the first time.

"Go out slow," he advised one man. "Save it up for Heartbreak Hill."

"Well," the man said, "last month, I ran a twenty-mile workout."

"Anyone can run twenty miles," my father said. "Not many people can run twenty-six."

When we got to Hopkington the next morning, a virtual sea of runners had flooded into the small park near the starting line. My father and I squeezed and bumped our way through them in search of a small patch of grass on which to stretch and loosen up. On an adjoining road, we saw some runners doing wind sprints. "Fools," he scoffed. "You run the first ten miles as a warm-up. The race doesn't begin until ten miles in."

There were more than a thousand runners that day. By today's standards, a puny showing. (Boston now limits entries to fifteen thousand, but when they lifted restrictions for their anniversary run a few years ago, forty thousand entered.) Still, it was a massive event back then. And as we moved through it to take our places, I lost him among the crowd of runners. Then as I found an opening well behind the starting line, I saw him again. He was about ten rows ahead of me, enveloped by the crowd and craning his head around to find me. "I'll see you at the finish," he yelled when our eyes met, before turning away to focus on the starting line. In a short while, I was off, jogging down a suburban road to Boston. Taking seriously my father's advice to "go out slow," I started at a relaxed pace, feeling nei-ther pain nor strain but wondering how I would feel in an hour or two. The tape recorder in my brain began playing all that my father had to say about marathons—the flip side of play.

In his philosophy, play was something of a loss leader—something that got the paying customer into the store. Once in, my father's readers learned that play was not all fun and games. Alas, there was also work involved or, at the very least, challenge. Agon or agony to the Greeks. Obstacles to be overcome. Impediments that strained and taxed your abilities. Without challenge, there would be no change, no growth, no peak experiences.

This absence of challenge in our lives had become one of my fa-ther's constant themes. It caused him to question the very nature of modern life. He questioned the comforts enjoyed by postwar Amer-ica and whether the trade-offs needed to attain them had been worth it. America had given its citizens an unprecedented level of wealth, and still unhappiness reigned. Instead of seeking challenge, we strove to anesthetize ourselves with drink and the options available to us at the flick of the TV clicker. The problem seemed to crystallize for my father when he read a conversation between the poets John Berryman and James Dickey.

"The trouble with this country," Berryman said, "is that you can live your entire life and not know whether or not you are a coward."

Dickey had written *Deliverance,* the story of some Atlanta busi-nessmen who try to recover lost challenge on a canoe trip into the backwoods. My father was no risk taker or thrill seeker, but he be-lieved that in choosing the easy life, you were choosing your own soft demise, and he often quoted a poem by Robinson Jeffers: "In pleas-ant ease and comfort, too soon the soul of man begins to die." If our lives had been emptied of challenge, clearly this spiritually bankrupt modern world required us to create our own. To my father, the marathon posed the most potent challenge of an unchallenging age. And the Boston Marathon was the greatest of all. As I passed through the suburban towns, I thought of how traversing the road ahead might be like fighting in a war or being lost at sea—or at least like being dropped off in a bad neighborhood with no money. If I made it to the finish, I would never gloat. There would be no mastery of the marathon—only survival.

Ten miles was no problem. At fifteen, however, my legs tightened, and at seventeen miles I began to struggle. All the while, my father's thoughts and sayings continued to fill my head. This wasn't about competing against other runners—he always stressed—it was about demanding the best from yourself. "The struggle the Greeks called the 'agon' is there for winner and loser alike," he had written, "—as are those brief, splendid moments that accompany them when we reach our finest potential." On the other side of agon, my father promised "arete," the Greek word for excellence, the end product of struggle. In describing it, my father always quoted Ortega y Gasset: "Life is a desperate struggle to become in being, in fact, that which we are in design." Arete made it all more than an exercise in mere masochism. It promised a complete awakening of the body and spirit.

At eighteen miles, I knew nothing of arete. I knew only pain. I was in Newton with eight miles to go, and I felt as though I could not take another step. The day had turned sunny and then hot. My stony legs reverberated with pain with every foot strike. One foot had blistered. And still I heard my father, quoting the great running coach Percy Cerutty, saying, "If it hurts, make it hurt more." And then, his most recent favorite: "Reach for what you cannot."

That, I knew from the dinner table back home, was the credo of

Nikos Kazantzakis in his autobiography, *Report to Greco*. My father had talked about emblazoning his marathon shirt with that phrase, which he never took the time to do. But I heard it in my head, now that I was considering dropping out. And I remembered what he had said to the runner in the lobby. "Anyone can run twenty miles. Very few people can run twenty-six."

With five miles left, I went up Heartbreak Hill. It really wasn't much of a hill by training standards but it loomed mountainous in my condition. I didn't know why I was going on. My mind felt like an airy stranger to my pain-racked body. Somewhere below me, I thought, my feet are moving and eventually this will end. Perhaps I plodded on just to please him. Or perhaps I was trying to prove something to myself. If I could finish maybe I would be a hero. Or at least I might know that I wasn't a coward.

In Brookline, I was in a world of pain. I could see the Prudential Building and the rest of the skyline in the distance but only in miniature. Every once in a while, I looked up hopefully but it grew no bigger, got no closer. With every step now I heard myself cry and groan, but I plugged on. I trudged through Brighton and then into downtown Boston. The city's canyons grew dark and loud with the people filling the sidewalks; the streets were wet and littered with paper cups discarded by runners. Police on horseback patroled the final blocks of the route. As I crested a small hill, there was a turn, and at the bottom of a slight incline I saw the finish. I hobbled and winced to the end, crossing the finish line with strides barely quicker than a walk.

Then I discovered the unfortunate truth: once you finish, the pain doesn't end. I was still in pain, and also lost. I was wandering through the crowd, squinting into the sky, when I heard the voice of my sister Sarah. "There's Andrew," she was saying to someone. "Andrew," she called. "Andrew." I saw her forge through the crowd, my father behind her, and when he reached me he put his arm around my shoulders for the first time I could remember. "Wow, baby, way to go," he said. "You're fantastic. Fan—tastic."

If he had felt the same pain, he had already recovered, and now he was beaming with satisfaction over my effort. As we hobbled back to the hotel, I still didn't know if all those things he had said about the marathon bore any relation to me. I didn't know about reaching my potential or even about not being a coward. But for that brief moment, I felt I was at one of those special father-son junctures: I was the son catching his first big fish or making his first solo flight. I had met the challenge, and at least for that time and that trip, I had joined the world of my father.

THE FOLLOWING WEEK, my high school track team had a dual meet. I went to the track that day, but I couldn't run because my legs were still too sore. So I watched trackside, handing out water and shouting encouragement to the runners. It was a close meet, and our team lost by a few points. At the end of the afternoon, my coach called me into the locker room.

Ours was the kind of rich suburban high school where the cars in the teachers' parking lot looked like junkers compared with those in the parking lot for the seniors. In my time there, I had gotten the sense from more than a few teachers, including our track coach, that they bit hard on their tongues at the unearned opulence. The coach was an ex-Marine loyal to his crewcut, and though he never said it outright, I sensed he resented me as a hippie and a snot-nosed kid. During the fall he coached junior varsity football, and he coached track the same way. In his view, both were team sports, and in both, winning was paramount. When he sat me down on a bench in the locker room that day, he was clearly angry that the team had lost. If I had run the mile, he told me, we would have won.

"Clean out your locker," he said. "You're off the team."

I was shocked, nonplussed. "But, why, Coach?" I managed to ask.

"If you wanted to run that marathon, you should have asked permission," he said. "Now, clean out your locker and get out."

"But, Coach, I didn't even know I was going until Saturday. There wouldn't have been any way to get permission," I said.

"Well, that's something you should have considered when you decided to go," he said. "Now, clean out your locker and get out."

A few minutes later, I was leaving the locker room in the late-afternoon sun with my arms full of running equipment. I walked home in a daze, and that night when I told my father, he was clearly distressed. "This is my fault," he said. "I'll call him. I'll write him a letter and get you back on the team."

By that time, however, my shock had turned to anger, and my anger to defiance. I told my father not to do anything. I wasn't going to kowtow to any coach. When I told my father this, he stared back at me sadly, trying to sway me with his pleading eyes. But while he didn't like my decision, he knew it had become a matter of principle for me. I wouldn't grovel, and he wouldn't interfere.

In the days and weeks that followed, I told myself it was a minor thing, this being kicked off the team, and I acted accordingly. To my father I espoused hippielike thoughts about how it was better to run for the sheer joy of running and renounce competition. In reality, however, the hurt was big, and my anger even bigger. Who was this coach to take away the only positive thing in my life? How could he summarily cut my lifeline? I had nowhere to put the anger, and nowhere to put the hurt. So I merely acted as though I felt neither. My father was hurt as well but equally powerless. I knew he felt guilty and complicitous about his role in my dismissal, and though he never expressed it openly, I knew he was angry at his inability to resolve things.

But without track, there was a void in my life and a void in our relationship. We had now lost our one common pursuit. No longer were we striving together for arete. When I told him about my new laissez-faire philosophy of running, he'd listen but he couldn't muster up any excitement. What was worse was that he couldn't tell me how bad he felt, although that was clear in his baleful eyes. Neither of us possessed the language of emotion. And so, after a time, we hardly talked at all—not about my getting kicked off the track team, not even about my running. The incident and all the bad feeling it engendered didn't go away, it just hung in the air between us.

Without practice to go to, I started spending afternoons with my pot-smoking friends again. Over the next months my father and I talked less and less as we drifted back into our separate lives. Neither of us wanted to engage the other, even as the signs that I was slipping became increasingly hard to ignore. My grades were bad again and most nights I barely uttered a word at dinner. On weekends I was out late, past the time my parents went to bed. In the morning they would find me sleeping fully clothed on top of my bedcovers. If they had any suspicions about drugs, they did not confront me. But in my father's silence I sensed a great disappointment.

Then one day in the kitchen the uneasy silence was broken. My father had long suffered from a stomach ulcer, with shooting pains and heartburn. Often, I'd see him grimace, doubled over in pain. To relieve it, he had begun taking a tincture of belladonna in a glass of water. I had read that belladonna was a kind of narcotic, known also as "deadly nightshade." As I watched my father putting drops of it in a glass, I unwisely made light of it.

"Hey, Dad, you'd better watch that stuff," I said. "It can be bad for you."

My father turned around and glared.

"Who are you to tell me what to do?" he said.

My older sister Ann, who was home at the time, tried vainly to intercede when she overheard this exchange.

"Dad, he's only trying to make a joke," she said.

"He's challenging my medical knowledge of thirty years," my father said. "Where does he get off?"

Ann tried further but only made matters worse.

"The kids," she said, "they just know that belladonna is some kind of a drug."

With this my father flared red. "Yeah, that's right," he said, "he knows all about drugs." Then he walked over to where I was sitting and put his face close to mine, and with his voice shaking, he said, "You miserable speck of humanity." Then he walked out of the room. I sat there stunned and dropped my head. Ann put her hand on my shoulder. "He didn't mean that," she said. "He's just having pain from his ulcer." But his words were already like a lead weight in my chest.

Soon after, I came upon what I believed to be the perfect solution: I would leave the house, and my parents wouldn't have to deal with me anymore. I would go overseas. The American Field Service was offering an exchange with a family in Italy, and without telling my parents, I applied, becoming a finalist. I told my mother, who thought it might be a good idea for me to get away. But when I asked my father, the response was different.

"No," he said, curtly.

When I asked him for an explanation, he said, "If you go we'll have to take in an exchange student and then I'll be expected to make donations. That's the way it works. The answer is no."

I just sat in silence and lowered my head. I was out of ideas, and I couldn't muster a thing to say. The silence felt long.

"Look," my father said at last. "You've come at the wrong time."

That was the end of our talk. In the silence that followed I could hear his words reverberating in my head: *You've come at the wrong time.* It was odd, but right then and there, I knew the exact meaning of those words. It wasn't just that this Italy idea had come at an inopportune time; my father was saying something much more global than that. He meant that I had been born too late. I had come along with the younger children, after all the love and the patience had run out. It's tough luck, my father seemed to be saying, but there's nothing to be done about it. He had other things to do now.

⚭

LOOKING BACK ON THOSE miserable days, I'm tempted to chalk them up to an adolescent's penchant for drama. And yet, if I climb back into my skin at the time, I can still feel the cold wind, and I shudder. It's hard now to put a name on it, but looking back I know that in those high school years, I was in some serious pain. And even though I may have romanticized that pain, that doesn't alter the fact that I felt a lot worse than I could cope with. What the problem was I couldn't have told you then and am still uncertain now. I recall a feeling of hollowness and loss—there was the loss of my old girlfriend and the loss of my old friends. But there was an even greater, unnameable sadness—a feeling that nothing was right in the world, at least not for me.

Then, a concerned teacher in whom I had begun to confide sent me to the school's psychologist, but I didn't cooperate. After two antagonistic sessions, he said, "We're going to have to have your parents come in."

*My father as a young boy. He's Little Lord Fauntleroy
on the right, with his mother in the center.*

*My father's father,
George Augustine Sheehan.*

*My father's family on the Jersey shore.
He's in the striped shirt. Fourteen kids
and two parents.*

Brooklyn Prep Cross-Country Team.
My father sitting next to Coach Giegengack.

My father in his
Navy dress blues.

My mother in the early 1940s.

My parents early in their marriage.

"World's Holiest Boy" with parents—First Communion, December 1963.

My father running in the backyard in Rumson.

Me in high school.

My father running in the Boston Marathon.

The "Hair Picture" family portrait in middle 1970s.

Me finishing the Boston Marathon, April 1972.

Me in my early newspaper days.

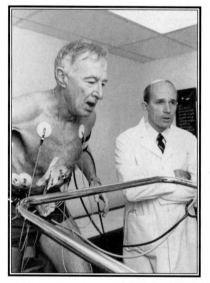

My father with Dr. Kenneth Cooper.

My father speaking at his farewell dinner.

My mother and father in their final years.

My father's last swim at Rehoboth.

My mother in the early 1990s.

My family. Emmet, myself, Abigail, and Eamon.
After the "Pittsburgh Great Race," September 2000.

"This has nothing to do with my parents," I told him.

"We know from our studies that the kinds of problems you have go back to your family," he said.

The psychologist called my parents, and when my father, my mother, and I arrived at his office, I was told to wait in the hall. A half hour later, the psychologist called me back in, and when I walked into the room, it was obvious that both of my parents had been crying. My father had his face in his hands and could hardly look at me.

"I'm sorry, baby," he said. "I'm really sorry."

The sight of him there, red-faced and sorrowful, made me greatly uncomfortable.

"You don't have to be sorry," I told him.

"No," he said. "I let you down. I wasn't around for you. My father wasn't there for me, and I wasn't there for you."

It was a quiet, uneasy drive home. My mother told me later that the psychologist believed I was severely depressed and potentially suicidal. During that week, my father and I didn't talk much. As the days wore on, however, his kindly eyes began to glower, and when we went back to the psychologist's office the next week, it was a different story.

"I have no apologies for you," he said to me in the psychologist's presence. "You are your own responsibility."

"That's right," I said.

Then he announced that what I needed was to be reined in. There were to be new rules in our house—rules about smoking ("Who do you think you are smoking cigarettes?" he asked), rules about school, rules about when I could leave the house and when I needed to be home. We rode home in a silence far more ominous than the uneasy quiet of the week before. After that, we hardly spoke.

For a time, things got worse. With the rules left to my mother to enforce, I did even more drugs, and more serious ones. I did entertain thoughts of suicide, and there came a night when I really did believe I would kill myself. I had heard that if you injected a vein with air, it sent a bubble through your arteries and stopped your heart. I took a syringe from my father's valise and locked myself in a bathroom. But when I sat down on the toilet and held the syringe in my hand, I broke down in a fit of tears. In the matter of suicide, I had exposed myself as a pretender. I wasn't really serious about killing myself; the fear of it was just too overwhelming.

It became clear that night that I wanted to live, and that in order to live I had to change. I sobbed, and as I sobbed I began to hear my own cries echoing against the tile walls, like echoes in a chamber. It was bottom for me, and it would also be a turning point. In the coming days, I stopped smoking and stopped taking drugs. For weeks I didn't sleep the night through, waking up with convulsive coughs. I know that coughing awoke my parents, because I could hear them talking about me in the next room. Still, they never asked me about it.

Soon, I began running again. I ran both farther and faster than I had before, and as my junior year came to an end I began serious training. By the summer, my father and I were talking, and we returned to Takanassee, where I consistently beat him in the races. One night, I heard his trademark groans coming from behind me on the final straightaway, and I pushed against the pain in my chest and ran faster. At the finish, we both collapsed on a small bit of grass between the road and the bank of the lake, panting and staring up at the summer sky through the branches of trees. As we once again shared our post-race lemon ices and sunset swims, it seemed the bad times were behind us. And even though we never acknowledged their passing, we started to enjoy each other's company again.

In the fall I ran cross-country, and after practice, instead of smoking pot with my friends, I went home. On those late-fall afternoons I would drink tea at the kitchen table and stare out the window, watching the sky grow dark. My mother would sing sweetly as she cooked dinner, and as I became enveloped by the warm smell of her food and the gentle timbre of her voice, I felt comfortable and at home. My father began showing up at my cross-country races, and at night he would counsel me as my coach. In that counsel, I was sure I felt his desire to get closer, to heal the hurt between us.

Just prior to the conference championship, I was running better than I had in my entire life. And on the blustery late-fall day of the race, I joined four hundred other runners in a line one hundred yards wide, on an open field at Monmouth College. When the starting gun fired, I tried to get a good jump, but the field condensed itself around me, leaving me somewhere in the middle of the pack. Still, I knew I was in great shape, and moving steadily and quickly, I began cutting my way through the great throng of schoolboys. The pack cornered a bend and ran into the street, and once on the pavement, I moved wide and passed people at will. I was neither laboring in my stride nor taxed in my breathing.

When I heard my split times, I knew I was running close to five minutes a mile, faster than I ever had in a three-mile race. Yet, instead of fatigue, I felt myself getting stronger. I was running at full stride without effort or need to concentrate; my feet seemed only to brush the ground as they touched it. It was as though something outside of me was doing the work, and I was merely a passenger. I wasn't actively running this race; it felt more as though I was presiding over the running. This was it, I realized. This was that effortlessness, that efficiency in movement, my father had always talked about. "Like pulling the sword from the stone," I had often heard him say, and now I heard the words in my head as I ran fast and free. We circled the campus, then came back through the iron-gated portal, back to the big open field and the finish. With a half mile to go, I was passing boys I recognized as the best runners on the shore. When I saw that there were only two ahead of me, I made a play for them. But I came up short, and another kid passed me at the finish. I came in fourth, which amounted to a stunning personal victory—I had run the best race of my life.

A few races like that were good enough to get me on the all-conference team. That winter, my father took me to the award banquet, and I went up to get my plaque. I remember that all through the dull keynote speech, he kept looking down at the plaque and touching the gilded runner on its face. Again and again he ran his hand over the runner. It seemed to me that he was touching it to see if it was real. It was as though he was trying to affirm to himself that I was going to be all right.

CHAPTER EIGHT

I T SHOULD HAVE BEEN the best of times.

Over the years, my father's solitary foot strikes through the town had been joined by the paces of others. Initially by a few, and then by hordes—tens of thousands, followed by millions. By the mid-1970s, his influence could be seen merely by looking out any window in America onto the streets below. We were the new running nation. People of all ages and body types were jogging and running with a complete lack of self-consciousness. They blended into the traffic of modern life as unremarkably as the cars, the postmen, and the people waiting for the bus.

In the middle seventies, America witnessed what was called a fitness revolution, replacing the political one, which had fizzled. American weekends began to revolve around road races. The terms "5K" and "10K" began creeping into the national lexicon, and every day people began to embrace the crazy pursuit of marathon training. Suddenly, seemingly everyone was running or beginning to run or planning to begin. An estimated 30 million people had taken up the sport and every last one of them was an expert—an expert in training, an expert in shoes, an expert in the mental, emotional, and spiritual benefits. But the chief expert on a national scale was my father.

It's never been clear to me whether he was a major catalyst or whether he was just in the right place at the right time. But probably they come down to the same thing in the end. What was clear was that he had somehow anticipated something that was about to be discovered by the world, and by the time everyone else arrived, he was sitting there like Buddha, waiting for them. They started calling him the Guru of Running. And people seemed to hang on his every utterance for clues to the fulfillment they were seeking.

At home we saw firsthand how demand for my father increased steadily, incrementally, week by week and month by month. At night there were the phone calls from reporters from all over the country. My father took the calls at the kitchen table, where he settled into his standard over-the-phone interview with ready quotes. ("We say the spirit is willing but the body isn't. Well, we have that all backwards. . . .") Then, there were the New York radio and television appearances, invitations to speak in other parts of the country, appearances that might be hitched to a second or third city on the same trip. Departure mornings typically found him in the kitchen, one hand frantically patting his breast pocket. "Where are my plane tickets?" and, "Where's that itinerary with the phone numbers?" My mother, of course, had it all together. His suitcase was packed, his running gear was stowed in another bag with clean socks and shorts, and his tickets, itinerary, and all other pertinent items were tucked neatly into a folder. They kissed lightly as he headed out the door.

But if my mother was adding travel secretary to her list of duties, she was not doing so happily. She had unanswered questions. Where was all of this leading? What would she do when he got there? While she clung to the same commitments she had always had—to family, church, and community—he was on a different mission now: he was in the business of self-promotion, though to what end she did not know. She continued to struggle with his message, straining to understand his ideas just as he tired of trying to explain them to her.

On his trips to California, my father spent time at places like the Esalen Institute, where running had taken its place next to Transcendental Meditation, primal scream, and Rolfing as one of the fad therapies of the moment. Once, my parents disappeared together for a long weekend of Gestalt encounters, after which my father, at least, seemed transformed, entering the kitchen as Mr. Natural himself. With his arms spread open, he attempted to compensate for a lifetime of no physical contact by hugging each of us. It was so foreign to us that my sister Nora accepted her hug with something of the mien of Lot's wife, standing stiffly erect and grimacing as though my father were performing some unpleasant medical procedure.

My mother's entrance was quite different. Showing the wear of the encounters, she immediately sank into a seat at the kitchen table and folded her arms across her chest. There she joined the rest of us, watching my father pacing across the floor, telling us all he had learned.

"It's all about being the real you," he was saying, "getting in touch with who you are."

To our collective amazement, he now proclaimed himself ready to be emotionally open, to take risks of intimacy—ready, he said, to be a new kind of father. Each of us stared at him in silence, watching him pace back and forth across the floor, not daring to look at one another for fear we would respond the wrong way. Waiting for a reaction and finding none, my father turned to my mother.

"How about you, Mary Jane," he said. "Do you see yourself changing in any way?"

My mother simply sat there with her arms folded.

"I am who I've always been," she said.

Perhaps taking a clue from the encounter sessions, he challenged her. "Why don't you want to take risks?" he said. "I mean, just look at your body language. Your arms are folded, your legs are crossed, you're all knotted up," he said. "Your body is saying, I don't want risk."

"I'm sitting very comfortably," she said, with a tremble of anger in her voice. "This is the way I like to sit."

"Well, why don't you want to try new things?" he said. "Why don't you want to change?"

Feeling badgered, she blurted out, "Because I'm fifty-two and you're eighteen. That's why."

We all began breathing a little more easily when the days of "new Dad" turned out to be short-lived. Within a few weeks normalcy returned in the form of his usual opaqueness, and he surrounded himself once again with his books and legal pads. But while most things reverted to pattern, the relationship between my parents seemed to be steadily deteriorating. In the end, the encounter week had served only to bring their differences into sharper relief: one wanted change, the other didn't. Nonetheless, the fact that their marriage was at a possible breaking point was lost on me. We were not people of divorce. It was not an option in our family. Even if my father was not really a Catholic anymore, surely he would never leave. But looking back, I wonder how I could have missed the signs. His writing alone should have prepared me for what was to come.

Circulation of *Runner's World* was taking off at the time, and his columns were a centerpiece. The magazine decided to turn that writing into a book. His friend and editor, Joe Henderson, organized his columns by topic, and together they wove the individual pieces into chapters. Throughout 1974, he worked on that first book, *Dr. Sheehan on Running*—which was, among other things, a call to middle-aged men like himself who felt dissatisfied with their lives. He began the book with that image of being on the train and pulling the emergency cord to disembark, thus rejecting the life that heretofore had been such a grim ride, not of his own choosing apparently.

"The previous me was not me. It was a self-image I had thrust upon me. It was the person I had accepted myself to be, but I had been playing a role."

I had never heard the term "midlife crisis" back then, but in the years following, I heard it used all the time in relation to my father. While his message was intended for all ages and genders, it had particular resonance with middle-aged men. At races, they gathered around him, and he told them to tune out the voices that told them to be someone else—those same voices, he said, that had told him to marry, raise a family, make money, and throw parties.

"When I was young, I knew who I was and tried to become something else," my father wrote. "I spent the next four decades with these feelings of being unworthy and incomplete and inferior. Combating my own nature. Trying to be something I was not. Concealing the real me under layer after layer or coping and adjusting and compensating. All the while refusing to believe that the person I initially rejected was the real me. All the while trying to pass as a normal member of a normal society."

To those men, now facing the second half of their lives, he held out a promise that they no longer had to force themselves into a mold. They could break out as he had, and in those first strides on the blacktop near their homes, they could declare themselves free of the nine-to-five servitude, free of the finely tailored straitjacket, free to discover the miraculous, creative being under all the grim layers of convention.

"Running," he wrote, "was discovery, a return to the past, a proof that life did come full cycle and the child was father to the man."

For his fellow travelers who had jumped off the slow train, my father promised a whole world of possibilities. You could become what you "are in design." In running, he said, you would become three things: the artist, the child, and the saint. As the artist, you would rediscover the creative side of yourself, though dormant for years. As the child, you would find your sense of awe once again. As the saint, you would become more emotionally in touch with yourself and thus with others; you would grow to care about other people and become empathic.

But on this last point, his promises stopped short, perhaps even foundered. My father had to equivocate on the saint part. Running, after all, might not make you a nicer person. Running was a kind of life-changing force that people unloosed into their lives at their own peril. "Running can break up families, destroy friendships and kill ambition. It can also, of course, rebuild families, create new friendships and inspire ambition," he wrote. Ordering from his own Chinese menu, my father would feed his ambition, reject his old friends, and put his family life in peril.

AFTER HIGH SCHOOL, I decided to get as far away as I could from my parents and family, so I ventured out into the frigid cold and anonymity of the Midwest. Like my father, I wanted to be a writer, and so I enrolled at the University of Iowa to attend the Writer's Workshop. At Iowa, the workshop actually has two parts: the graduate-school workshop, where young writers spend all their time working on first novels, and a lesser known undergraduate workshop, which consists of only one course in the English curriculum, where students like me generally work on their first short stories.

The fact that we were just the little kids of the writing community didn't prevent me and my fellow workshoppers from imagining ourselves young Hemingways and the Iowa River we strolled along as it wound its way through campus as our River Seine. We talked always about the great writers, and often at night we went to hear them read: Cheever, Doctorow, Burgess, even the great Borges came to speak. We had the temerity to ask them questions on style and structure, and afterward, we discussed writing at all hours. If we never did much actual writing, we certainly talked about it a great deal—every night over pitchers of beer.

If Iowa didn't teach me to become a writer, it certainly did teach me how to drink. There in the grip of a frigid winter I came to terms with the fact that I didn't much like drugs after all. Pot, I finally conceded, made me paranoid, and at the freshman dorm at Iowa I soon rediscovered that after a few hits, I retreated into a shell, overcome by an inability to speak. On my dorm's floor, the smell of it wafted nightly through the corridor, the smoke seeping out from beneath the closed doors of rooms stretching down the hallway. The rooms with the biggest stereos became the smokiest chambers—the gathering places where the boys from Peoria corrupted the clean-cut Iowa farmboys with the lure of the bong. Every night, there was the flashing of lighters, the bubbling of smoke, and the rolling and laughing on the floor. All the while, Black Sabbath and Yes egged them on at deafening levels. For me, pot had ceased to hold any allure. I was now a veteran of the drug wars, and this was no longer my scene. I liked to drink instead.

My would-be writer friends and I were mostly serious students and spent at least the early part of the evening at the library. That, however, didn't prevent us from meeting every night at our favorite bar. Even on the coldest nights, we trudged across the quad and down the dark side streets to find our little shoebox of a tavern. Inside, the amber-toned light and the rumble of conversation welcomed us as if we were refugees off the moors. The wooden booths, the bratwursts spinning on rotisserie spikes, the Hamm's Beer sign above the bar made it feel like home to me.

As we began our literary ramblings, I would hold forth without any self-consciousness, and I loved this about drinking beer, the way it empowered my speech instead of strangling it. In conversation, it would be my ally for hours on end as I prattled on with what I assumed to be clarity and daring until, of course, my tongue thickened and my words began to slur. By then it was usually closing time anyway, so we bundled up to face the outrageous cold once more. But I would always faithfully return—if not the following night then the night after that—to that bar where I felt so at home that it in many ways became my home.

When I called my real home in New Jersey, my father would answer with his standard Iowa joke: "Well," he said, "have you gotten used to the tall buildings yet?" In other calls, however, there were hints that things weren't great at the other end. Often he was away, giving speeches in distant cities. My mother rallied at each phone call, but underneath her bravado I could detect a sadness. I envisioned her sitting at the end of this long telephone-line tether, alone and unhappy.

That summer, when I went home to the Jersey Shore, my father's book had just come out, and there was a flurry of excitement around him. The book had been published by the magazine, and despite limited distribution and promotion, it was selling quite well. The calls from reporters and invitations to speak and to appear on TV all picked up. He had already attracted a big-deal agent and the interest of some major publishing houses for any future books. In anticipation, he was already writing feverishly to meet the demand.

The serene aura he wrote about in his book was completely absent. Rather, my father seemed perpetually rushed. When speaking with him, I was always conscious of the clock, aware of being fit in as his schedule would permit—as though I was taking him away from his primary focus. He was making up for lost time. Having wasted so much of it getting to this point, he was determined to seize what remained to him. "Carpe diem," he would say. This would be his time—the middle 1970s, as it turned out.

∞

I HAD STAYED A HIPPIE at Iowa, and I had a fair amount of success coaxing like-minded girls into my dorm room with sensitive talk and Jackson Browne playing on my stereo. ("Do you like Joni Mitchell? I have her, too.") But when I came home that summer, I found that being a hippie was no longer cool.

Growing up on the shore, my brothers and I always worked summer jobs in the seafood places that dotted the coastline for miles. Their big, lit signs displayed their faux nautical names: The Rum Runner, Barnacle Bill's, Captain This and Admiral That. We walked the greasy kitchen floors, under the bright fluorescent lights, amid the clatter of metal pots and transistor radios playing the AM hits. We were dishwashers and busboys in our early teens, waiters, cooks, and bartenders when we got older. In working those jobs, we had our first peek outside of our sheltered existence, getting to know the barflies, the sport gamblers, and the small-time hoods.

When I came home that summer my friend Steve was cooking in a restaurant, and he tried to get me a job with him. I had never been a cook and the Greek owner was dubious. "No 'schperience,' " he said. But Steve was also Greek—we called him by his Greek name, Stavros, like the detective on Kojak—and as Stavros he prevailed and got me in.

It was the beginning of the disco era, and it had become a very unhippie-like scene. Times had changed, and we hadn't kept up. At the restaurant, we harbored fantasies about the pretty young waitress we worked with, reading amorous intent into her every kindness. If she brought us a Coke or a beer from the bar to our broiler, surely it must be love. Imagine then our discontent when, peering out the kitchen doors, we saw, sitting at the bar, the real objects of her amour—Italian guys with shirts flared open to reveal gold coke spoons nestled in black chest hair. They were what was hip, and we were suddenly anachronisms.

Stavros and I were equally out-of-place in this new scene. He had been a high school folksinger, and his Greek parents had raised him on yogurt and Ian and Sylvia records. We despised these garish new times, the coke-snorting and wife-swapping and blatant promiscuity. Oh, the depravity, we moaned. It offended us not only as hippies but as Catholics. Never mind our own excesses.

Every night we slaved in front of the broiler, cooking steaks and fish in the unconscionable heat. After, we headed out to the bars to throw down as many beers as we could before closing time. We loved the bars, loved stretching out our bills in small piles in front of us and watching the bartender reduce those piles to nothing as he brought us our beers. We loved the magic of the bars—the noise, the sideshows, the ample material for commentary. During the day, we walked the streets of Red Bank engaged in high-minded denuncia- tions of the decadent world we lived in—two Cassandras predicting the fall. Every night, we sat on our barstools as though we had front-row seats on Armageddon. After the bars closed, we hung out in his apartment over Broad Street and continued drinking, sometimes till dawn. All those nights, slowly sinking down in our cups, we looked down upon the town as if we were looking at the streets of Sodom and Gomorrah.

∞

BUT WHILE STAVROS AND I FELT like throwbacks to another era, hanging back warily, my father was running to catch the bus, ready to claim his share of attention. This new phase made me wonder about him. It seemed so antithetical to what I viewed as his true nature. He was an ectomorph, wasn't he? So, who was the real George Sheehan? The retiring introvert or the gadfly clamoring for fame? He was a walking contradiction, and nothing seemed quite as contradictory as his newfound speaking career.

He gave speeches ("talks" he preferred to call them) on the nights before the marathons or the major road races that were springing up in cities throughout the country. They were inspirational talks, meant to motivate. But the prospect of each one struck him with terror. I knew he had a terrible problem with stage fright, but I needed to accompany him to only one such talk in Manhattan that summer to see just how tormented he was. Backstage, with his hands shoved deep into his pockets and his torso bent forward, he paced back and forth between repeated stops at the water fountain, trying to tame his fear. Time and again, he pulled his notes from his back pocket and looked at them in his quivering hand.

Once on stage, he didn't so much give a speech as molt—like a crab trying to cast off its shell. When introduced, he skulked onto the stage, presenting himself to the clapping audience without even a wave. His shoulders were hunched and his hands clenched together, and his voice squeaked with the opening words before settling into a dull monotone. At the beginning of his talk, he seemed to struggle against himself, forcing a few awkward waves of his hand, struggling to throw off his cloak of fear while sinking under the weight of it. Then, mercifully, he got a few laughs. He straightened up, began to gesture more freely, and walked around the stage. And when his act finally kicked in, he came unbound, flailing with full arms until the messenger mirrored his message—the excitement of play and its potential.

His nervousness seemed to evoke empathy in his audience, perhaps some identification with him. From the beginning they seemed to root for him to hit his stride. He and his audience had developed a symbiotic relationship, one born out of reciprocity and mutual generosity: my father was willing to bare his soul, and his audience was willing to give him safe harbor, claiming him as their own. As the laughter and applause made him looser, less inhibited, his vision became more compelling, more convincing. "If I can do these things and feel these things," he told them, "just imagine what you could do." They believed him, for they had just seen him transform himself in front of their very eyes.

After the exhilaration of these successes, he endured any amount of nervousness to feel it again. And now that his columns were reaching a growing cult of runners, the audiences at these talks were getting bigger and bigger. They swarmed around him afterward, asking questions of their guru. It was as though you could hear a distant drumbeat. Slowly but steadily, fame was coming for him.

❦

IF YOU WISH TO TAKE the national stage, you cannot take it timidly. Rather, you must swagger, worrying not so much about embarrassing yourself as about keeping your energy high and your message clear. You must desire the attention at almost all cost and be prepared to show your audience complete commitment, even to the point of playing the clown. By the mid-1970s, my father was ready in all regards. In his conversations, his writing, and his public talks, I always felt a seriousness and silliness, as though some part of him wished to entertain even at his own expense. Like Shakespeare's Falstaff, who noted, "I am not only witty in myself, but the cause of wit in other men," my father seemed aware of the tension he created and began to use it, theatrically. He expounded new theories, the wackier the better, especially when he was applying medical and biological science to sport.

Once, he proposed that athletes didn't need to shower. This grew out of an avowed contempt for the use of athletes as pitchmen. "I can put up with Madison Avenue using athletes to promote beer, even men's perfume, but when I see athletes in commercials for antiperspirants and deodorants, I rise in protest," he wrote. His theory held that there are two types of sweat—athletic sweat, and nervous sweat. The former doesn't smell but the latter does. Nervous sweat— the sweat that smells—comes from apocrine glands. It is produced by "the guy with a top-heavy mortgage, rebellious kids, an irritable boss and depressed wife." In contrast, he said, athletic sweat is "a dilute salt solution of minty purity" and thus has no odor. There was no need for showers after workouts, and he, in fact, quit taking them. After an hour's run, he would simply towel off, put his street clothes back on, and go back to work, smelling only of that "minty purity." The nurses at the hospital had a different view.

In his columns he also ruminated on the quality of his bowel movements and his desire for a good firm one prior to a race. Pre-race jitters would assist in this, he said, by stimulating the gastro-colic reflex—the fear that makes you want to crap. Only my father would have thought to put such matters into historic context. "The effect of apprehension and anxiety on the gut has been well established," he wrote. "Such reports go back to biblical accounts of the Assyrians' charge and the effects on the gastrointestinal tracts of the Israelites."

And, if the pre-race anxiety was not enough, the reflex would be aided by a cup of coffee, my father's guaranteed solution. Before that it had been trial and error. The results of one experiment with a quart of orange juice and a quart of milk were set down for the benefit of the reader: "I had a satisfactory movement before the race and was two miles into the woods when I developed an uncontrollable diarrhea. I finally had to stop and let my pants down and perch on a rock while the rest of the crowd streamed past."

My mother read these things in horror, and my sisters told him he was debasing himself. Such comments did not faze him. "If you wish to win at anything," he said, "you must go a little bit berserk." And the more outrageous his writings, the more affirmation he seemed to get. When he finally got his chance, he was prepared to go to any lengths to command the public's attention. And as soon as he began to get that attention, he seemed to crave it all the more. It was as if he had some bottomless hole to fill; no matter how much he got, it would always be too little.

∞

THE LAMENT OF THE CHILDREN of the famous is not a new sound in our skies. It has filled books and talk shows, with the "victims" droning on about unresolved grievances. The kids of famous people have grown wearisome. Whatever their complaint, it does not evoke much sympathy. As with fame itself, people on the outside of it believe they would gladly endure whatever problems arise, for surely anything beats obscurity and the mundane. But when fame is visited upon a family member, it doesn't extend its mantle to everyone else. It is not something that is transferable from head to head.

Even if fame could be shared, my father did not seem inclined to share it. Fame was for him alone. And it made him even more oblivious to the needs of others than before. Ignoring the effects of his new life on his wife and children, he bullied on, growing ever more self-confident and self-satisfied, even as his marriage became ever more fragile.

After that summer, I went back to Iowa, but over the winter and spring my mother could no longer hide the trouble at home, even over the phone. "Dad and I aren't doing well," she said, as if to prepare me before I headed back home for the summer of 1976.

"What's going on exactly?" I asked.

"We'll talk when you get home," she said.

When I got there, I discovered he was gone. He had moved out of the house, had taken an apartment and, apparently, a girlfriend. My mother told me he was now living a few miles away in Atlantic Highlands, on a bluff overlooking the ocean at the mouth of New York Harbor. He was calling this a separation. A time to think, and a time to write. His first book had been successful, and now he had an advance from Simon & Schuster for the second and was positioned to ride the crest of the running boom. But his time of triumph had become one of crisis for my mother.

I found her in the kitchen, cooking as usual. The first thing I noticed was a wrinkled puffiness about her eyes that had never been there before. And looking into those eyes, I saw panic and fear. Although she was peeling potatoes and draining lettuce as though nothing had changed, she seemed tentative, as if she could no longer claim even this space as her own. Unlike my father, she had never aspired to anything beyond what she already had. She said once that when she was in first grade, a nun had told the class that God had a plan for everyone, and that if they had faith, the plan would be revealed. My mother's beliefs had a continuity unbroken since she was a little girl, and she thought she'd known her role. There was no hand wringing or search for deeper insights.

In the phrase of Eliot, she had always walked through the world "assured of certain certainties." Now that that world was gone, she couldn't sleep. Some nights she walked around the house like a phantom until dawn. Daylight brought new afflictions, as she tried to ignore the sidelong glances of the women lunching at the beach club, whose voices grew silent when she passed. One day she turned and walked directly over to a table of women she knew.

"George and I are having trouble," she told them. "It's not worth talking about."

She was worried about the effect of the separation on me, but especially worried about the younger ones—the three still in grammar school and high school. They had taken the brunt of the decaying marriage and now there was this gossip to contend with. If all of us in the second half of the family had suffered from inattention, Stephen, Monica, and Michael had suffered more.

One day in early July, I took Stephen to see our father at his new apartment. It was the day the tall ships sailed into New York Harbor, and when Stephen and I arrived, my father was outside holding a pair of binoculars. There, from the top of the bluff, we could see the great three-masted ships sailing to America's big party. His new neighbors were there too, sitting on folded beach chairs in the backyard, drinking beer. When they asked us to join them, I retreated indoors. I didn't want to join my father in his anonymous new community. Neither did I want to join the extended family of America in their celebration.

I began feeling vaguely nauseated. But my father seemed to soak it all in with the sunshine. Following me inside, he drank his Tab and talked to me about his writing and his book contract. Nothing more. I couldn't bring up the separation or my mother, and clearly he wouldn't broach the subject unprompted.

"Would you like to see the apartment?" he asked.

"All right," I said, even though I didn't.

Why in the world would I? As I walked around the sparsely furnished rooms, I felt lost, as though I were now cast in a role I was ill-prepared to play, with lines I hadn't memorized. I felt even worse for Stephen, who seemed to sleepwalk through the visit without talking. Of all the younger children, Stephen seemed most hurt by the changes. I thought it was monstrous that my father appeared so unaware of the silence that had engulfed his son.

When we returned home that day, entering through the kitchen, my mother peppered me with questions. What was his mood? His physical appearance? Did he mention her? When it became clear that I had no new insights, she went back to her cooking and the two of us lapsed into quiet. Suddenly she broke the silence.

"Did Stephen see the ships?" she asked, gazing out the window over the kitchen sink.

"The ships?"

"Yes. Did Stephen see the ships?" she asked again.

"Yeah," I said, "you could see the ships. They were pretty far off, but you could see them with the binoculars."

"Did Stephen look through the binoculars, too?" she asked, concerned.

Her questions seemed odd, but I answered anyway. "Yeah, Mom," I said. "Stephen saw them."

My mother continued to stare out the window and in a faraway voice said, "Stephen always loved the ships. Ever since he was a little boy."

After she said this, I began to cry. My mother knew her boys. She had always known us in ways we would never know ourselves. Even then, locked deep in her own pain, she saw into ours. Her deep knowledge of us touched me so much at that moment that I began to weep—for her but also for me. I was almost twenty-one. Too old, I had told myself, to be affected by all of this. Still, the departure of my father—as distant as he had often been—seemed to signal the breakup of my family. We were all beginning to spin off like planets into the void, each one alone, and the realization of our aloneness frightened me, hurt me.

My mother maintained an open-door policy with my father, allowing him to come for occasional dinners and family events. Sometimes he got a cold shoulder but there were few if any confrontations. Perhaps he took that as a sign of acceptance, because he seemed not to notice how uncomfortable we all were when he showed up. My mother, though clearly shattered, somehow maintained faith that things would eventually work out, and even went so far as to decorate my father's apartment for him. She appeared to be operating on a kind of invisible assurance from an unknown source that things would eventually return to normal.

"Your grandfather has gone away to find himself," she told her grandchildren. "And when he does, he'll come back."

He showed no sign of returning, and he was quite public about the affair, taking no pains to hide it or his girlfriend from his friends and relations. That summer, I was tending bar in the shore town of Sea Bright, and on off nights I would cruise other bars. One night I ran into him and his girlfriend as I was leaving one of the few bars in Rumson. I hadn't noticed them come in, but they were standing by the door, so I had to walk by them as I left. Our eyes met as I walked by him. "What do I say?" he asked in a pleading voice. I just shook my head wordlessly as I went out the door. For a moment, I stood dazed in the parking lot, unable to comprehend what I had just seen.

Unfortunately, the indignities didn't stop there. That summer he wrote a most remarkable column in the local newspaper, which seemed a veritable broadside against my mother. He dismissed the "old" ideal of womanhood, the women who devoted themselves to the triumvirate of "children, church, and kitchen." Instead, he held up the new ideal—an ideal I could only assume was based on his girl-friend—the athlete, the runner and independent thinker. He sang the praises of "the girl in the sweats," the young woman who, like him, was creating a world of her own. In that column, he also dis-owned his old friends, saying that it was necessary to make new ones. The old ones were no longer relevant.

One of those old friends was Schuyler, the New York ad man. The week the column appeared in the paper, he showed up at the bar where I was working. As he sauntered, half lit, into the bar, he looked around and smiled as though amused by the place. It was a cheap old shot-and-beer dive on Ocean Avenue, which had recently gained fa-vor with younger drinkers, who had turned it into a hard-rock juke-box. Schuyler asked if we had any "decent" scotch, so I poured him a Dewars. Sitting down on a stool, he said, "I read that column where he talked about getting rid of his old friends. My wife said to me, 'You know he's talking about you, don't you?' " It hurt, he said, to lose my father's friendship but he had figured they were finished long before the newspaper column spelled it out. It was my mother he was concerned about. He'd wanted to be there for her but wasn't sure whether to approach her, knowing her pride. We talked for a while, and when he finished his scotch he told me, "Your father is a very

sick man. You should pray for him." Then he turned and strolled out
of the bar into the steamy summer night.

∞

IT STILL AMAZES ME how we can go through our lives unaware of our
interdependence on one another. We tend to run 'round and 'round
that hamster cage of our brains, plotting our daily course as if we
were on some solo mission. We live in that inner space and peer out
through our scopes, developing our own strategies, divining our own
paths. We tend to believe that if we don't shoot or rob anyone, our
lives are our own to live and that they affect no one else's. Nowhere is
this less true than with family, but my father seemed completely
oblivious to that reality. My sister Nora tells a story of sitting down
with my father at a restaurant one day, mustering up all of her
courage to speak with him about a family member who had fallen
into a deep depression. As she talked, my father doctored his ham-
burger, carefully placing tomatoes and onions on top and then pouring on the ketchup and sprinkling massive quantities of salt.

"You don't think that has anything to do with me, do ya?" he said
as he chomped down hard on the burger.

He seemed incredulous that his decision to leave could be inter-
preted as a rejection of his family. As far as he was concerned, it was a
matter between him and his wife, not something that should affect
his children. His obliviousness, however, had its own effect, causing
most of his children to position themselves, squarely and unequivo-
cally, in my mother's corner.

Today, I look at my father's leaving from at least two perspec-
tives—that of the young man I was then, and that of the man I have
become. At the time, I was a needy young man and an angry one, although I didn't realize that I was either. If I needed my father's pres-

ence and guidance, I couldn't admit it to myself. And yet, deprived of those things, I grew angrier than before.

Even now I sometimes feel the anger rising when I think about my father, but it's tempered by my own experience in the intervening years. I've lived to know the stresses of work, the claustrophobia of a bad marriage, the desperation of feeling trapped by circumstances. So I can imagine the feeling of liberation he must have experienced when he began to break out, the joy of finally having found something for himself: the running, which made him feel alive, and the writing, which gave him adulation from a world with which he had hitherto been at war.

If my father was opting for a chance at another life, I should perhaps give him his due. Who am I to judge? But to this day, it is the way he went about it that still bothers me. It was not just the column about "the new woman," although that was the most public and irresponsible outburst. And it was not just the fact that he took his girlfriend out to places where he was bound to see people he and my mother knew. No—it was not just that he was bent on leaving but that he seemed bent on punishing my mother as he left.

His growing fame only worsened things for us. Far from enjoying the warm glow that now surrounded him, we shrank from it. Whenever any of us met people who realized that we were related to George Sheehan, which happened almost daily over a period of years, we had to listen to eager testimonials about how his books and columns had changed their lives. "How lucky you are" to have such a great man for a father, they would say. "Yes, we're all quite proud of him," I would dutifully reply.

The time soon came when I would do my best not to use my last name. Determined to distance myself from my father's celebrity, I decided to get far away, farther away even than Iowa. After the summer of '76, I decided that I would leave college and move to San Francisco to chase my Kerouac–fueled dreams of being a writer. Once there, I did very little writing. Instead, I got a job as a waiter and drank every night after work. This was the beginning of my secret life as a serious drinker. It was a life that became progressively grim, lonely, even desperate.

CHAPTER NINE

THE WHOLE SCENE FELT apocalyptic: a great mass of humanity waited, all of us huddled together, steam rising off our naked shoulders. Above us, six helicopters circled in the blue sky with a deafening chop and drone, hovering above the first mighty stanchion of the bridge. The great hum and chatter of the runners rose toward them and blended into a featureless cacophony of sound. We stood somewhere in the middle of the runners, my father and I, bouncing up and down, trying to stay loose, shaking our naked legs in the cold. We were joined by 9,875 other pairs of naked legs at the Staten Island tollgates of the Verrazano Narrows Bridge. Somewhere out in front of us, invisible to all but those in front, the bridge's span, vacant and carless, awaited the start of the 1978 New York Marathon.

In the preceding hour we had assembled in the adjoining park at Fort Wadsworth, where I had seen a most unusual sight—a slanted trough, stretching fifty yards, with hundreds of runners peeing into it. I peed there myself, adding mine to the fast-moving stream of yellow urine. When I leaned forward to look upstream, I saw a runner thirty yards away taking the same measure of things, leaning forward in a row of runners that stretched out of sight. My father and I had daubed ourselves with the requisite Vaseline and discarded our Salvation Army sweats, giving up hope of ever reclaiming them. We began moving with the enormous crowd to find a place on the bridge, blending with this substrata of human body odor, heat, and steam, which rose and dissipated in the October chill. As I walked alongside my father, I felt like his attaché. Everywhere we went, a knot of runners surrounded him, heaping praises upon him and cajoling him to sign their numbers or asking for some last-minute advice. We moved through them until we found the smallest bit of open concrete. Then, as we awaited the start of the great event, he dispensed the time-honored advice to me. "Remember, we take the first ten miles as a warm-up only," he said. "Nice and easy."

A feeling of anxiety rippled through the crowd, and I began to pogo up and down to get a better view. I saw other bobbing heads doing the same thing, creating the impression of whitecaps on the ocean. Yet, in the middle of this huge, amorphous sea there were a few recognizable faces. I was keenly aware—as was he—that my father was not just a participant in this race, he was a primary attraction.

The starter cannon boomed, and above our heads you could see a great plume of smoke rising and twisting in the air. But despite the great answering roar from the crowd, we didn't go anywhere. The lead runners out in front were obviously under way, but it would be a long time before those of us in the back could begin to move. In front of me, I saw the legs, torsos, and heads of other runners moving up and down, but not forward; then, almost imperceptibly inching forward, the crowd began to disperse into its separate pieces, like a glacier beginning to thaw and break apart. Soon we were taking whole walking steps, and then mincing jogging steps. Finally, we began to run.

We covered the first half of the bridge in quick halting steps, mindful of the people in front and behind, careful not to trip and fall. As we neared the middle of the great span, the crowd began to thin out, giving us some running room. Suddenly there were open pockets of uninhabited space and I had a running back's inclination to sprint into the void. "Take it easy now," barked my father, cautioning against premature strain. "Remember, just a warm-up." But now we were being pushed forward by the throng behind us. It was hard to restrain my strides and harder still to contain my excitement.

Craning my head to the side, I could see the far-off island of Manhattan, and as we crested the midpoint of the bridge I could see the low-rise brick buildings of Brooklyn spread out before us. While I had seen those views from car windows, this was different—being out in the air, unbuffered, unmediated. Out ahead I saw another amazing sight: thousands of runners before us creating one unified stream as they snaked into Brooklyn and disappeared behind a row of buildings, like an invading army. But if this was an army, I thought, it certainly was a gentle one—though it emanated an undeniable power, accompanied by a slightly absurd but compelling sense of mission.

As we came off the Verrazano exit ramp and onto the crowd-laden sidewalks of Bay Ridge, an apartment window blasted the *Rocky* theme music, and my father began to be recognized. "Way to go, Doc," and, "Go get 'em, Dr. Sheehan," we would hear as we passed. Easy to spot, he was dressed in his standard, quite distinctive, marathon garb: a tattered shirt with JASPERS on the front and the tight-fitting skull cap he'd created by knotting a handkerchief at all four corners. Runners sidled up alongside him, and as they flanked him, he dispensed tips and medical advice like an ambulatory doctor's office. Mostly it seemed they just wanted to exchange a few words and match a few strides with him.

Maybe it was the excitement of the event, or maybe the added excitement of traversing the Brooklyn streets of his childhood, but my father couldn't contain himself. Early on, he had settled into an easy, relaxed gait, like a passenger on a long ride locking in cruise control. Not far into the race, however, he began running. Not jogging. He was no longer "taking it easy" as he had espoused, and I noticed him picking up speed as he moved through Park Slope. He was flying through the streets, waving to those who called out his name. At times, he stripped the handkerchief from his head and twirled it aloft, eliciting a roar from the sidewalk.

We were both back home now. I was back from San Francisco, living in New York and going to school at Columbia. My father was back as well, living with my mother again in Rumson. He returned before I did and was accepted back into the family with a minimum of fuss or rancor. Appearing properly penitent and calling his life away an aberration, he said his departure had been a flirtation with madness. He was back, and so this day was both a celebration and a triumph. It was a celebration for the family as well as a triumph for him, for he had reached the very pinnacle of success.

∞

DURING MY PARENTS' SEPARATION, my father had finished the book for Simon & Schuster. *Running & Being* had been published a few months before and was already on the *New York Times* best-seller list, though its success was somewhat eclipsed by the even larger success of another book by a runner/author named James Fixx. *The Complete*

Book of Running had spent the previous year at number one as a kind of one-stop shopping for runners. But while it was promoted as "the only book you'll ever need," it also contained a glowing chapter on my father, a tribute to his importance in fostering the running movement and an homage to his place in the sport. Even if Fixx had stolen some of his thunder, my father had little room to grouse. *Running & Being* was flying off the shelf.

And still, even as he approached the height of his success, there was something in his pursuit of fame that made me ache for him. He was so vulnerable, and so much of him was on the line. To me, he seemed an introvert hard-pressed to play an exhibitionist. In my heart, I knew him to be a person who craved solitude and liked best to be left alone. The very pursuit of fame seemed contrary to that, and I wondered how he would withstand the inevitable knocks.

Running & Being stayed on the *Times* list for four months, despite the paper's own caustic review. My heart bled for him when I read the scathing "get a load of this" treatment it received in the *Sunday Book Review*. The reviewer quoted copiously from the book in the interest of ridiculing it: " 'When I run the roads I am a saint. I am Assisi wearing the least and meanest of clothes.' Or, 'I am a descendant of . . . People of the mind. Men like Kierkegaard and Emerson and Bertrand Russell.' Or, 'But I am who I am and can be nothing but that.' Or, 'Today I took Truth and ran with it on the River Road.' Or, 'The distance runner is a prophet. Like the poet he is the antenna of the race.' (I could go on.) It must be all those long runs—they've scrambled the man's mind."

The reviewer did go on: "In case we question his relationship with Kierkegaard and Emerson and Bertrand Russell, he gathers together a large number of quotes from Great Minds such as Kant, Nietzsche, Plato, Socrates . . . Ortega y Gasset, Suzuki, and one Bertram S.

Brown (he's nothing if not eclectic). Their works are ruthlessly exca-
vated for material to buttress his thesis, to wit; or rather, witless: that
Running is Being, that Running is the Total Experience; that Body
Maketh Man and the Boston Celtics are saints." The exasperated reviewer concluded: "If this is what running does to you, we'd better go
back to crawling on all fours."

When my father read the review, he apparently winced and then
simply put it aside without comment. By this time, he had adopted a
kind of "just spell the name right" public relations stance, not reacting
to the jibes and mocks. Practically speaking, it was no matter anyway.
There was now an insatiable demand for running shoes and running
books and for him personally. He was the spokesman of the sport,
a sport that in many ways had become synonymous with the times.
Depending on how you looked at it, running was either the perfect
endeavor for those who wanted to redefine themselves and reach their
potential or, to take a dimmer view of it, running was the perfect activity for the shamelessly self-involved.

It had already been observed, most famously by Tom Wolfe, that
in the American culture there now seemed to be a burning urgency
of self. People doted openly and shamelessly on themselves—their
physical appearance, their health, and their sexuality. Wolfe had
dubbed the 1970s the "Me" decade, and although this constituted
rather a broad brushstroke of pop sociology, I figured he'd gotten it
basically right. For, all at once, it was suddenly okay to be completely
self-absorbed, and the self-help gurus stood ready to cater to that
most important of all people: You. By the mid-seventies, the business
of "me" had become something more than a cottage industry. It
seemed to have unlimited potential, and my father rode the same
waves, sometimes appearing with gurus of other spheres.

At one event in New York, people paid the unheard-of sum of

sixty dollars a head to hear an all-star lineup of self-helpers. *People* magazine called it the first "Me-In." The list included Wayne Dyer, Werner Erhard, and my father. It had been organized by ex-yippie Jerry Rubin, who called it the You-Me Mind-Body Day. To me, that about summed it up. One final nail in the counterculture coffin.

"Sixty bucks?" I asked my father, incredulously.

"It's already sold out," he told me with satisfaction.

"And how much will the ex-revolutionary make?" I asked.

"I imagine the ex-revolutionary will do just fine," my father said.

The event drew thirteen hundred to a Manhattan high school and merited this account in *People* magazine:

"Among the living founts of salable wisdom: hunger artist Dick Gregory (who flew in first class from California), iron pumper Arnold Schwarzenegger (who arrived on the arm of Sargent Shriver's voluptuous daughter Maria), marathon man Dr. George Sheehan (in 20 year old running shoes) . . . After a lunch of free Perrier water and a $4 sprout salad (tossed by hand in black rubberized trash cans), the multitude sat down for a rap session with sexologists Masters and Johnson. Soon participants were grappling for the microphone to blurt out details of their most recent orgasms. In the afterglow, Dr. Sheehan appeared to explain 'How to Get the Most out of Jogging.' "

My father was ebullient about the event and about his mention in *People*. While I felt I shouldn't rain too hard on his parade, to me it was part of the same gigantic letdown. It saddened me that my father's message, born of the counterculture, would be embraced by those who seemed so intrepidly self-involved, and that it didn't take much of a shoehorn to fit my father and his philosophies into their niche. During the late sixties and early seventies, I had really believed that the world was about to be transformed in bold and dramatic ways. The whole notion—as vague as it was—was dashed on the shore of commercialism. *Co-opted* was the word I used then to describe the marketing of all hippie regalia from jeans to waterpipes to Rolling Stones albums. Everyone was angling to market their piece of the crumbling subculture, including, to my dismay, my own father.

And still, if I wasn't quite convinced of his purity, I certainly admired his courage. I had heard it said that the truly courageous in war are those who are terrified and go into battle anyway. That, to me, described him—especially in his battles with his persistent stagefright. All that year, he hawked his book throughout the country, bouncing from city to city, speech to speech, television appearance to television appearance. First there were the local shows and then came the national ones. Only a few months before, my sister Nora and I had met at a bar in downtown Manhattan, where our friend the bartender turned off the jukebox so we could watch our father on television. There at the bar, we watched in surreal amazement as the curtain was pulled and our very own father slinked out onto the set of *The Tonight Show.* Dressed in a baby-blue sweater with sleeves pulled up around his slender forearms, he came out walking slightly bent over, as if he had been caught by surprise by the bright lights. He glanced sidelong at the camera as if to say, "I've really done it this time," and as he settled into the guest chair, I could see him swallow hard as he tried to appear comfortable. On the other side of America, I held my breath.

Johnny Carson was off that night, which was unfortunate, because I could imagine Carson loosening him up with a few jokes about the relative benefits of scotch to running. But the guest host, John Davidson, took my father straight, giving him full reign to explain why running had so captivated the nation.

"We have become the new aristocrats," I heard my father say in his low monotone. "We're like the Greeks, we have all of the money and time to be anything we want to be. We've been through that *nouveau riche* period when we were consumers and spectators. Now, we want to get out and be doers. I think that's what we're seeing. We see people going out and finding themselves, finding their bodies and finding it's good to do that."

Then he told the rest of the drowsy American public to "listen to your body" and take to the streets.

Davidson, a newborn runner, replied, "I listen to my body and it tells me to quit."

"It really doesn't," my father said earnestly. "You know we have this saying, 'the spirit is willing but the flesh is weak'?"

"Yes."

"Well, it's really the exact opposite. The flesh is willing to do anything. It will go out and run twenty-six miles if it has the spirit."

At one point, my father seemed distracted and I feared he might sink into himself, but then he rallied and scored with some more of his ready-made sayings and quotes. And still, he never stopped looking vulnerable up there. Or perhaps that was just me projecting. As I watched him, I felt as though I were up there with him, with no place to hide.

I called him the next day in New Jersey. He had taken the red-eye back from Los Angeles, thinking he had bombed. "I don't know what happened," he told me. "I just wanted to get the hell out of there." Still, that show and others had put his face in play in America, and soon it became impossible to walk the street with him without his being recognized. In running circles, he was an ever-growing attraction, and at races and marathons like Boston and New York, he was sometimes mobbed. The joy of that trumped any fear of missteps or failures.

By then he was so focused on his new career that he had phased out most of his medical practice, and at home he had pressed the entire household into service as part of his support crew. It was as though he was using the house as a kind of staging area in between his talks and appearances. This wasn't what my mother had expected when she took him back. When he had asked for a reconciliation, she told him she needed him to be more of a husband, and he had agreed. But once back, he seemed to want not a wife but an organizer of suitcases and a guarantor that he would get to the airline gate on time.

Taking our cue from her, we accepted him back on his terms. He returned from his trips and talk-show interviews wanting us to act thrilled or amazed, and for the most part we obliged him. But over time, we began to feel more like staff than family.

∞

RUNNING THROUGH BROOKLYN that day was like running through an Edward Hopper painting. The October sun slanted down on the red-brick buildings, casting crisp, dark shadows beneath a brilliant blue sky. Looking up, I could see people staring down at us, leaning out their windows above flowerpots and fire escapes, waving as we passed. In a matter of blocks, we crossed through several different worlds. In Bed-Stuy, the people partied as we streamed past, and we saw a few winos dancing as a Calypso band played. In Williamsburg, Hasidic Jews stared out from under big furry hats in stony wonder at this invading horde.

My father and I matched strides as our pace dropped down to seven and a half minutes a mile. In contrast to mine, however, my father's stride appeared unlabored, as he glided along like a bird under

his handkerchief crown. He seemed unbound, his every stride a celebration of his freedom.

I envied that sense of freedom as I began to strain just to keep up.
My breathing was already taxed, my stride already forced. As the race
wore on, my proximity to him made me feel more and more exposed
as the poseur I knew myself to be. I was running this marathon on
the cheap, having cut short my training and also having gone out
drinking the night before. I had also been out drinking the night before that, and the night before that, too. Truth was, I was now out
drinking all the time.

∞

I CONTINUED TO HAVE a genuine commitment to running, but it no
longer sprang from a desire for any kind of spiritual enlightenment. I
ran now out of physical necessity—to rid my body of alcohol. When
I went out running, it was to run off a hangover, to clean my system
of toxins, and to keep my head clear to do the things I needed to do.
It had become a purely practical matter, allowing me to continue my
favorite indulgence—the drinking of copious quantities of beer.

If I had not quit pot altogether, it had definitely taken a backseat
to beer. I had become a prodigious drinker, and when I worried
about the amount I drank, I told myself that beer drinking was hon-
orable, American, and stable. I loved beer, and I loved the taste of it.
In bars, I loved to watch the way it sweated the glass, the way the
light illuminated its amber color, the way the small bubbles climbed
through it like strings of little pearls. I loved to drink it in large swal-
lows and chase it with a hard pull on a cigarette. I loved it so much, I
couldn't imagine anyone else being quite as fond of it. For I could
drink ten, eleven, twelve, and perhaps as many as fifteen beers in a

sitting. It gave me a manageable high as well as some plausible deniability. If someone were to query me about my drinking, I had a ready defense. After all, I could say, it's only beer.

By the time I reached San Francisco, mine had become a sort of binge-and-purge existence—drinking beer at night and then running it off in the morning. I lived on the fringes of Haight-Ashbury, where the sun shining through the palm trees didn't abide sloth. I opened my eyes most mornings to a punishingly bright blue sky and a cement block of a hangover encasing my head. Immediately, I put on my running shoes for a six-mile spin through the magnificent Golden Gate Park, the concrete headache crumbling into sweat and heavy breathing. Sometimes I would stop for a cup of tea at the Japanese Tea Garden or a mango juice at the grocery. After a shower, I'd sit with a cappuccino and a newspaper at the corner café, feeling the cool sunlight on my newly unfettered head.

For a few brief hours, I would feel alive, in touch, and then I'd catch a bus and head downtown for my restaurant job. After eight hours of running down trays and plates, I walked out onto Van Ness and wandered past the gay boys on Polk Street. It was pre-AIDS San Francisco, and Polk Street was a Felliniesque carnival every night. But alone and heterosexual, I always felt cavernous and empty in the face of the stray laughs and midweek juvenilia. With the air cold and the dark streets often wet with rain, I searched for a late-night plate of fried rice or headed straight to a bar.

North Beach was my nighttime haunt. In my head, I was searching after dead Kerouac, penning my little poems in bars and cafés and dreaming large about the literary life. My grandiose fantasies soared even as the reality of my paltry achievements threatened to ground them. When drinking didn't produce much writing, I settled for mere drunkenness, wanting only the escape, something that would cushion the daily bumps and bruises. In drunkenness, I could be maudlin, sentimental, poignant, even contortedly heroic. It became a world of my own, a comfortable bower I could return to again and again.

Within a short time, the streets in North Beach became devoid of poetry. I was just walking them drunk—too drunk to write or to do anything but try to find my way home to sleep. Each morning, I promised myself not to drink, but the whole cycle started over again each night. In a twenty-four-hour day, I would get drunk, sweat it out, and then get drunk again. And still, I was somehow able to convince myself that this was a zero-sum game, that my life was somehow in balance.

I had come back to New York determined to cut back on my drinking, vowing to be a serious student. At Columbia, however, I found that drinking and serious study were not necessarily mutually exclusive, and the old pattern reasserted itself. I took afternoon classes so I could drink late at night without having to worry about getting up in the morning. I haunted the library for hours in the evening, but as the night grew late, I would squirm in the wooden chairs, thinking about the bars on Broadway. After forcing myself to hold out for one more hour and then one more, I'd eventually succumb; I'd put away my Keats, Shelley, or Byron and walk up Broadway.

Shakespeare was replacing Dylan in my personal pantheon, and in my drinking, I began to see myself in one of his characters—the slothful Prince Hal. Like Hal, I saw myself as debauched but still of promise, ever ready to throw off my wanton ways "by breaking through the foul and ugly mists of vapors that did seem to strangle." I was ready to throw it off at any time, I told myself. This drinking was but a temporary thing. I would prove myself worthy by "redeeming myself when men least think I will." And yet, after walking out of the library onto Broadway, I would find myself walking into the West End Cafe, once again to drink my beer and throw back shots. I would stare into the liquor bottles, all lit from behind, glowing amber and brown, and a line in *Henry IV* would come to me:

"If all the year were playing holidays, To sport would be as tedious as to work."

It had come to pass that I was treating every day as a holiday, and life was indeed tedious. And worse.

One night I went to a party down on Avenue A, where a few friends were crammed into a railroad apartment. We drank and smoked pot until the night grew light. Some people passed out on the couch, and I tried to grab some sleep on the floor only to wake a little while later with a stiff neck. Determined to find my way to my own bed uptown, I ventured out into the chilly Sunday dawn, and onto the gray streets of the Lower East Side. A few blocks away, I heard a siren or a horn, and then saw dozens of catatonic-looking men filing out of a building. Those dozens turned into more than a hundred, and I realized, getting closer, that they were homeless people leaving some kind of flophouse or shelter. I stood watching them for a while until I was approached by a middle-aged man. He was bearded and dirty but wearing a suit, and though it hung about him tattered, torn, and covered with dirt, its quality still showed through. The man himself was still youngish-looking with distinguished, angular features. Curious about him, I gave him a five-dollar bill.

"If you don't mind me saying this, you don't look like you belong here," I told him.

Then the man told me that he had been a broker on Wall Street, and until recently had had a wife, kids, and a big house in Connecticut. As was apparent, he had lost all of that, and I could see from his suit that the descent had been rapid, taking him by surprise.

"What happened?" I asked.

"What do you think happened," he snapped. "I like to drink."

The man began to eye me warily, and I could feel his shame turn to anger. It was clear that my five dollars would not buy much more conversation, but I forged on.

"Well, can I ask you one more thing?" I said to the man.

"What is it?"

"How do you live? I mean, what do you do all day?"

"What do I do?" he said. "I try to bum as much money as I can so I can drink as much as I can. So I can get as drunk as possible."

He then looked at me and his eyes widened.

"Okay?" he said loudly. "Okay? Okay?"

He shouted "Okay" at me until he was screeching it. I began to walk away and he began to yell, "What's it to you? What the fuck is it to you?" And then as I managed to put some distance between us, he screamed, "Hey, fuck you. Fuck you."

When I caught the IRT uptown, the drunk stuck in my mind and stayed there, accompanying me even as I fell asleep that night. He was still there when I woke up, and he would stay with me as a kind of measuring stick. In one way, he had given me a perverse sense of hope. After all, I wasn't in a Bowery flophouse or sleeping under a bridge; I was pulling A's at Columbia. And still, in the days and weeks that followed this encounter, try as I might to distance myself emotionally from him, I couldn't shake the feeling that we were more similar than dissimilar, that alcohol stood at or near the center of both our lives, even though I had not yet fallen as far as he had. In my head I kept hearing him yell at me, "What's it to you? What's it to you?" I knew but I couldn't say: I was doing research on alcoholism, seeing how I might end up.

Not that anyone noticed my slide. Not friends or family. In the big anonymous cities of New York and San Francisco, where people could do just about anything they wanted, there was plenty of cover. And in those days everybody seemed to be in pursuit of a good time. Once when we were walking in Red Bank, Stavros said to me, "In life, you become what you hate." I now believed him to be right, for I had become just one more party boy. I had no moral high ground anymore, since I could no longer differentiate myself from the people I loathed: glitter glam guys, disco roller skaters, leather boys in the West Village—all of them, like me, completely self-involved. One night, I even let myself be dragged to Studio 54, where my friends and I waited outside under the stony gaze of the doormen, who deemed us not hip enough to enter. We were only part of the great unwashed. I was ashamed to be standing there, ashamed that I was allowing myself to be judged. But having been judged, I was ready to accept the judgment of my own worthlessness. I walked away and as I did I saw Andy Warhol and Bianca Jagger coming toward me on the sidewalk.

"Hey, Andy," I said as I passed.

Warhol stopped, turned, and said in his famous whine, "Who's that?"

"Nobody," I said and kept walking.

∞

I STAYED ALONGSIDE MY FATHER but by about the twelfth mile, in Queens, I could no longer keep up. My shortcut training coupled with the drinking the night before had become a debilitating combination. The beer had left me dehydrated, and no amount of water seemed to slake my thirst. Already tired and not even halfway to the end. I was worried whether I would be able to make it. My father, by contrast, looked as if he were out on a stroll. "You go ahead," I told him. "I'll see you at the finish."

As I slowed and fell behind, I watched him pull away. I watched the back of his shirt, his birdlike skullcap disappearing up the street. I could tell he was still dispensing his wisdom to his fans, his philosophies pouring forth for the benefit of those running around him. He seemed barely to have registered my absence. If he was a hawk ascending, I was on a certain descent. Our lives were on different paths, but he seemed oblivious to what was happening to me. Running slowly through Queens, I moved along with the anonymous crowd of runners, unnoticed now that I was no longer at my father's side. I was on my own once again.

As I plodded through the marathon, the futility of it began to overwhelm me. I rallied briefly as I passed over the Queensboro Bridge, trying to pull myself together for the beautiful women lining the Upper East Side blocks along First Avenue, but I felt more like some Roman entertainment. From then on, I knew nothing but pain. Up to the Bronx, then down through Harlem and onto the roadways through Central Park, until finally the finish loomed close, and I tried to rearrange my contorted face to meet the great crowd that had gathered on Fifty-ninth Street outside the Plaza. At last I found myself crossing the finish line, and falling to my knees on a barren spot of dirt in the park.

Afterward, my father and I hooked up with a few of my sisters and we all went downtown to the Lion's Head on Christopher Street, where, under the low oak-beamed ceiling, a group of literary cognoscenti-turned-runners clustered around my father over Rolling Rocks, eager for any of his spoutings. You couldn't get near him. I left—half lit and alone—and descended the subway steps at Sheridan Square. Heading uptown on the IRT, I felt my legs stiffening below me, and my wafer-slim sense of accomplishment quickly slipping away.

I wanted to get drunk; more accurately, I needed to get drunk. And I did, alone, at the West End, as soon as I exited the subway at 116th Street. It was Sunday night. There would be classes in the morning but I sat there among the Sunday-night people, a dozen or so lonely souls I had seen on other Sunday nights. They either needed to be there or had no other place to go, and I was one of them. That day, I had run twenty-six miles, but I could not outrun myself. Sitting there alone in my sweats, plying myself with beer and shots, it was clear to me that this had nothing to do with celebration. It was surrender.

CHAPTER TEN

I T IS A SOMEWHAT SUBTLE but definitive change: the change in a person who has gone from anonymity to fame. Suddenly, features once so familiar take on a whole new cast as you look again and try to see what others see. To all of us, my father suddenly became bigger, more formidable. Suddenly he seemed to have wattage. You could see it in the way the camera light played off his skin: he loved that light, and the light seemed to like him. Once he felt the warmth of it, he only wanted more.

When you walked the street with him, people stared. Or you could hear them say his name as he passed. Often, they stopped him and he was always happy, even grateful, to engage them. It wasn't a trifling attention. It was the touch-the-hem-of-your-garment–type attention, the "you don't know me, but you changed my life" kind of attention. It convinced him that he was on to something big, that he could turn off the naysaying voices in his head. He would stop when approached, and he would stay, becoming a willing captive to the latest outpouring of the standard litany. Always it was some version of how a life that had been dull and flabby was now transformed, thanks to my father. The self-sameness of the tales caused my father to quip, "Every runner has a story, and I don't want to hear it." But in fact he did want to hear it, and he never really tired of hearing it, especially the part about him.

Running & Being was regarded by some devotees as a kind of sacred text. They carried it around with them, and often in these chance meetings they would produce the book itself from a backpack, gym bag, or briefcase. This to my father was the greatest thrill of all. "When someone asks me to sign one of my books, and I find it dog-eared and underlined; when a runner tells me that reading my book is like looking in a mirror; when someone tells me whole paragraphs of my book had been written in his mind before he saw my words in print, then I know happiness. I have the feeling that I must write another book to express it."

But even as he felt himself the anointed one, he could hear the rising voices of the cynics down below. The giddy heights are never secure. The running backlash came early and hard, with Frank Deford firing the first salvo in *Sports Illustrated*. "I am sick of joggers, and I am sick of runners," Deford wrote. "I don't care if all the people in the U.S. are running or planning to run or wishing they could run. All I ask is, don't write articles about running and don't ask me to read them.

"I don't ever want to read about the joy of running, the beauty, the ecstasy, the pain, the anguish, the agony, the rapture, the enchantment, the thrill, the majesty, the love, the coming-togetherness, the where-it's-atness. I don't want to hear running compared to religion, sex, or ultimate truth."

"Ouch," I whispered to myself. If the sports trades didn't completely embrace him, neither would my father find safe harbor among the intellectuals. He became the target of an undeniably funny parody of *Running & Being* published in *The New Yorker*. It was called "Z-ing and Being: a Horizontal Alternative to the Bestseller by Dr. George Sheehan," by staffer Daniel Menaker.

"I have made a vocation of slumber because I am not much good at anything else. When I was younger, I was a somnolent outsider . . . I was always trying to explain myself, to make excuses for myself. Those who listened to me always ended up saying, 'Why not give it a rest?' but I fooled them. I took them seriously. I became an endurance sleeper."

Menaker ended his parody by paraphrasing Falstaff: "He was not only sleepy in himself but the cause of sleep in others."

My father made photocopies of the Menaker piece and gave one to me. "You'll get a kick out of this," he said. And after reading it, I shook my head and smiled—hesitant to appear to get too much of a charge out of it. My father smiled, too, being a good sport. He could easily afford to be one, for he was at the height of his fame. Still, he was by nature a worrier, and he had that "uneasy lies the head that wears a crown" look about him, the anxious look of the front runner. Never letting up on his brutal writing and speaking schedule, he was hyper-vigilant in his effort to stay on top lest fame elude him. Fame was now his highest priority, and he would try to keep it no matter the cost.

When I graduated college, I stayed in New York, working as a waiter in Manhattan and trying to find a newspaper job. Starting in leisurely fashion and at the top, I began collecting rejection letters in a descending order of newspaper mastheads: the *Times*, the *Post*, the *Globe*, and then the smaller papers. Soon I was willing to go anywhere for a job—anywhere but home. When I went down to the shore for an occasional weekend, questions about my future mounted. My father, who had always adopted a laissez-faire attitude toward his children's careers, had suddenly begun expressing concern.

"What are your plans now?" he asked.

When I told him I was applying to newspapers, he wanted to know which ones. His attitude not only struck me as odd but irritated me as well. When I had wanted attention from him, he had always parceled it out grudgingly, but now that I was deciding my future in my own fashion, he was suddenly taking charge. I decided to stay away, and I took a trip up to Gloucester, Massachusetts, where Stavros and some of my other friends were working in restaurants. During the day I went for long runs followed by swims along the beautiful cove at Good Harbor Beach. At night we cooked fish and drank beer and watched the fishing boats sail in and out of the inner harbor, while Stavros held forth on this or that problem he had with modern America. His views seemed to get darker with every passing year.

This was the place, I decided. I could stay up there, do some restaurant work, try to do some writing, and look for a newspaper job at my own pace. When I went back to New York to collect my things, however, there was a message for me. It was the editor of my hometown paper on the Jersey Shore—the paper for which my father wrote his weekly column. I returned the call with trepidation.

"I'm very displeased with you," the editor told me on the phone. "Your father tells me you're looking for a newspaper job and you haven't so much as given me a call."

I immediately knew the implications of the conversation that would follow. I was boxed in. I couldn't very well tell him that I didn't want his job, because it wasn't clear whether any other paper would have me. If he was offering me a chance at a job, I would need to take it.

"Well, I was about to drop you a line, Art."

"Really, I'd hate to put you out. I mean, of course, if you don't want a job here . . ."

"Oh, no. Really, I'd love the opportunity," I said. "I guess I was just taking my time about it."

"Well, if you don't want a job . . ." he said.

Suddenly, I was applying for a job at a paper where I would be working in the same office as my father. When I took the train home from the interview, it turned out that the job was pretty much mine for the taking. And in case I had any thoughts of backing out, there was a letter from my father waiting for me at my apartment in New York. "I want you to take this job," he wrote. "You'll see it will be a terrific opportunity for you." The letter bore a curious resemblance to an order, and things became even more curious when I visited my parents that weekend. Scanning the apartment listings as I sat at their kitchen table Sunday morning, I noticed my father eyeing me warily.

"Aren't you going to stay here?" he asked.

"I don't think so," I said.

"Don't you want to save money?" he asked.

"I want a life," I said.

The following week everything came into sharper focus. I began working at the newspaper and living at home, and my father moved out. I returned from work one night and found my mother at the kitchen table, crying. "He's gone," she said. "He's gone again." She was devastated—a victim of her own false hopes, and of his indecisiveness, his failure to know himself. Try as I would, she was not to be consoled.

The following days would mirror the year ahead. As I left work I would see my mother, up all night and sleep deprived, sitting at the kitchen table staring blankly into a coffee cup. When I returned after midnight she would still be there, wondering out loud, and asking questions: Had I seen him? What was he thinking? What did I know? I knew nothing. I knew only that she needed me to be there and that my father had to know that as well. I realized suddenly that I was there by design, that he had gotten me to take this job so I could be home, so I could be with my mother once he left. A few scant weeks before, I had hitchhiked up to New England with no specific plans for the future. Now, I had a job and an even greater obligation: to fill my father's shoes and take care of my mother.

After this turn of events I heard nothing from him until he showed up in the newsroom one night to hand in his column. I shot him an angry look across the room, but because I was under deadline, I went back to typing my story. A while later, he showed up at my desk. "I don't really have time, now," he said. "We'll have dinner next week." I barely broke stride in my typing, refusing to look up.

∞

WHY DID I DREAD that dinner so much? So many feelings churned inside me. Anger, yes, but also fear—of what, I didn't even know. And yet every time I thought of the dinner, I thought the fear might well up and strangle my words—words that now needed to be said.

There was an Italian family restaurant in Red Bank where my brothers and I did much more drinking than eating. It had a thick oak bar that was lined with autographed photos of the New York Giants going back to Tittle and Gifford. In the restaurant part, there were wooden booths, gingham tablecloths, a bowl of pickled tomatoes on each table. Today, there seem to be fewer and fewer of them left, but at the time, New Jersey was still full of these places—sometimes called "buckets of blood" in tribute to the big pot of tomato sauce that simmered in the kitchen all night long.

When my father and I met there, he ordered spaghetti and started to inhale it as if he had not eaten for days. He then launched into what seemed like a prepared statement. "Your mother and I have philosophical differences," he said by way of getting things started. "It's no one's fault, really. We just don't see eye to eye."

He went through his version of it all as though reciting one of his travel schedules, stating the facts as he saw them. He and my mother saw the world differently: she was of the old world, he of the new. They had been growing apart for several years, and now there was little left to keep them together. But as he went through it all methodically and logically, I couldn't get his initial utterance out of my head: *Philosophical differences,* I repeated to myself. Was that really what he thought this was all about? It struck me as so beside the point, so dismissive, so easy. I kept repeating it in my head until suddenly I flashed hot with anger, and I thought of challenging him, but I hardly knew where to start.

"You're having an affair," I said finally. "I imagine you and Mom have a philosophical difference about that."

I stammered to say more but suddenly I began to cry, unable to continue. A long silence followed. The depth of my response shocked my father, and may have shocked me even more. To my astonishment, I couldn't stop crying.

"I didn't think you would take it so hard," he said. "I didn't know that our splitting up would have this kind of impact."

The truth was that before I began to cry, I had convinced myself that my parents' relationship no longer had much of an impact on me. After their first separation, I told myself, I had no complaint. Kids, maybe teenagers, have a grievance. Not adults. After all, my parents had stayed together until I left home, and now I was grown. Still, the pent-up emotions flowed out as if a sluice, long dammed up, had suddenly sprung open.

"That seems to be your problem," I told him at last. "You don't think anything you do has any impact on anyone else."

My father kind of stared at me and fumbled with his hands. He was unable to reach out to me, because he had always been unable to reach out. So, he stared on helplessly in silence. "I thought . . ." he said, and stopped. "I thought you wouldn't be as judgmental as the others."

"Well, maybe I am," I said. "Maybe I am judgmental."

I told him that I had come to some grudging respect for his generation—not so much for the choices they had made but for their resolve to stick by those choices. People stayed in dull jobs and bad marriages; they held firm and showed their class. They put their kids through college when they probably wanted to take their secretary to the Bahamas. "We like to throw things away," I said of my own generation. "But now, I see it takes courage to stay."

"You don't think I've tried to do that?" he said. "You don't think I wanted to leave years ago? Well, I have tried, and I don't think I can do it anymore."

He then went on to tell me that he had sunk into a very deep depression. One night before he left, he had sat alone in his room, and he had even thought about killing himself. He knew then that he had to take some sort of action for change. He began to reiterate a theme he'd been writing about for years, but it surprised me to hear it directly from him—that his life had not been of his own choosing.

"All my life, I never made a decision for myself," he told me. "It was decided where I should go to school, that I should go to med school, that I should marry and have children. I never felt these were decisions of my own making."

In his view, he had fulfilled his duty to my mother and my family, and now he needed his freedom to survive. He could no longer be saddled with a role and an identity so antithetical to what he yearned to be.

"I thought you could understand that," he said to me. "You've already done a fair share of searching."

We stared off in silence as I thought about what he had said.

"I can understand that," I said after a time. "But it seems unfair that you would ask me to understand."

He nodded in agreement, offering no other solution.

"You're right about that," he said. "I shouldn't ask you to understand me. I have no right to expect it. I don't know why I would ask."

No nice, tidy resolution would come out of our dinner conversation. He felt one way, and I felt another—neither of us had to like it. But I did learn something important about my father that night. He may have done his best to avoid the truth, but once confronted with it, he did not flinch. He did not deny it. In fact, his self-appraisal could be the most brutal of all. Later that month, this new insight into my father would be confirmed after he had a similar meeting with my mother. She told me how she had confronted him with all the questions that had been tormenting her during those long nights alone. Why had he left? How could he do this to her? To his family?

"How can you do these things, George?" she pleaded.

He responded simply, "Because I'm not a good man."

That is how he saw himself, plain and flat. He did not duck her judgment, and that night in the restaurant he didn't duck mine. When we said goodbye after our dinner, it was clear that our conversation had changed our relationship. He seemed now to be asking for my friendship, and in asking for it, he was abdicating his right to authority, giving me equal standing. What he seemed to want most of all was my acceptance. But it would be some time before I felt any desire to give it.

∞

WE WENT TO THE SAME PLACE of work in a suburban office-park building with huge plate-glass windows, a parking lot, and a small spread of grass bordering some scrub woods. Occasionally a rabbit or deer wandered into the light and looked at us sitting at our computers. They were one reminder among many that this was not the hyperpaced, big-city newsroom of my longing.

Most of the time, my father wasn't there. There was just his empty chair and a nest of papers piled high on his desk, along with stacks of books about philosophy and medical science. Only once or twice a week would he suddenly appear in the midst of it, usually around 10 P.M. I would hear the metal tip-tapping of his manual typewriter anachronistically violating the computer hush of the modern newsroom. Then I'd look up to find his great nose and balding head floating above the mess. If we happened to pass each other, we didn't venture much beyond "What's up," or "How's it going." Still, I could feel him reaching out for contact—contact I was consciously withholding.

Typically, after work I would try to make last call with some other reporters. But no matter how late it was when I went home, I always found my mother awake. Sitting down with her, she would cover the same ground, asking the same questions that seemed to haunt her. "Why did he leave?" and "Why do men cheat?" I soon realized that she wasn't looking for answers, just for the chance to unburden herself of this reservoir of pain. After a time, I became fearful of the gauzy questions that spun from her in what seemed a detached and ethereal way. It was as if she were speaking from another world, and after a time, I became afraid she wouldn't make it back.

Meanwhile, I pictured my father living his life unfettered and free, and I seethed with resentment that he seemed to be able to escape all consequences. I found myself hoping he would get his comeuppance, and one night in the office I fed a piece of paper into my father's Royal and typed a line from a John Lennon song: "Instant Karma's gonna get you." That was it. A line on a blank piece of paper, which I wrote and forgot about. A few days later, a friend in the sports department told me that my father had become very upset upon finding it, asking everyone in sight if they knew who would write such a thing. He never did confront me, even though I was the most obvious suspect.

I began to feel as though we had switched roles. Now I was playing the distant father to his role of wild son. And though I felt I was carrying the mantle of manhood bravely, it was soon to become apparent that I was not. There was tension now both at work and at home, so the bars seemed the only safe haven, the only escape. I began to drink even more.

Surrounded by a group of first-time reporters fresh from college, I wasn't alone in believing that hard drinking was essential to the newspaper life. We thought of ourselves as young Breslins or Hamills, and this allowed us—impelled us, even—to take our drinking up a notch.

I worked mostly at night and often carried on drinking into the morning hours. Some nights after my mother went to bed, I would walk around the backyard and smoke a joint, then I'd return to Dylan playing softly on the stereo and another bout of drinking into near oblivion. I needed to smoke cigarettes when I drank, and I needed to drink when I smoked, but I never seemed to finish them both at the same time. So, I'd pop another beer or light up one more cigarette, traveling solo this way into the morning light.

During that year, my mother was unable to turn the corner on her grief. Sometimes I would be awakened by noises coming from downstairs, and when I went to investigate, I would see her pacing around in the dark in her nightgown. It was painful to see her that way. Such a strong woman, always before the very model of self-composure and decorum, now rudderless and wandering in the night. In attempting to assuage her pain, I began to tell her things I doubted.

"He'll come back, Mom," I told her once.

"He doesn't want me," she said. "He only wants you people—the family."

My father faltered as well. Despite his continued success, he seemed a tinderbox of suppressed resentment. One night at the paper, he flew into a rage at having one of his columns cut. Shouting, slamming books, and threatening to quit, he stormed out. The whole scene shook me deeply, and I sought cover in the office of Doris, an older woman who wrote editorials for the paper. Unprompted, I unloaded secret tales of my home life and my concern for my mother if my father never came back.

"You can see what it's doing to her, Andy," she said. "But can you see what it's doing to you?"

I couldn't see, and I refused to blame my parents' problems for my own state of affairs. I knew only that I was unraveling, and the kindness and concern of her words touched me in a place that was undefended, and I once again began to cry.

∞

I LOOKED FOR ANOTHER JOB, but while collecting rejection letters from America's premier newspapers, I stayed. I saw my father from time to time. Always the lone hawk, he would fly in suddenly, materializing in his newspaper nest. I'd hear the typing, and swivel around to find him there, eyes intent on his fingers, pecking away. He appeared so solitary, so driven, so determined to stay on top of this running thing, lest he blow his chance and let his fame slip away. Having now closed down his medical practice, he no longer had a safety net. I realized then that it must have been a terrifying thought—the end of fame. Even as fame itself was becoming more burdensome, even as he became less and less enamored with it, he was hellbent on keeping it alive.

He published a new book with Simon & Schuster trumpeting the same themes. It was an even louder and more virulent call for people to follow their own drummer. I didn't have to look past the dedication to feel the stridency. There was no cuddly thank-you to family or friends; rather, he addressed it to the readers: "to those who will weigh and consider what is contained herein—and will test it against their own truth." This book proved not nearly as successful with the public as *Running & Being*.

Though the running wave had not yet crested, people seemed to be running more and reading less about it. While running was still gaining in popularity, the runners themselves seemed no longer to need an authority to explain the experience. Or, more to the point, they had all become experts themselves, dispensing advice to their fellow runners on training, diet, and shoes, and waxing philosophic on the emotional and spiritual benefits of the experience. On the rare occasions I entered a road race those days, I'd hear the competing voices at the starting line, trying to out-expert one another.

But with 30 million runners out there, my father's audience didn't just shrivel up overnight. He was still on the circuit, traveling to speaking engagements in San Diego, San Francisco, and Seattle one week; Austin, Chicago, and Boston the next. He was, in effect, running harder and harder to maintain his fame, and in those faces and audiences he met in far-flung cities, he found reassurance that his fame was secure, that he was still vital, still popular, still known. He seemed to need reassurance even from me, and although at times I thought it would have been far easier to erect a wall and keep him out, I could never sustain my anger. Truth was, I more often felt sorry for him. Whenever I saw him, he appeared so overmatched by it all: the fame—so antithetical to his natural shyness and ever threatening to disappear; the money—once so plentiful and now being spread so thin; the estranged family—moving ever further away from him; and the abandoned wife—still wanting him back. Then, of course, front and center, there was the new woman and her demands. Just to look at him, to see the strain in his eyes, was to know how heavy his burden had become. In searching for freedom, he seemed to have found its opposite.

My anger toward him ebbed as it became apparent to me that he was merely a man—a flawed man admittedly, but a man just the same. And wasn't I the same kind of selfish, insecure, fear-driven human being fumbling forward in the dark? A nightly inebriate shuffling through the day toward another night of drinking? Some part of me knew that if I judged or rejected him, I could just as easily be judging and rejecting myself, and that I would end our relationship at my own peril. I saw myself in him and sensed how lonely he was. One night when I was working at my newspaper desk, I became aware of a presence nearby. I looked up to see him standing at my desk, looking down. "Any words from the others?" he asked, referring to my brothers and sisters. As I started to give him an account of where everyone was and what everyone was doing, I looked again at his face, and I saw incredible sadness in his eyes.

He missed his sons and daughters. While he was always hungry for news of them, most had chosen to have little or no contact with him during that period. He did see them on occasion, because my mother still invited him to the family events—Thanksgiving, Christmas, Easter—and he appeared without fail. Once the awkwardness passed, the stern lines of his face always seemed to crack and soften at the stories and the mimicry. On Christmas Eve that year, the evening rose to a great crescendo of laughter, but then culminated in a sudden silence. Midnight found him still sitting there. The odd man out. It was time for him to leave, but instead, he lingered.

"Isn't it about time for you to go?" my mother said.

"I don't really feel like making the drive," he said sheepishly.

"Well, you're not staying here," she said.

Amid a few timorous laughs, we watched him slink out the door, a lonely and pitiable figure disappearing into the cold night. When he had gone, we imagined him alone behind the wheel, his car rolling over the frigid, empty roads. A few of my sisters began to cry.

∞

IT STARTED WITH an occasional dinner together and then some beers after work, but gradually he and I began to renew our contact with each other. Although I was noncommittal about what I was offering, his eyes showed deep gratitude for any kindness extended. We mostly stayed on the plane of ideas, talking about news and writing. As muted as it might be in our suburban beat, he thrilled at the drumbeat of the newsroom, and it made me think that if he had had any choice in the matter, he would have been a reporter from the start. He loved to talk the scoop and was conversant with the details of even the most minor stories. Being both voracious and indiscriminate in his hunger for knowledge, he knew the political battles in the local towns just as well as he knew Civil War history. And he longed to be a part of the camaraderie of the newsroom. On my birthday, he was clearly delighted when I invited him to a local steakhouse with the other reporters, his eyes following our banter as closely as if it were a tennis ball in a tennis match. At the end he insisted on paying the check for all of us—some dozen or so—and as he signed the credit card receipt he said, "This is for my son, in whom I am well pleased."

If he had once been concerned about my career, my first few articles seem to have reassured him on that count. He liked the way I wrote, and I guess he felt I could always make a living doing it. From then on, our talks about my job were writer to writer. My father always advised me to "get the good quotes." Since I liked to write features, I always searched for the vanishing characters of the shore: the fishing-boat captains, the cabbies, the saloonkeepers. And I always made sure to get at least five quotable quotes, so that the quotes would generally write the story.

We were now fellow journalists, and we shared the same insecurity about our writing, the same need for praise. "To us," he told me, "our bylines shine like the North Star. But no one else seems to notice." I also discovered something else I had in common with my father: an expanding ego. Perhaps we were both covering up the same radical insecurity, but after I found that I could break page-one stories with regularity, I developed my own newsroom swagger. This wasn't lost on my fellow reporters.

∞

EVEN WHEN WE WEREN'T SPEAKING I could always take my father's emotional temperature by reading his column. And I thought it telling at this time that he began writing about anger. At last he had begun addressing something that had haunted him all his life, something he now attributed to being Irish: "The history of Ireland is a story of frustration, of anger concealed," he wrote, adding that letting that anger out "is the only time, save being drunk or joking, when we can tell the truth." But searching other columns for deeper insights, I was disappointed. Here again, he rejected any real probing in favor of the easy answer. Basically, what he had to say about anger was: if you're angry, run it off. In one column on anger he wrote: "When I am in a situation when the usual advice is to count to 10, I run 10—miles that is. I take off and run until that heat dissipates, and when I get back, I have usually forgotten what upset me. I am pleasantly fatigued. I have what the psychiatrists call a global feeling of well-being."

Running had brought him to the dance, and it was to running that he would remain ever faithful. His columns took a predictable shape: first he would diagnose a problem of modern life—stress, boredom, disenchantment—and running and physical fitness would always be there at the end as the solution. The long run on the roads would always be the trip to Lourdes. His writing imbued running with ever greater restorative and life-altering powers. "The fish keeps getting bigger every time you tell the story," I told him once, a comment that drew a menacing stare. If I didn't want to help, he seemed to be telling me, at least don't throw stones.

We never really got drunk together (after his earlier bouts with alcohol he drank very little), but the times we came closest to talking about what was really on our minds were always over beers. We'd go to bars, where I drank and he sipped, and he'd get that far-off look in his eyes and talk about his life and the directions it had taken, spilling his doubts and his fears and wondering out loud about the major decisions.

"Maybe we should have never moved to Rumson," he would say. "We never fit in there."

It was as though he was trying to explain to himself how the two of us could have found ourselves sitting together at this outpost, two stray vestiges of a family now falling apart. He told me that his own mother had given him what-for about his leaving my mother. Her barrage had shaken him, and then Granny Sheehan had even broadened her indictment of her favorite son.

"What's this about not being a doctor anymore?" she asked him sharply. To my grandmother, a doctor who was no longer a physician was something akin to a priest who had left the priesthood. "George, I've never heard of such a thing," his mother told him. "I think it's disgraceful."

Her high-pitched emotion took him by surprise.

"You never know what people will feel strongly about," he said sadly, sipping his beer.

As we talked those nights, I realized that I was becoming one of his last links to his past—to a life he kept thinking he might want to return to one of these days. The night I told him I wasn't sure that going back was still an option, he was visibly shocked. It stunned him to think that he might not be welcome anytime he chose to return.

Although it was difficult to hear, I allowed him to talk about the problems he had with my mother, but when he wanted to talk about his girlfriend, I drew the line. I knew almost nothing about her and preferred it that way. She was at least twenty years younger than he, and they lived together. That was the sum of my knowledge and all I wanted to know. I didn't even know what town they lived in. From time to time he would slip her name into the conversation, but from the look on my face even he could tell that this was out of bounds.

∽

AFTER A YEAR WITH MY MOTHER, I moved out of the house and into an apartment with some local rockers. It was the beginning of the punk era, and on weekends we wore thin ties and went out nightclubbing in the punk scene on the Jersey Shore and in Manhattan. It suddenly felt incredibly liberating to say fuck-all to everything. On Saturday night, we'd hightail it up to the city, and hit places like CBGBs and the Mudd Club, trying to look like we weren't from Jersey. "Faster, louder," we'd yell at the bands. "Faster, louder." We'd pogo and shake our heads up and down, like paint cans in a shaker, trying to knock loose all sensibility, eager for the oblivion of the noise and the heat, the sweat and the alcohol.

On weekdays, it was a straight life. Notepad in hand, I made my way around the dying seashore cities of Long Branch and Asbury Park, checking police blotters. At night, I drove to council meetings in tract-development towns that had sprung up out in the cornfields. All the while I thought about the drinking I would do later on. I'd try to get my stories filed before the bars closed, but often I hit a speed bump in the form of my father, who would be there working late into the night, increasingly worried about the state of his life.

"It's over," he began saying of the running boom. "I'm finished."

He continued to brood about the flimsiness of his fame and the loss of his family. Still, he seemed never to figure out whether the family was obstacle or goal. I had grown impatient with his Hamlet–like indecision and was more interested in making last call. My mind raced past my father and his problems. Where could I still get a drink? Did I have any beer at home? Was any place still selling six-packs? How was I going to get drunk tonight if he kept on talking?

My father went home once again in 1981. My brothers and sisters and I waited to see if he was staying or just putting his feet up. It began to look like a serious commitment when my parents decided to sell the house in Rumson. They had found a new one in the old oceanside town of Ocean Grove, where my mother had spent some weekends with my sisters in support of her broken heart. It was a small Victorian hotel that they were now converting into a home for themselves, using the proceeds from the sale of the Rumson house for a major renovation. When it was finished, it was spectacular. The second-floor living quarters featured a panoramic view of the shoreline through wrap-around windows. On sunny days, it felt like being aboard a great ocean liner.

Recently, I found a book of poems my father gave to my mother when they moved to Ocean Grove in 1981. He inscribed it: "To Mary Jane as we begin our new life by the sea." The new life turned out to be short-lived. Except for the change in scenery, the same tensions prevailed, and their marriage remained more business arrangement than love match. While she provided the organization and the family, he merely had to be there. Within the year, he was gone again, leaving my mother alone once more, this time in a cavernous house by the sea. At last, it seemed he had made his final decision; he told my mother he was ready to proceed with the divorce. He moved back with his woman—or perhaps it was a new woman. Even now, I don't know. At the time, I didn't care to know.

My tolerance had run out. I began watching him again from a distance, ignoring him at the office, checking in with him only through his columns. Unwaveringly, he went on writing about the virtues of running. Yet, in his own life, it was increasingly apparent that running was not the cure-all that he professed, that he couldn't run off whatever ailed him, couldn't outrun his demons. Let him try; I knew what I had to do, and it no longer involved him. My responsibilities were clear: give moral support to my mother and get on with my life. Besides, I had better things to do than play confidant to my father: I had fallen in love.

CHAPTER ELEVEN

S HE MANAGED A BAR. And the fact that I picked someone who worked in a bar to fall in love with said a lot about how little I understood my relationship with alcohol. To me, her job seemed merely fortuitous—an added bonus. She kept the books in an office upstairs, and for more than a year I went there most nights after work. I would sit at the bar and stare up at the door to her office on the chance that she'd come down to check the cash register tapes. I was always ready with small talk, in the hopes of getting on her radar.

She liked to drink, and she already knew that about me. One night when she turned on all the floodlights to get the customers out, I began standing up to leave, but she patted me on the hand. "Sit down," she said. "You can stay." In the empty bar, she set me up with another beer, and we talked as she inventoried the liquor.

A tall, lithe beauty, she had long chestnut hair and large almond-shaped eyes, and it was thrilling just to be alone with her as she looked over the bottles behind the bar and wrote numbers down on her clipboard. At the same time, I knew this was a fool's paradise, for I'd heard that she had a boyfriend of long standing, although my sources said their relationship was on the rocks. When she made herself a drink and sat down with me, I knew not even to hint at being anything more than friendly.

Still, our after-hours drinking at the bar became a regular thing, and then there was a concert. I knew she was crazy about Joe Jackson and his *Night and Day* album. So when he came to the Meadowlands, I got tickets.

"Okay," she said, at last, but insisted on paying for her ticket.

"Suit yourself," I said.

After the show, we went drinking and ended up at her place, listening to "Breaking Us in Two," and rolling around on the couch together. Then she sat up, pushed her hair back over her forehead, and sent me home. The next day, she called.

"That shouldn't have happened last night," she said. "It can't happen again."

"If you don't want it to happen, it won't," I said.

It did, of course; and together we shared a year of nights like it, drunken hours of intimacy in barrooms and bedrooms around the shore. To me, it was love, and I loved her in detail. Perhaps they were only the surface details, but I loved the way she threw back her head and laughed, I loved the way she flipped her hair behind her ear, and I loved the doe-eyed way she looked at me when she was in her cups. Though she liked to drink, drinking had not dimmed her lights and her spirit was untrammeled. And still, she was that rarest of women—a beautiful woman who liked to drink and who let me drink the way I wanted without judgment or recrimination. She became my sweet bower away from the world, until it came time that I had to leave.

In the late spring of 1983, another newspaper job finally came through for me. The *Pittsburgh Post-Gazette* offered me a job, and even though we hadn't really talked about it, I was sure she would come with me. So I was crushed when she said no.

"I like living here," she said. "You're free to stay."

I couldn't turn down the job. I had already spent too much time at the small paper where my father worked and it was time to move on. I tried to reason with her, hoped to persuade her to come, but she never wavered. "She wasn't in love," was my mother's assessment, but I believed otherwise. It was a different world from my mother's: women no longer needed to follow their men, perhaps the men should follow their women. Still, when I went back two months later for a visit, she already had a new guy. I returned to Pittsburgh in the middle of a brutal summer without even an ocean to throw myself in. Of our dreamlike love affair, only the drinking remained.

∞

IT'S HARD FOR ME TO DETERMINE when I crossed that blurry line between drinking heavily and becoming a bona-fide alcoholic. Somewhere in my past, there must have been a line that, once crossed, prevented any return to moderation. Perhaps I crossed it the very night I experienced that first warm glow of drunkenness as a teenager. In finding myself suddenly at home inside my own skin, I seemed to consign myself to the ceaseless attempt to re-create that sodden state of well-being. Perhaps alcoholism became an inevitability from that point on, though the physical addiction probably took hold well after that. Whenever or wherever I had crossed the line, I probably was not aware I had crossed it until I was well beyond it. Regardless, I think it would have been hard to step off at any place along the way.

Shortly after moving to Pittsburgh, I found a bar on the city's Northside that became my new home. Though I would stop briefly at my apartment after work, I spent most of my nights at that bar. Sometimes, when I returned from a trip out of town, I went directly there from the airport, and they stashed my suitcase behind the bar. George, the bartender, became one of my best friends, and when I walked through the doors every night, he and the waitresses seemed glad to see me. The owner regarded me respectfully, and I was invited to all of the bar's picnics and private parties. I became part of the family.

Not long after I found the bar, I moved into its neighborhood, a sketchy section of town with some beautiful but decayed streets of turn-of-the-century row houses that were being gentrified. The bar sat at the end of a blighted business street that was dark and tinted gray at night and traveled mainly by street people. At the end of that row of squalor, it always emanated an inviting yellow glow, impossible for me to resist. Inside was everything I wanted in a tavern. It was an old-time place with a polished oak bar, a tile floor, and a pressed tin ceiling. Television was on only for sports, and the sound was kept off except for the big games. The bartenders and waitresses never made me wait for a beer and always kept my ashtray clean, providing a soft world of comfort removed from the harsh one just outside the door.

Each night, I would sit and look at myself in the mirror across the bar and ply myself with a dozen or more beers. Early on in Pittsburgh, the rationalization was clear: alcohol was unguent for a broken heart, a balm for my pain and my loss. But as the weeks of heavy drinking turned into months, and I tried to coax my new newspaper friends along for the ride, I found that not everybody thought this bar, or any bar, to be the best of all possible places. Shockingly, they had other things to do. On the nights they did come with me, no one seemed to drink as quickly, and no one wanted to stay as long. On the nights they didn't come, I drank there alone. Some nights, I would look up from my beer and find the entire bar, raucously filled just moments before, completely empty. It would be only myself and George attending to the last details before locking up.

Then came the nights when the bar and the drinking were no comfort at all—nights when the reality of my drinking dependency weighed heavily on me in a shameful way. It had become almost impossible to deny the salient fact that once I had even one beer, I was unable to stop. As I stared in that mirror and tried to convince myself otherwise, I knew that alcohol controlled me and not the converse, knew that alcohol was driving and I was merely the passenger. On and on it drove, night after night, as I sat there powerless to get up and leave.

Such a realization is devastating, so I suppose it sounds like a supreme rationalization to say that I believe my drinking and drugging began as a kind of spiritual search. And yet to this day, I believe this to have been true, at least in the beginning. Not only did alcohol and drugs make me outwardly confident, they began to fill the cavernous hole inside me—the great need to be connected to something outside myself, to grasp in some way the great otherness, the hidden order in things.

There were nights when my friend Stavros and I would drink until dawn, talking about church mystics like St. John of the Cross and St. Theresa, and pondering the nature of God. To us, drinking and smoking seemed somehow sacramental, as if our beer were communion wine. Other times late at night, I'd sit alone listening to Dylan, plying myself with alcohol and chain-smoking cigarettes, and to me the experience seemed transcendent—as if my mind and spirit were breaking free from the clamor of the quotidian to a fleeting glimpse of what lay beyond. "A vision of the street as the street hardly understands," was the phrase from Eliot I repeated to myself over and over, grasping its meaning faintly in the smoky haze. In time, I could grasp it no longer.

They call alcoholism a progressive disease, meaning, I suppose, that it only gets worse. I'm not sure if alcoholism is a disease, a predilection, or a weakness, but it certainly seems progressive. Early in college, and most definitely by the time I went to San Francisco, I drank purposefully, ever pursuing that quasi-mystical state even as it receded, becoming more and more elusive. As time and creeping addiction advanced, there was only drunkenness. When I returned to New York in the late seventies, I had resolved to cut back on my drinking. Despite my resolutions, I drank myself senseless, finding myself in increasingly bizarre places; one time, it was a Hispanic bar at four in the morning, all salsa dancers and strobe lights. Other nights I ended up walking the streets of the Upper West Side at dawn or riding the subway alone, all the way to New Lots Avenue in Brooklyn, the end of the line.

I may not have looked like the bums on the street or like the man I met that morning in the Bowery, but deep down, I knew we shared the same dependency on alcohol. The homeless drunk who was always wandering into the bar I frequented in Pittsburgh was another reminder of my link to this netherworld. "Get out," the bartenders would yell every time he came in. "Turn around, and get out." I would see his mad eyes vainly seeking the same comfort I sought there, and each time the bartenders put him back on the street, I felt his shame. Just like that bum, I needed the alcohol, I needed to reach that state where the madness would be tamed. I was just better at hiding my need.

When I was no longer able to deny my addiction to myself, it became an absolute necessity to hide it from other people. In New Jersey I had lived in a house of rockers, so there had been little need to dissemble. But in Pittsburgh I was supposedly a respectable city newspaper reporter, and while being known as a hard-drinking reporter was fine with me, having a reputation for chronic drunkenness was not. The chinks in my image could be suffered only around the edges. Where "heavy drinker" would only sting a bit, "problem drinker" or "alcoholic" would be devastating. Thus began my life of alcoholic stealth: the need to procure alcohol and drink it prodigiously, and all the while to try to keep it hidden from everyone else.

Every morning, the same battle would begin—the same thoughts and questions rising to the surface shortly after coffee. "Should I drink tonight or shouldn't I?" "If I am to drink, I'll need to start early, so I can have my fill before a reasonable hour." "If I decide not to drink, I'll need to hold firm. I can't allow myself to cave in later on." The decision not to drink was never firm. Throughout the day, I would revisit the decision time and again, turning it over and over like a hamster on a wheel. As the afternoon grew dark, my resolve generally weakened, and I looked for one rationalization or another to placate my guilt. "If I allow myself to drink tonight, I won't drink again until the weekend." Or, "If I drink tonight, I will get to bed before two." And so on. These deals and calculations dominated my waking life.

Every night required a new plan for drinking. If I was meeting other people, the plan involved a sleight-of-hand. Arriving at the bar before everyone else, I would have three or four drinks before they came, and knowing I would need more later, I would have made sure there was beer or whiskey waiting for me back at my apartment. When we all left the bar together, I appeared sober enough, but I was really close to the edge of drunkenness, and I would return home to finish myself off. Within the web of my own strange logic, I would generally post a win. That meant I could get up and go to work the next day and I might even break a front-page story. But in effect I was leading two lives: a drunken life and the life I lived to cover that one up. My existence had become a shadow play, a duplicity, an elaborate fake.

Though I continued to fight it, to stay sober a few nights a week, it was a losing battle. Each night I succumbed, it was like the little nick of a blade on my heart—the disappointment of another defeat. Immediately, I would set the alcohol to its work of assuaging my guilt over it. But with every little nick, I felt as though I had died a little. They were small deaths leading perhaps to the great big one in the future. In trancelike steps, I felt I was walking there; if not into a literal demise, at least into a life where my spirit would be so deadened that life would become only an endurance of time. And still, there seemed to be no other way.

If alcoholism is a disease, it is one of loneliness. It is the disease of the dark secret you try to keep from yourself. And failing that, it is a secret you keep from others at all costs. I did my best to keep my secret hidden, and despite a few raised eyebrows here and there, I was successful. Until I was ready to address it, I kept it secret from even my closest friends. And yet I was always thinking, how could they be close friends if they were unaware of the central fact of my life, the maintenance of which occupied all my waking hours? In my family, I was perhaps viewed as a middle-of-the-pack drinker. No one in my family confronted me, lest—I later realized—such a confrontation might hold a mirror to habits of their own. So, I let my drinking blend with their drinking, and if my habits were a little more extreme, I could confidently assume that I would not be called to task. In that safety, however, there was an even deeper loneliness, because I knew now that in a very unromantic way, I was doing myself severe harm. It was chilling to realize that those closest to me were complicit in my descent, the rules strictly forbidding any discussion.

This extended to my love life as well. If I dated a woman, it was as though she had to accept the presence of my mistress—alcohol. Any date was a threesome—the two of us and my drinking; it would have to at least end, if not begin, in a bar. When she failed in changing the venue for even a single night, one woman I dated during that period told me, "You're an alcoholic." I became so infuriated, I drove her home and then returned to the bar to get really drunk. The absurdity of my defiance was clear even to me. And as I drank my beer and stared at myself in the mirror behind the bar, I said these words softly: "You're a drunk." When my mind didn't rally in my own defense, another thought occurred: so be it. I might be an alcoholic, but I was not ready to change, to commit myself to what even then I knew would be the only possible "cure"—lifelong abstinence. To be an excommunicant of bars seemed tantamount to a death sentence.

And so I was forced to marshal all of my powers of rationalization against it. Perhaps the greatest of these rationales was that when I was drinking, I was actually doing work. I drank with cops, politicians, city workers—anyone with a potential story. In the morning, I would search my dark memory bank to retrieve whatever information I had coaxed out of them the night before. More often than not, I could turn that information into a story, and that evening I could read it— basking in the immediate gratification of the early edition. Another cause of celebration, another reason to tip a few and savor.

And there were still nights when I seemed to play it right. Holding up the bar with a few other reporters, I would stand in the middle laughing and telling the war stories of newspaper life, the drinks fueling the hilarity. What would I do without nights like that? I wondered. How could I go to a baseball game and not drink beer? How could I go to a rock club sober? Drinking seemed my only reliable source of fun and good times. For the life of me, I could not imagine enjoying a single evening without it. So, in the contorted logic of alcoholism, the power of denial showed its strength. All evidence to the contrary, I could still rationalize that alcohol was not the cause of my problems. Rather, for all of its faults, it was still my only relief. Although I had begun to know that a day of reckoning must come, and that I would have to either stop drinking or face some very dire consequences, I responded in my mind to the notion of reform with the words of St. Augustine: "Not yet."

∞

MAYBE IT'S ALCOHOLISM, perhaps it's just being Irish, but the people in my family have always seemed saddled with a radical need for self-sufficiency. No matter how great the problem, there is almost a knee-jerk need to insist that it's under control and no cause for concern. I know at least for myself, and most likely for my father, it would have been a very hard thing to admit that we were in trouble or that we might need some help. It definitely did not occur to me to seek him out at this time, and he wasn't seeking me out either. Once he'd left my mother again, after all the talk about a new life, I'd distanced myself from him, and although I would generally see him when I went back for visits, it would never have occurred to me to confide in him about my drinking or my broken heart. Since he had become just as unlikely to share any intimacies with me, it was only through my mother that I learned shortly after I left for Pittsburgh that he had had a cancer scare.

One of the great ironies of my father's life is that he didn't believe in doctors. Whether out of fear or principle, he never wanted to be a patient. Rarely would he consult anyone else for sickness or pain, and even less frequently would he submit to an examination. He had troubled eyesight, but, refusing to see an optometrist, he would go to

Woolworth's, where they kept a bin of three-dollar glasses. I remember watching him once, trying on pair after pair, looking down his nose at a newspaper, until he found ones that satisfied him. As his vision worsened, he would merely return to Woolworth's to find a stronger pair.

He had waged a kind of private war against the medical establishment. Though a doctor himself, he didn't believe that most doctors did much besides treat the symptoms of sick people. Fearing and distrusting doctors as he did, he promoted fitness as a way not to get sick in the first place. But his belief in prevention did not extend to checkups. He never had a regular physical, not every other year, not every five years. It was something he would come to regret. "I have made major mistakes in my life," he would write years later. "But none equal to this one. I gave no thought to being checked for cancer."

In the early 1980s, he was in Houston visiting early mentor and running pioneer Dr. Kenneth Cooper, who maintains perhaps the most elaborate physical-fitness laboratory in the world. Also there was my father's friend and writing competitor Jim Fixx, the author of the two-year best seller *The Complete Book of Running*. Cooper suggested that while they were in town, both Fixx and my father have complete physicals. Years before, my father had told Fixx: "Annual physicals are a waste of time," and that day he turned down Cooper's offer. Fixx declined to be tested as well, even though his family had a history of coronary problems. Five months later, Fixx died of a heart attack while running through the woods near his home in Vermont.

Despite being a competitor, Fixx had been a good friend to my father, someone who shared the same passion and, at the height of his success, had also been willing to share the credit, making sure to give my father his due. Now, with Fixx's death, my father felt alone and besieged. For the next two months he defended running, taking phone calls from press all over the world, fending off assertions that running was in fact dangerous. He began making his first concessions to the idea that physicals, even for seasoned runners like himself, might be warranted. In 1984, he was back in Houston with Cooper, who this time wouldn't take no for an answer. "I'm not going to lose another one," Cooper told him. And my father assented to the physical.

A few weeks later, I read my father's account of how he stripped down to his running shorts, hopped on the treadmill, and proceeded to run a few miles at a six-minute pace. As he sped along the moving tread, he broke his age-group records and landed in the 99th percentile of all the thousands Cooper had tested over the years. "Afterwards, as I lay on the recovery table," he wrote, "I felt that I had joined the immortals." But as he lay there prone, Cooper began giving him the physical he had promised, and in his probing he felt an enlargement of my father's prostate. When Cooper told my father this, it struck him with sudden terror. "The sense was paralysis," he wrote. "I had just joined the immortals, and suddenly I was aware of my own mortality."

I got a call from my mother, saying that my father was flying to Cleveland for tests. "He told me to tell you not to worry," she said. "But he wanted me to let you know." A few weeks later, he sent me the article he had written while awaiting his test results in the hospital. "Whether this nodule turns out to be benign or malignant, my life has been unalterably changed. The lesson: I've made every day count. But what I have not done is make every person count." It sounded like a stunning moment of clarity. After neglecting friends and family, he appeared to be reaching out for our forgiveness. He had arrived at this juncture in his life unprepared to face any illness, let alone a life-threatening one. Now as he waited, he didn't even need to hear the test results. The brush with serious illness had already shown him who and what were important in life.

I read all this in the article, but I never heard from him. My mother told me he had called to tell her that the biopsy showed the tumor to be benign. And that was the last she heard from him. If he was reaching out to the people who counted, those people seemed not to be us. We knew only that he wasn't leaving his girlfriend or abandoning his new social circle, which consisted entirely of people much younger than he. But years later, when I read one of his final books, *Personal Best,* I learned that this brush with cancer had left him with a pervading awareness of growing old—a realization that he could not go on beating back age indefinitely.

He did not return to us or to his old friends at this time; but unknown to us, his new relationships had begun unraveling as he looked to them for a sympathy and understanding that were not forthcoming. "I live in social circles that are one and two generations younger than I am," he wrote. "I had never felt that difference to any great extent and neither did they. But lately, I'd become resigned to being no longer contemporary in body or even in mind. I had become a bore, and I'd found that I was even boring to myself."

His girlfriend, according to that book, proved particularly demanding. As he had exhausted the goodwill of his family, he had become dependent on hers—notwithstanding the fact that she didn't have our soft spot for his weaknesses. Having lived together in an apartment for two years, they had traveled the country and the world and had a committed relationship. But short of a marriage proposal, she grew impatient and exasperated. The time came when she told him to get out. It devastated him in ways that were worse than the threat of cancer.

"I was injured—and for the moment—mortally," he wrote.

Suddenly, with the breakup knocking him completely off his moorings, he was adrift. He wrote of an emotional pain so acute that it bordered on the physical, and he pleaded with her to reconsider. It was pleading that was as shameful as it was futile, and he concluded: "There is nothing more piteous than the wail of a man who has been told to pack up and go."

It amazes me that although my father had tremendous difficulty speaking of his emotions, he had no similar compunction against putting them down on paper, revealing them to his readers. It was as one of those readers that I learned—though not until years after he wrote about it—how hard it had been for him to deal with a broken heart, and saw how closely his despair had mirrored my own in those days.

On the fourth day of the breakup, as he wrote, he was determined to thwart his pain with some resolute action. "I collected every reminder of her—letter, photos, and gifts—put them in her final (and prophetic?) gift, a suitcase, and left them on her porch." It felt over and done, but predictably it wasn't. For a while he thumped his chest, saying that he welcomed this new challenge and that the new round of suffering would make him stronger still. But eventually he folded under the great weight of it: "As the days become weeks, and the weeks become months, the dominant emotion is loneliness."

And it would be a new kind of loneliness. Having always touted the virtues of being alone and the freedom of self-sufficiency, he now felt only the hollowness of it. He had always had people—lots of people—around him. Though he may not have communicated with them at the time, they were always within reach, within earshot.

"I am a loner, but I am rarely alone," he wrote. "Being alone is my natural state. I seek solitude to think. I isolate myself to write. I need no company. I retreat into my mind, and there I do what I do best. There, I am content—never less alone than when alone.

"But now that she's gone, all that has changed. I cannot stand the solitude, I cannot cope with the isolation. I have a desperate need for company. The retreat into my mind is now a painful journey from which I want only escape. I no longer seek privacy, I no longer want to think. I have never been so lonely in all my life."

He pined away, and then glorified his affair, elevating it to the level of supreme love: "It was she and I, not so much against the world, but becoming the world. In her I found myself completed. She was everything I needed from my fellows on this earth. I could then seek everything I needed from myself. The physical, the mental, the spiritual . . . I have lost the love that gave me the freedom to live a lover's life."

Friends assured him it was only a matter of time before his depression would lift. Some told him to find a new woman. One friend, however, recognized that the changes he needed to make were internal, not circumstantial.

"Look inside, George," the friend told him. "There is a reason this has happened, but you alone will know it."

And for a while, it seemed, he took his friend's advice, using his writing as a form of self-exploration. He sought to understand what had gone wrong with his relationships with those he loved.

"Being the self I am is easy. Being the self I could be is quite difficult," he wrote. "It is a task never fully attempted. I have honed my talents, perhaps, but I have done nothing to eliminate my weaknesses—my lack of sensitivity to the feelings of others. I have not used my self-knowledge to create a self that can sustain a relationship with a fellow human being."

Soon, he felt he had found the answer to his friend's challenge.

"I know now there is a reason," he wrote, "and I see it, clearly enough to make out the major features: the failure to live up to my own beliefs. The failure to develop them further. And the failure to see that my concentration on the mind and the body had atrophied my life with others.

"In seeking a sound mind in a sound body, I neglected my soul."

When I returned for my occasional dinners with him, I knew nothing of these ruminations. As we had been doing for years, we talked mostly about the business of writing. Tomes on running had been relegated to the sports shelf, no longer occupying the best-seller section in the front of the bookstore. "It's over," he lamented. "I'm finished." While his practical advice on health and nutrition could still sell, and he did more and more of that kind of writing, there seemed to be no market for his philosophic sorties on running, let alone the brokenhearted keenings of a man in his late sixties.

Still, if there was a change that I could discern in him, it was that the waning of fame and prestige no longer seemed to frighten him. Years before, he would have sunk into an obsessive spiral. Now he seemed detached and strangely unburdened, resigned to writing what people wanted him to write but refusing to curtail his new interest in self-analysis.

In keeping with the new persona he was cultivating, he was now going to the theater and hanging with a more literary crowd. He seemed to fancy himself a kind of bohemian or even an artist, free of conventional living arrangements and about to change completely his direction in life. He was floating as if his life were on the precipice of some kind of unseen but imminent change. Then suddenly it did change, cataclysmically and irrevocably.

In March 1986, a doctor found a growth on his prostate. When they tested, it proved to be malignant. My father thought it was the same tumor that had been found sixteen months before, and that it had been incorrectly biopsied as benign. "I think they goofed," he told a friend. By this time, the cancer had metastasized and had spread not only through the prostate but into his bones. It was inoperable and life-threatening, and the doctor who diagnosed him didn't pull punches. He told my father that 85 percent of people with this diagnosis died within two years.

There was no way around it this time. He might try chemo and radiation, but the cancer had set upon its march. In his mind, he saw the end. "I always wondered what I would die of," he told my brother Peter. Now my father knew. He was paralyzed with fear and depression. There would be no reprieve, and there would be no cure. When he called to tell me the news, his voice was heavy.

"For the first time in my life," he said, "I have no idea what to do."

He canceled his speaking trips, revised his will, and broke off relations with yet another young girlfriend, whom I hadn't even known about. In his view, he was sparing her the aggravation of ending the relationship herself. "She didn't need a sixty-seven-year-old man, and definitely doesn't need one with cancer," he told a friend. Then he began looking around for people to console him and found few shoulders to cry on. He wanted desperately now to be with his family, and he was resolved to return home to my mother—if she would have him.

CHAPTER TWELVE

IT DIDN'T HIT ME like a sledgehammer; it was more of a pin-
prick, the news that he had terminal cancer. When I first heard it,
in a telephone call from my mother, it echoed back to me not as a
roar of terror but as a light whisper in my ear. "It's time," it said.
"The time has come." Although a few of my sisters sobbed at the
other end of the phone, it did not register that way with me, perhaps
because it simply wasn't registering at all.

In Pittsburgh, away from my family, I felt removed from the reality of what was going on. Of late, my father had been dwelling only
on the fringes of my radar, relegated to a peripheral blip. But as the
facts gradually started to hit home, his face and body began dominat-
ing my thoughts. From afar, I kept thinking of his cancer on its grim,
unstoppable march. I wondered how he would look when I saw him.
I wondered what I would say. I wondered if he would go back home.

When I returned to Ocean Grove in June, however, he was not
only living there, it was as though he had always been there, had been
in the same place his entire life. As I walked to the top of the stairs, I
immediately saw that his books and legal pads had taken over the

dining-room table again, and from the living room I heard the blare of an afternoon Mets game. I heard his voice speaking loudly over the play-by-play, talking about revisions to an article, and then I saw him turn the corner, a cordless phone cradled between his shoulder and his ear.

"Listen, I have to get off now," he said. "My son's here from Pittsburgh."

He looked no different at all, though the very fact of his interrupting a phone call to greet me told me he was different. There was perhaps a trace of sallowness in his face, but otherwise he looked as fit as when I'd last seen him. "Hey, Andrew, baby," he said. "Great of you to come." And as he walked toward me, he smiled broadly and gave me a surprising hug.

"I'm sorry about things," I said.

"Oh, that," he said. "I'm gonna be fine. No need to worry about that."

"But, I thought . . ."

"Oh, we can talk later on," he said. "We're past all that. Everyone's tired of talking about it."

Whatever drama had surrounded his return, I had clearly missed it. "He's not coming back here to die," my mother had stridently told me on the phone only two months before. He could not simply waltz back into her life, and she would not be his caretaker. But here he was, and soon I heard her coming up the stairs, arms laden with groceries, once again having settled into the role of innkeeper. "I see you've found our little lost sheep," she said to me as she appeared in the doorway, and we all laughed.

That was as deep as the face-to-face recriminations would go, though in private her bitterness lingered. He had begun daily injections of Gn-RH, the hypothalamic hormone that blocks the production of testosterone, which stimulates prostate cancer. The thwarting of testosterone slowed the growth of the cancer but also performed a chemical castration, atrophying the gonads. He didn't tell me about this, but when I asked my mother, she confirmed. "And it couldn't have happened to a nicer guy," she said. I looked at her and said nothing. After all she'd been through, I called no fouls.

Having emerged from his latest depression, my father was back speaking, back running, and had already braved the frigid early-summer ocean. Throughout the house in Ocean Grove that week I could hear the tip-tapping of his manual typewriter, signaling that he was here for the duration. And he was back, I discovered, with nary a word of dissent from any of his sons or daughters. We all deferred to the will of our mother. If she wanted him back in spite of it all, who were we to judge?

And for all her protestations, my parents, it seemed, had turned back the clock, resuming their lives together as though the separations had never occurred—and no harm had been done. She fed him breakfast, lunch, and dinner. At night, they sat in front of the TV together on the couch, and at bedtime they walked up the stairs with their arms around each other. As I watched the two of them, I became aware that their relationship was more complex than a tally sheet of transgressions and kindnesses. In their wordless communication, through sidelong glances, the rolling of eyes, and increasingly frequent laughter, there was something more than familiarity—there was a deep knowing. They both took an obvious comfort in being together.

She knew his foibles better than anyone, and, despite the hell he had put her through, she had somehow never stopped believing in his higher angels. For his part, he seemed to understand that she knew him better than anyone else, in many ways better than he knew himself. She had once confronted him on his cheating, and he had told her, "I am not a good man." Whether she believed him or not, she knew honesty to be his strength, perhaps had known that his life away from her would eventually cave under the weight of self-deceit.

Cancer had stripped him of all the rationalizations he had once used. "I'm the problem," he told me later that weekend. "The problem has always been me." There would be no more time for dodging. He was now willing to accept all responsibility and suffer any recriminations from his family. The fact that we offered virtually none didn't prevent him from a harsh self-appraisal: "I wanted to blame everyone else, but the problem has been me all along."

As in every time of transition, he had hitched his wagon to a philosopher. This time it was Epictetus, the first-century Greek, who would be his guide through terminal cancer. Through Epictetus, he tried to find some measure of acceptance. Epictetus said one should not worry about anything outside of his own power. "I have learned to see that everything which happens, if it be independent of my will, is nothing to me," my father said, quoting Epictetus. In his cancer, my father would try to apply the Epictetus test to every problem. If he could do something about it, he would. If it was beyond his control, he would try to let it go.

With cancer, my father's dictum that "there are no bad experiences" would be put to its most extreme test. He hoped to learn the reason for his hardship, hoping further to be transformed by it. What all that would mean in practical terms was unclear, but he had already gone public with it. He had informed his *Runner's World* readers that he had inoperable cancer, and that they could expect to be taken along on this life-altering (if not life-ending) trip. He expected that cancer would be a kind of crucible in which his soul would be transformed.

"It is the difficulties that show what men are," he wrote, quoting again from Epictetus. "Therefore when difficulty falls upon you, remember that God, like a trainer of wrestlers, has matched you against a rough opponent. For what purpose? you may say. Why, that you may become an Olympic conqueror."

My father seemed ready for a stripped-down life. In his columns at least, he disavowed interest in his career, saying it would now take a backseat to his own survival and the well-being of his family and friends, and quickly finding a role model in Massachusetts Senator Paul Tsongas, who had recently quit the U.S. Senate after being diagnosed with cancer. "He had reexamined his life and then determined to live it in a different way," my father wrote of Tsongas. "He had discovered there were people in his life more important to him than his position."

If he now meant to repair his damaged relationships with his sons and daughters, the manner in which he chose to do it, once he set his sights on me, was not welcome.

"Andrew, you need to change your life," he announced one day, out of the blue.

"Excuse me?"

"Your life will not pass muster," he said loudly. "Do you know what muster is?"

"Military inspection," I said.

"Well, at some point, you have to ask yourself: does your life pass muster? You have to give yourself a rough going over and examine your life. And, Andrew, let me tell you, your life will not pass muster."

A jolt of anger shot through me. What made him think he had the right? If fingers were to be pointed, they surely should be pointed at him. Since the family had given him a free pass, he could at least do me the small courtesy of returning the favor.

In reply, all I could come up with was: "I suppose you think your life passes with flying colors?"

The most startling fact was that he was not just the first but the only person in my family to intuit that I was in very serious trouble. He may have been absent from my life at many times when I needed him, but now he could see through my apparent successes, could see that my life was off track. Although the word *alcohol* was not mentioned, he had put me on notice. I left the room without saying anything further, but his salvo had hit its mark. Not that anything changed at the time.

Before returning to Pittsburgh, I took a trip to Gloucester to see my friend Stavros, but the visit did not lighten my mood. He had been sick of late with mysterious ailments, which he ascribed to having a rare blood disorder, and his views had turned from cynical to bitter. One night we got drunk together, but his searching diatribes had been supplanted by a melancholy droning about how all the cards were stacked against him. His eyes were lifeless, and there was no hint of his old acerbic humor as he drank himself to sleep, sitting upright at the table. Drinking is destroying him, I thought—while telling myself I was far better off than he.

But back in Pittsburgh, my drinking nights grew longer, often following some crazed circuitous path into dawn. In a less benign city, my adventures through after-hours clubs and the often squalid apartments of perfect strangers could have been fatal. Still, I always woke the next day, lying unscathed in my bed, with vague memories of the night before. I'd spend the day piecing it all together. One midsummer Sunday I woke at 3 P.M. under the sticky covers of my bed. I was unclear about the night before and suddenly afraid. As scenes from the night returned, I realized that though no damage had been done, either to myself or to anyone else, I was sinking lower and lower into my pit of shame. And yet I also knew that this was not the bottom. I knew I would be out drinking again that night. I didn't even bother telling myself, "That's it. I'll never drink again." Rather, I told myself, "I need to put some order in my life." Then a thought occurred to me: "I need to get married."

My life in Pittsburgh had become one of serial relationships, small flings of brief duration, lasting only until I passed judgment on the woman or she on me. A few didn't like my drinking habits and cut things short, though I was usually the one who did the terminating, deciding one woman was too provincial, others too controlling or too plain or too something. Always too this or too that. After our first few dates, it appeared that my relationship with my future wife would meet the same fate.

Before I arrived in Pittsburgh, she had been an intern at the *Post-Gazette,* and after I started working there, she returned to a staff job. When she walked in the newsroom on the day of her return, everyone flocked around her, this beautful, delicate-looking woman with a knockout smile, like a young Audrey Hepburn. I knew immediately I would ask her out when the chance presented itself.

When we went to dinner a few weeks later, it turned out she already knew about me, that she had read and liked my articles in the two years I had been at the paper. She even seemed nervous to be out with me—as if I intimidated her. Afterward, I tallied the reasons that mitigated against seeing her again. For one, I had to work with her; if it didn't work out it would be awkward. But above all that, she was too interested in me. I was only interested in women who—initially at least—showed no interest at all. I only wanted those who were inaccessible, unattainable.

And yet, she was undoubtedly beautiful both inside and out, and I couldn't help seeing, and admiring, her goodness. She was funny and deeply intelligent, and what impressed me most were her insights into people. She seemed to know them intimately, seeing their struggles and pain, where I could see them only on the surface.

We continued to go out, now and then, as I continued to see others. When she became aware of that, she refused my advances. When I persisted, she agreed to meet me for lunch, where she told me she would no longer see me outside the office. "I don't want to share myself with someone like you," she said. And when she said that, it struck a deep chord. I saw her insight into me, and I saw her strength and resolve. Now, I wanted her badly. I wanted to prove her wrong about me. I wanted her to see that I was a good man. After she agreed to see me again, we eventually moved in together, and finally we married.

In retrospect, I think she was always wary of me, waiting to see if I could be trusted, waiting to see if I would cut and run. Still, I could find no greater supporter and no greater defender. At the paper, I had a growing reputation for brusqueness and an inflated sense of my talent, but she defended me against those who called me conceited and self-centered. She knew it was all a cover; she knew that underneath, I was wounded and in pain. They were wrong about me, and she would prove it by finally accepting my proposal. In marriage, she hoped to make me whole. "Give him plenty of love," my mother told her on our wedding day. "Because he never got any."

In my own mind, it seemed we had made another bond, another kind of pact. I would protect her from what I saw as her vulnerability, and she would defend me against the accusations of arrogance. For me, the arrangement was easy. Demands were few, since it seemed I could do little or no wrong in her eyes. If my wife believed that I had a problem with alcohol, she chose not to confront me. And though not a drinker herself, she didn't voice any objection to sitting at the bar with me and watching me drink. Even if I had a dozen beers, I was still the one who drove us home. Often she preferred to stay home at night, but she gave me free rein to go out whenever I wanted. The trust wasn't misplaced. I was only going out for the drinks, nothing more.

Not surprisingly, my drinking didn't end, it only got worse. Sometimes in bed at night, I would wait for her to fall asleep, then go down to the back porch to drink, smoke cigarettes, and look at the stars. In time, my drinking excesses became harder and harder to conceal. I used to stash empty beer cans in various crawl spaces and crannies in the house, and then on garbage night I would collect them and spirit them out to the curb in one large garbage bag. Then, the city of Pittsburgh began a recycling program requiring that cans be bagged separately from other trash. Twice monthly, I had to haul bag after bag of the empties out to the curb, dreading the watchful eyes of neighbors and the comments of the trashmen. When I found this public display too humiliating, I stopped taking all the empties to the curb. A backlog soon developed as the cans began piling up in my secret places. One basement closet was filled to the top with them.

The shadow play of my drinking life had carried over into my marriage. Every day demanded the same duplicity, the same care in getting drunk and hiding it—even as the task became more and more difficult. Though my wife never complained, and for the most part seemed not to see the way I drank, it was not something we shared and it was not open for discussion. It seems that we were locked into our prescribed roles. Where once I had felt I was her protector from the world, I eventually came to feel that I was protecting her from myself, from the real me.

Rather than relief, marriage only brought my loneliness into sharper focus. I now had structure: the house, the yard, the job, and a hundred people to call friends. But to me it felt like an elaborate jail, a kind of golden cage. I seemed to know how my father must have felt in his early days back in Rumson, drunk at his own cocktail parties, secretly resentful of his guests, his putative friends. Although I hung with my friends, drank with them, laughed with them, I dared not reveal my dissatisfactions or my secret alcoholic fears. I would not confide in my wife, either. I drank after she went to bed, and, after a while, I would sneak out to the bars, where, not surprisingly, I found women who "understood" me.

I always drew the line at flirtation, but even as I eyed other women, and chatted them up, I couldn't believe I was doing it. Only a year before, it would have seemed unfathomable that I could act so despicably. And even though it didn't go further initially, the die was cast. I was looking outside my marriage to fill that unfillable hole. Predictably, over time, one attraction turned serious, and then turned obsessive. There were secret rendezvous, secret talks, secret longings expressed. When we finally gave in and kissed outside a bar one night, I felt as though I were falling in space, twisting and turning in freefall.

Our affair would never quite take off, manifesting itself only in more stolen kisses and parking-lot gropes. She ended it before it could go any further, heaving me into a world of loneliness, remorse, and despair. I would drive home at night, praying for my wife's car not to be in the driveway, so that when I walked in the door I could drink myself into oblivion. Or, if she was there, I would steel myself, like an actor playing a part, hiding myself from her at all costs. I was getting drunker and drunker, until it seemed that I couldn't even get drunk anymore. One night when my wife went to bed, I sat on my back porch drinking copiously. "God, help me. God, help me," I said to myself in a desperate whisper. I was in a world of hurt, and I saw no way of freeing myself. "God, help me. God, help me," I repeated over and over again like a mantra.

A few days later, in early November, I told her that I was depressed and deeply dissatisfied with my life and with the marriage. Worse than that, I told her in complete honesty that I had no idea what to do about any of it. The comments struck her deeply, and she was devastated.

In many ways the marriage as we knew it ended right then and there. For weeks afterward we passed each other in an uneasy silence, which was broken from time to time with rage. Then one afternoon there was a phone call. My friend Stavros was dead. The last few times I had seen him, he had seemed set on a path of self-destruction. Now my friend on the other end of the line said that Stavros had become anemic, contracted pneumonia, and died. His blood disorder had finally gotten him. But that's not how it struck me. Whatever name they wanted to put on it, I knew alcohol had played a role, and I believed that but for alcohol, Stavros would have lived. I didn't know if Stavros was an alcoholic, but at that moment, I knew that I was.

"I'm going back to New Jersey for the funeral," I told my wife. "I'm going to get drunk with my friends, and when I come back, I'm going to quit drinking and go to AA."

"Is that what you think?" she said. "That drinking is your problem?"

"It's a problem," I told her. "It's the only problem I can do anything about."

∞

BACK IN JERSEY, we drank and cried, but of all of my friends, it seemed as though I cried the most. I sobbed when the old priest limped out to the altar and sobbed harder as he said the rites over an inquisitive Catholic boy who had left grade school full of hope and good intentions only years before. I cried for Stavros, for his promise denied, but mostly I think I cried for myself. How had we squandered our lives and our gifts when there was no enemy visible?

My plan had been to get drunk this one last time, and so I was drinking. I drank after the funeral with my friends, I drank through dinner with my family, and late that night I ended up drinking with my father in the kitchen—although it's probably more accurate to say that he sat and watched me drink.

"I never understood him," my father said of Stavros. "I never understood how someone so intelligent could find life so embittering."

"Because maybe life isn't supposed to work out," I said.

"You see, I just don't get that," he said.

I was angry in my drunken haze: angry with Stavros and angry with my father, and angry with myself and my life. Under the cover of being in my cups, I eyed my father, and I became determined to let him have it in some way. I watched him through my stuporous gaze and, like a punch-drunk boxer, I looked for an opening to land my verbal punches. But on his face I couldn't see an enemy; there were only those blue-gray eyes looking back at me with sad concern. He was concerned for his drunken son, concerned that I was worse than drunk, concerned that I was coming apart.

Then I broke down and told him about my marriage, and about the most recent of my illicit obsessions. He listened as if unsurprised, and he began talking in an oddly abstract, philosophical manner.

There is something within ourselves we don't want to face, he said, and so we look for someone or something outside ourselves to cure it. We look for someone new, someone who "understands," but we really just get a whole new set of problems.

I listened, and in some part of me I understood that he was trying to throw me a lifeline, but nothing he said seemed to make sense—only that he seemed to have figured things out in his own sweet time and now was offering it back too late. I told him I resented his advice after he'd been absent most of my life. Emboldened by my drunkenness, I began to list his failings as a parent: the distant father of childhood, the angry father of my high school years, the father who had left me to take care of his wife. Then, I told him I doubted the authenticity of his present life. "The only reason you're here is that you're castrated," I said.

He winced and laughed a little. "You might be right," he said.

I expected him to call it a night, but he stayed.

"I know I haven't been a good father," he said. "I've learned things the hard way, and if I can give you anything, it's the benefit of what I've learned."

It was lost on my drunken self. After he left, I pulled myself off the chair and dragged myself to bed. I haven't had a drink since.

∞

IN MANY WAYS, the stories of all alcoholics are the same story. Although there may be tens of millions of variations, they are really only variations on a single theme. It is not until you sit through your first hundred AA meetings that you realize this humbling truth. Your story is nothing special at all. Garden variety, you are told. It unfolded according to the same predictable script, proceeded along the same predictable trajectory, and ended with the same inevitable crash. The only thing exceptional—and what is exceptional in all of the stories—is that you, and so many others, were able to walk away before completely destroying yourself.

When you sit in those meetings and hear the stories, you hear your own story told back to you. It's usually the story of a child lost in the shuffle, sadly overwhelmed, shunted aside, in many cases abused. There is a sense that while everyone else seemed to know what was going on, you were somehow absent when it was all explained. There is always, from the beginning, this feeling of being sadly out of step, a disconnectedness that continues into adolescence and beyond. Enter alcohol. Then, all is miraculously changed. There is the taming of fear, the calm confidence of feeling at home in your own skin. Then, there is the arrogance of inebriation. Inferiority becomes superiority, and in your high, you see yourself as usurper, conqueror, greatness itself.

Naturally, you return to the bottle again and again, seeking to re-create that high, that feeling of ease. The occasional becomes the usual, and the usual becomes the addiction. There comes a time when all reformed drinkers say that "drinking stopped working for me." Play becomes work: the labor of drinking every day. In drinking, there no longer comes release or escape—only the need to fill a hole. Then comes the long, slow descent: the car crashes, the broken marriages, the lost jobs. It's no longer a question of whether you will descend, it's only a question of how far down you will go.

The story is always pretty much the same, the same basic tale. Yet even though you hear it time and again, it never bores you. You are always amazed by just how far people will sink before they are resigned to change or get help. Is it the fourth car wreck? The second liver transplant? The third divorce? You sit and listen, and you think you've finally heard the *thud* of the speaker hitting bottom, but almost invariably it is not yet time. More drinking is required. More damage must be done—not just to themselves but to those around them. This was true for me. In my marriage, all would come tumbling down under the weight of an addiction unfaced. I would learn that mine was not a solitary affliction, but that I was fully capable of ruining another person's life.

Probably the saddest, and most destructive, part of being an alcoholic is that it makes you incapable of loving another person. Perhaps it's because you can never really love yourself. Deep down, there is self-hatred and self-contempt, and you are convinced that anyone who loves you must be seriously flawed. You can neither value that love nor trust it. They'll tell you in AA that when alcoholics get married, they "take a prisoner." Rather than an invitation to a life together, you really offer only a sentence.

When I came back to Pittsburgh, I didn't drink. Within a few days, I went to my first AA meeting. There in a church basement, businessmen and street people, grunge rockers and housewives, all somehow comfortably congregated under the fluorescent light. When the first speaker told his tale of how his life had spun out of control and how he had slowly identified drinking as the main culprit, I determined his to be a much greater problem than my own. I was still unconvinced that demon alcohol was the genesis of my sad state. But while keenly aware of the differences, I couldn't avoid the similarities. I saw myself in this stranger, and I resolved to keep going to the meetings.

I think my wife wondered whether my nightly trips to the meeting hall weren't just another way of not dealing with the problems in our marriage. Every night I would dutifully slip out the door to go to my AA meeting, and when I returned she would ask me if anything was "getting better." I had the feeling that she thought of AA as a kind of ruse on my part, an elaborate avoidance. "I'm not going to sit in this house while you go on your search," she told me.

In the midst of this, I received a remarkable letter from my father. He laid down on paper the things he had tried to tell me when I was drunk that night in the kitchen. He was trying to help me save my marriage.

Dear Andrew,

I am writing not so much to advise you but to tell you my own hard earned experience. I discovered that the truths I have been told by those who should know were really truths.

Several friends living and dead warned me against leaving your mother. Only after years did I finally accept what they told me, which in the words of a Hollywood attorney, is "the worst marriage is better than the best divorce."

The fault, as it always turns out, was in me. I married your mother because she was perfect. I wouldn't accept less. And, of course she wasn't perfect. Nobody is. And she was a woman; which made living together impossible without accepting the difference between her and me.

Chesterton said he had seen many a happy marriage but never a compatible one. I blamed that incompatibility on your mother and left her only to discover that every other woman I took up with was also incompatible.

Not at first of course because I was in love, which is akin to be-ing drunk and temporarily insane. Being in love is something that can happen on a regular basis. When contact with the loved one is limited it may last for years. However, marriage quickly leads to its disappearance. A Wednesday–weekend relationship will last considerably longer than anything day by day. What must come next in a marriage is the realization that you must love—an act of will—this less than perfect being you have taken your oath to love and cherish until death.

This is an act of will and can—as the saints have shown us—be extended to any one of God's creatures including this most difficult person you are living with.

My playwright friend knew this. When I told him I was leaving home to live with another woman, he said, "take good notes, in three years you'll be doing it all over again." He was right.

My physician colleague told me I was not facing the real problem inside. Most men were in the same situation and dealing with it. "If every man in this town who wanted to leave home did so, this town would be empty."

Ultimately, I found I was the problem. I learned how to live with a woman, and when I did that I came back home. Mencken said a man could be happy with any one of a dozen women—but it takes a sense of humor and a realization that men and women are two different species to do it. Even until now I've never admitted I was a fool. And I was one . . . because I never understood that I had to accept, and accept with tolerance and humor, this person I was living with. It takes two to have dissension and anger and disappointment.

I'm beginning to understand the futility of trying to change another person—and even more important that such a change is unnecessary. I am in control of myself as Epictetus and Marcus Aurelius and Arnold Bennett had been telling me all along. Not the event but my reaction to it.

I'm telling you things that took me eight years and a lot of grief and sorrow to learn. You will have to accept these fundamental truths sooner or later. It's up to you, as it was to me, how many people are hurt in the interim.

Love,

Dad.

I read his letter over and again, and with my newly sober head, some of it began to sink in. My father was telling me that other people are outside my control. That I should not try to change them, but rather I should try to change myself, face my own problems. I should not be looking for some perfect human being as a kind of cure-all.

My father believed love to be an act of will; not just a feeling, but rather a commitment you live up to. Only in accepting another human being could you accept yourself.

I wrote him back, saying that I was in a world of pain and crushing guilt. I was afraid for myself and afraid for my wife but without a clue about how to make myself whole.

The next week, I received a new letter from my father, offering his support.

Dear Andy,

I have said that I have twelve children and my wife had thirteen since I was like every other child in the house. I have never felt I was a positive force in any one's upbringing so I have been reluctant to be proud of anyone in the family. We create ourselves, no matter how much our parents do or don't do.

One thing that has always buoyed me up, however, is how good every son and daughter is, and I think there is not a mean spirited, selfish or boorish member of the family. Even at their worst they are good people. I hear it all the time.

Your letter is more evidence of your basic honesty and desire to do your best. I felt very proud to read your letter and see in it a person who is trying very hard to cope with the human situation and do it without hurting anyone. I'd be happy to have you on my team.

The life game—the infinite game—requires first of all class. Then a sense of humor, and then all the things we need in doing our thing. Discipline, patience, concentration, concern. I see all those things in your letter. When things get tough, said Epictetus, it is because God has singled you out as someone capable of becoming better and better.

Love,

Dad.

The arguments between my wife and me grew more heated. She accused me of having an affair, and though I denied it, my self-defense was half-spirited and sounded unconvincing even to me. In a few weeks' time, she left to stay with her folks. The house was suddenly empty, and I was alone and sober. Not long after that she filed for divorce.

I was a chance she had taken. I was someone she loved and believed in, but I was always someone she secretly feared. Now that things had exploded only a year into our marriage, she felt it right to end it. One day, I came home to find our wedding pictures torn up and strewn through the house. But my wife had left whole several pictures of my father, which were now prominently displayed in every room. She had left them there as a reminder that I was my father's son.

CHAPTER THIRTEEN

I T'S NOT AS THOUGH time slows down. It's more like time stands
still. The noise stops, the people are gone, and you are alone. Time
surrounds you, static and motionless, and you are stuck in its silent
maw. It drips from the coffeemaker and hums in the refrigerator, an-
nounces itself in the children playing outside. It is always there—
past, present, and future in one indiscriminate heap. You are sober
and alone, and time is frozen. You have broken the world, and everything has come to a halt.

It may be the toughest thing to do—to quit drinking. It's like
pulling off the bandages and exposing an unhealed wound to the elements without even your skin for protection. You quit drinking because your life has never been so bad, and then you are suddenly
sober, only to see those problems in an even clearer light. They have
not diminished. If anything, they are more real, more haunting. But
you've deprived yourself of the one thing you used to blunt them—
alcohol. You indict yourself as foolhardy. Why would you decide to
face the nadir of your life without the armor you have relied on for so
long? You are the worst of fools.

Suddenly unprotected, you feel your doubts and regrets flood in at will and threaten to overwhelm. You had used alcohol to fill that gaping hole in your chest. Now there is no alcohol, and the hole not only remains but the grim truth pours in unimpeded, unchecked. For me the truth was that I had made a wreck of two lives: mine and my wife's. It was a truth I seemed unable to bear.

In our last days and weeks together, my wife and I went to the Christmas parties of our friends. Relegated to the sidelines, I would sit on the kitchen counter and watch everyone drink. Only weeks before, with a few drinks down, I could have stepped to the center of the floor, told jokes and stories, performed my imitations. Now, I could barely mouth words. Trying to hide in plain sight, I felt like a plate-glass window through which everyone could see the car wreck inside.

There were times in those first weeks when I felt panic, a sense of being unable to cope. At night, I was often engulfed by unnamed fears that came in waves. I could neither understand my fears nor explain them to anyone else. I wanted only to be alone. When we split up, my wife was gracious enough to move out and let me stay in the house. The friends, however, I bequeathed to her, distancing myself from almost all of them. Cocooned in the empty house with all its fresh reminders of a marriage destroyed, I played Springsteen's *Tunnel of Love* album over and over every day, seeking comfort in his anguished songs of love and loss. Every night, I ventured out to my AA meetings and tried to find another kind of comfort there. Try as I would, however, I couldn't rid myself of the notion that it was some sort of cult in which strangers spewed out the intimate details of their lives to other strangers. It seemed inappropriate, and yet it also seemed that I was out of alternatives. I stayed in AA, but I stayed on the perimeter. After the meetings, I'd return home to the empty house each night and try not to think of all the damage I had done. When I went home to New Jersey for a week, my father tried to console me.

"This doesn't make you a bad person," he said. "You did what you could."

When I think back to that first year of sobriety I sometimes get a chill, as though from a sudden wind blowing open a door. I feel brushed by fear and a familiar pain. And yet if I sit with it awhile, I feel other sensations as well, the other side of early sobriety. There's the gradual awakening of your brain and your senses, the feeling that the world is opening itself up to you. I discovered Saturday morning, something I hadn't been on the right side of in fifteen years. For someone who couldn't remember seeing a Saturday morning without being hungover or still downright drunk, a cup of coffee and the backyard sunlight proved no minor blessing. In those clearheaded hours, I could smell the grass and sit in the sifted light of the trees. In the bird-chirping stillness, there was nothing dramatic, but there was at least a hint of freedom, and a burgeoning sense of adventure—as tepid as that adventure might appear.

Early sobriety also seemed pregnant with strange opportunity. I was the vanquished, and yet, for some odd reason, there seemed to be a freedom in that, too. At least I no longer had to carry on a charade, no longer had to pretend that I was the happily married man or the affable friend to legions. Most important, I no longer had to pretend that I wasn't a drunk, and it was as though I had put down a weight that I had been carrying for a long, long time.

I had spent the first couple of months disavowing the advice of people in AA, who told me to change old habits. Instead, I continued to hang out at my old bar, ordering club soda after club soda, watching the regulars get drunk. The bottles behind the bar—those ambers, browns, and clears—held me suddenly in awe of their contained power. Mercifully, the craving for alcohol had, for the most part, disappeared within the first few weeks, so it felt somewhat empowering to be sitting at a bar without feeling the lure of a drink. At the same time, I began to wonder what I was doing there, and it dawned on me that this was no longer my place to be. As I listened to the stories people told, I realized that I had heard them all before; I realized, too, that I now had a choice; that, with my drinking days over, I wasn't chained to the stool. One night, I felt myself rise and walk out the door to the street. I never went back.

Alcoholics Anonymous may have been a safe harbor, but it didn't feel that comfortable either. In response to my gut-wrenching laments, fellow drunks offered an inexhaustible litany of trite, boy-scoutish sayings like "One day at a time" and "Easy does it." Or worse, the rhyming ones like "Fake it till you make it" and "Have an attitude of gratitude." Everyone engaged in the same recovery-speak and seemingly everyone from the recovering cabbies to the recovering waiters to the recovering executives was a Zen master. Each held the philosopher's stone, and each was quicker than the next with the simple, ready answers. Still, I knew that I would tune them out at my own peril.

The joke about AA is that there are no rules, only suggestions. Those suggestions outline an arduous process of recovery in very simple terms. The process is hard, and the odds against you—odds made only greater by the fact that alcoholics hate authority. As a rule, alcoholics hate being told what to do, and they like to find their own way. AA somewhat disingenuously reserves judgment. Those who carry the philosopher's stone only laugh when you tell them your ideas about staying sober. "Good luck," they say. "We'll welcome you back after you get drunk."

Simply put, AA is about getting honest with yourself, prescribing a simple program of "rigorous honesty" with very little room to wiggle. I kept wishing the philosophy were more layered and textured, more appealing to my sense of myself as a thinking, intelligent being. Then it became clear to me that the last thing my overworked brain needed was complexity. What I needed was for everything to slow down. Resist as I might, I needed to take it "one day at a time," because on most days, that was just about all I could do. Had I thought about the prospect of staying sober for days or weeks at a stretch, I would have gotten drunk, without a doubt. When some bright-eyed, recovered drunk told me I needed to "make sobriety" my "highest priority," I began to see that despite the sudden jolt of resentment I felt, he was probably correct.

And then, almost in spite of myself, I began to like the meetings. I began to find them strangely comforting and calming. At least for that hour or so, I enjoyed some peace of mind. It could be fleeting, lasting perhaps only the hour I was there, but when I went into the meetings, a deep sense of calm descended over my thought-twisted brain. It was like a tangle of knots slowly unraveling and slackening, or a kind of decompression, as though steam were escaping through my ears. This remains a mystery to me, but I believe it has to do with being in the presence of other drunks.

What seems most central to AA is this belief: a fellow sufferer, another drunk, is better than any doctor or therapist. AA is based on the relationship between two people who have the same problem, neither superior to the other, just equals sharing a common experience. This is the healing dynamic, and it is replicated all over the world in individual relationships and groups, among the millions of people who go to AA meetings. The creepy cult feeling dissipated when I realized there was really no organization at all. AA has no charismatic leader, no hierarchy, no big foundation, and no public relations program. It proliferates only through this central relationship. Drunk to drunk. How odd it was, after meetings, to find myself hanging out in coffeeshops with other recovering drunks. I would find myself sitting there late into the night and think: have I walked the earth to end up here, divorced and alone, sharing jokes and intimacies with virtual strangers? At the same time, it would occur to me that this is where I needed to be, trying to make contact, trying at long last to get honest.

∞

WHEN I BEGAN FINDING this relationship with my fellow drunks, I began looking for it with my father. We were, after all, two people in roughly the same boat, albeit his more leaky than mine. In telephone calls now, at least twice weekly, I confided in him, sought his advice, for my trials were nothing he hadn't experienced firsthand. Always he seemed attentive, concerned about my condition and my spirits. When I came home again that fall of 1991, we went for runs on the boardwalk, and we talked more—but only about me. There was no reciprocity of confidences. All my attempts to inquire about his health were invariably met with a curt "I'm fine." It became the answer that had to suffice.

And it seemed on the surface to be true. To look at him, you would hardly guess that he was dying of cancer. Most of the time, he seemed uninterested in the cancer and interested in just about everything else in the world. His multimedia overload came blaring from all corners—from television and radio, and from a new source as well. He never owned a computer, and the Internet would remain a rumor to him until the day he died. But he had latched on to his own low-tech version: shortwave radio.

I'd see him in the corner, a spindly headset pinching his head, his bony fingers punching numbered buttons on a small black box. Every once in a while, he would tell me the news from Ireland, Japan, Spain, or Italy. It came in especially handy during those months leading up to the Gulf War, as he tried to glean more and more information about what was happening in that part of the world. Relentless as ever in his pursuit of knowledge, he was soon toting around a copy of T.E. Lawrence's *Seven Pillars of Wisdom,* which had spawned the movie *Lawrence of Arabia.* From it, he hoped to cull historical perspective. "We should at least try to understand these people before we bomb them," he said, quoting from its pages to whoever would listen.

In him, there still beat the heart of a leftist—and an antisprawl environmentalist as well. In drives around the county, he'd grimace at the proliferation of malls. When a sign announcing yet another mall popped up in front of a wooded area where we had once run cross-country races, it was one mall too many. "I'm going to paint a sign saying 'Why do we need this?' and stand out in front," he said. He never did, but whenever I pass that strip mall today, I picture him standing in front of it like a wooden Indian, holding his placard.

He was now in his fourth year of cancer, looking a little thinner, running a little slower, napping a little longer, but otherwise his same old self. When we went out running on the boardwalk, he could still push as hard as ever. So his cancer, though real and growing, could easily seem an abstraction—to us, anyway. I didn't know what it was like for him, and he wasn't saying.

After the initial despondency lifted, he began casting about for a cure. He dived into the study of oncology and became an expert. He read about radiation, chemo, shark fins, peach pits, and anything else that offered a glimmer of hope. "During these stages," he would later write, "I spent most of my time searching for a cure. There were newsletters and support groups that had information on various programs around the country. I spoke with or visited experts with the most prestigious institutions. I learned that every now and then they had an exceptional result—but these exceptional results were truly exceptions."

In the course of his searching, he discovered an experimental treatment in Virginia, and went down to try it, but the injections sickened him and left him sluggish. "I don't think I want to live that way," he told me. "It's not worth it." So, he quit. More interested in quality than quantity of life, he quickly decided against anything that undermined his day-to-day existence. In fact, for a time he became more concerned about his diminishing capacity to run than about the prospect of dying. When I would call him and ask about the latest cancer reports, he would shuck them off and instead talk about how poorly he was running.

"I've lost a minute on my mile time," he said.

"So what?" I said. "You have cancer."

"I'm not interested in cancer," he said. "I'm interested in performance."

He was so interested in performance that he began to cheat himself on the Gn-RH hormone injections his oncologist had prescribed. In the absence of the hormone, his testosterone level came back up, and his muscles became stronger. He began running faster and harder, and began to have more success in running his local 5K races. Amazingly, he was trading the slowing of his cancer for better race times. He told me about this on one of my trips home, and I was as incredulous as I was angry.

"That's more than a little insane," I said.

"Well, if you're going to be that way about it," he said, "I'll keep this information to myself."

Soon, however, it would not be my words but his body that would knock sense into him. The pain came back vengefully as his tests began showing the aggressive advance of prostate cancer in his blood and bones. The bones were becoming more brittle, and his doctor told him he would risk breaking his leg if his running wasn't curtailed. Though he had made a life of flouting doctors' orders, he would now have to face the reality of his cancer: there would be no outrunning it, either literally or figuratively. He went back on the hormones, but sometimes when I spoke with him on the phone, he sounded sluggish and despondent.

"I'm starting to run out of gas," he conceded.

Thankfully and perhaps inevitably, he started to slow down. Now when I called, he talked less about his running and more about his bicycling and his walking, activities less punishing to his legs and hospitable to a different kind of introspection. As he had once spoken of listening to his body, he now spoke of listening to his disease. Cancer, he told me, was becoming his new teacher, and he seemed to be open to its truth.

Since his chosen philosopher, Epictetus, said that God, that almighty wrestling coach, had matched him with this opponent for a reason, my father decided to make a project of finding out just what that reason might be. He had said in the past that there are no bad experiences in life, and so cancer had become the ultimate challenge, one that he would explore in much the same way as he had explored running. He would ponder its workings, philosophize about the transformations it wrought, and write down his ruminations about this final phase in his life.

In an odd way, he began seeing his cancer as an opportunity—albeit one with a narrow window. Having always said that life was an experiment of one, he would be his own laboratory once again. "One should never write about things they haven't experienced firsthand," he had said of running marathons. Now, he could write about the ultimate experience, that of death and dying. He adopted a sports metaphor. His engagement with cancer became a "blood sport," like a bullfight; it was a sport in which one of the participants would die. He knew that it was he who would die, but at the same time he decided to do all in his power to stay alive. He wrote about staying physically fit with his cancer, vowing that "I may die of prostate cancer but I'm not going to die of anything else." In his mind he was cutting down the ring, limiting the areas from which the cancer could attack, taking control of what was in his power and leaving the rest to fate.

At the very minimum, the cancer would provide a wealth of new material, and there could be no bigger or more mysterious subject. Soon, his former zeal for running was supplanted by an unlikely enthusiasm for dying. Where his columns once broadcast the benefits of fitness, they now touted the even greater life-changing potential of terminal disease. In public at least, he gave no hint of sorrow. When someone asked my sister Sarah how my father was doing with his cancer, she replied, "Oh, he loves it."

CANCER MADE HIS WRITING more personal, more probing. And still between us there were walls. Now that he was dying, there were things I felt we needed to talk about, and it occurred to me one day the following March when we were running on the boardwalk that he had never asked me about my drinking.

It was another gray and windy day, and, more frail now, he was being visibly buffeted by the winds. As we loped slowly along, I began asking him about his drinking in the past. Decades before, when his friend told him he was one drink away from being an alcoholic, was he really that close, I wanted to know. When I asked, I found that he attached a great deal of shame to the subject.

"I never wanted to become one of those people," he said.

I was somewhat taken aback. Surely he must have known that I was "one of those people." When I protested, however, he took exception, saying he wasn't talking about people like me. Rather, he was referring to Bowery bums, or to businessmen he had known who started their days in the train-station bar. "Real drunks," he said. "People completely defeated by life. I would never admit that I was defeated by life."

I understood, but at the same time I was smarting from the sting of his words. Here, it seemed to me, was the root of denial in my family.

"*I'm* a real drunk," I said sharply. "I've admitted defeat."

My words surprised me with their conviction and their anger; they shot from me as if trying to break a conspiracy of silence. It was important to me to be completely up-front with my father about my alcoholism, and disturbing that he couldn't hear what I was saying. Central to AA is the Zenlike paradox that you gain control of your life only by admitting that you are no longer in control of it. Only when you admit that you have become powerless over alcohol can you find the power that gives you the strength to resist it. That power could be God or it could be just the support of others. But you have to admit defeat and abandon the self-reliance that almost killed you. Running beside my father that day, I began to realize how much of this philosophy had already sunk in. "For me not to admit that I'm an alcoholic would be like you not admitting that you have cancer," I told him.

Drinking had become in the end a lonely and shameful experience, and I told my father how hard it had been to admit defeat. Now, as I was trying to get beyond drinking, I told him how I continued to struggle, and how I was still in some ways at odds with AA. I believed in God, but I wasn't quite willing to turn myself over to this philosophy—not completely. I wasn't ready to give up control, and I didn't entirely know what giving up control meant. "I'm trying to let go," I told my father. "It's a hard thing, but I'm trying. I'm trying very hard."

My father remained uncharacteristically silent, apparently focused on the boardwalk before him, but when we slowed to a walk in front of the house, he put his arm over my shoulder. Later, he passed me in the kitchen and said, "Let's have some more talks like the one we had this afternoon."

Perhaps our talk struck him because the AA philosophy so closely mirrored that of Epictetus—the idea that we should concern ourselves only with things we could control. Or maybe it was the simple honesty that appealed to him. But in the days after our run, my father became fascinated with AA and wanted to know more. Was it applicable to him? To his cancer? In the week that followed, he peppered me with questions. Was it like a religion? he asked.

"Well, they say it's not a religious program but a spiritual one," I told him.

"What does that mean?" he said.

"I don't know," I said. "I'm still working on it."

He didn't see religion as a pejorative. What was wrong with it being a religious program? When I told him about an alternative sobriety program that had been in the news, which did not rely on any kind of spiritual awakening, my father rejected it out of hand. "What's the point of getting sober, if you don't have a spiritual awakening?" he said. He even dismissed my concerns that I might be going to too many meetings, developing a new reliance, replacing one addiction with another: alcohol in exchange for meetings. "People go to church every day," he argued. "We don't say they're addicted to church."

Bill Wilson said that AA had two fathers: one was the psychologist Carl Jung, and the other was William James, who as it happened was one of my father's seminal philosophers. Jung had said that in his treatment of alcoholics, only those who had had a conversion experience were successful in quitting, and James had written about these transformations in his book *Varieties of Religious Experience*. When I told my father about James and AA, he became even more interested.

Although he wasn't sure if it would be appropriate, he wanted badly to go to an AA meeting. He wondered how he might introduce himself if it became his turn to speak. Then he told me his solution: "I could say, 'My name is George, and I wish I were an alcoholic.' " I never did take him to a meeting. But sometimes when I'm sitting in one now, I imagine him there with me, standing up and announcing that he wished he were an alcoholic, too, and I have a private laugh.

∞

IN THE SPRING he arranged to give a talk in Pittsburgh, but I think he just wanted to spend some time with me. We went for runs on the bridle trails in Schenley Park, ducked into used-book stores, and wandered around the city like tourists. It seemed not to matter what we did as long as we were together, making jokes, trying out theories, looking for small adventures. Together, we were experiencing something we'd rarely shared in the past: we were starting to have fun.

One day we were listening to NPR in the car when a commentator was saying something less than favorable about Sting's new record.

"Leave Sting alone," my father protested.

I was shocked that he even knew who Sting was.

"They should get off his back," he said.

As it turned out, he had read an article critical of Sting for writing songs inspired by the books he had read. Sting's modus operandi, it was alleged, was to read a book and write a song. To my father, that was a perfectly acceptable practice. "What's wrong with that?" he wanted to know. Of course, the criticism had hit close to home, since he had for years followed roughly the same practice—turning books he had read into the stuff of columns.

I looked at him, finding it all but incomprehensible that I was discussing Sting with a seventy-two-year-old man. But he was always an indiscriminate sponge for information, and his interest in all subjects, no matter how unlikely, seemed to know no bounds or boundaries— even then. In fact, his appetite for ideas and information seemed only to have been piqued by the awareness of death. All knowledge informed other knowledge, he said, and none of it was useless. He gleaned it from every source. His books, the morning papers, all-news radio, the Met and Yankee games, all-sports radio, the transmissions off the shortwave—he took it all in, and he seemed unable to turn away from any of it, perhaps fearing that he might miss something.

Our conversations were like a game—an open-ended game where the outcome was always uncertain. He'd bounce from topic to topic, exploring the similarities and the differences, reaching some synthesis and moving on again. It was play, and it was fun. When we talked, the subject seemed not to matter. Maybe it was a report I was working on or a book I had just read; maybe just a thought or some nascent theory. Regardless of what it was, I could always feel his excitement at being engaged by something new. I got the feeling that to him, playing around with an idea was very close to his notion of why we are here.

One afternoon that week he spent with me in Pittsburgh, we sat in my backyard and ate calamata olives and feta cheese. As we talked, I came to a conscious realization of something that I had already begun to take for granted: We were now completely at ease with each other. I felt us to be companions, exploring unknown terrain together. When he asked me for some help with the book he was writing on death and dying, I mentioned Elisabeth Kübler-Ross, a woman whom I knew my father had quoted before but whom he now seemed to have forgotten.

"She talks about these stages of dying," I said. "You know, shock, denial, anger. All those emotions before acceptance."

In AA, too, I told him, they often talk about the necessity of acceptance—accepting life on its own terms, accepting that there are things beyond our control. I wondered if the same wasn't true for his cancer. Wasn't there freedom in acceptance? Wasn't he beginning to feel a freedom in accepting his own death? Later, he approached me with his legal pad.

"Okay," he said. "Give those back to me."

"Which?"

"The stages," he said.

"Shock," I said.

"Right," he said, as he began writing.

"Denial," I said.

"Certainly," he said.

"Bargaining," I said. "You don't want to accept things, so you make a deal with God that you'll accept something lesser. Kind of like a plea bargain."

"I've had that," he said. "Go on."

"Anger," I said.

"Well," he said.

"Depression," I said.

"Lovely," he said.

"Grief," I said.

"Right," he said.

"Acceptance," I said.

My father sighed at the daunting list, then let out a laugh. But clearly he was already well embarked on his travels through these stages. Until recently, I had expected the anger that had so dominated his life to well up and consume him, expected that he would rail against the cancer that was pulling him down despite all his efforts to stay young and fit. The opposite was true. He had moved beyond anger, it seemed. Illness had indeed been his teacher. He seemed to be more comfortable inside himself, less self-involved, more gentle, more concerned with how everyone else was doing.

They tell you in AA that anger is a secondary emotion and that the primary emotion is fear. Anger is a cover for fear. In hiding our fear with anger, we allow ourselves to believe that we are avenging a wrong, when actually we are simply covering up our fears. Initially, this made no sense to me. Fear had never been my problem. After all, I had always allowed my drinking to place me directly in harm's way. I was recklessness incarnate. In time, however, I realized that I had always been afraid, and that fear was so ubiquitous a presence in my life that I had ceased to be aware of it.

Rather than cover that fear, the AA-ers tell you to "walk through it." Face it as it is, allow it to demystify, and let it fade into a vapor. I saw my father doing that, allowing himself to see the reality of his situation, unvarnished. "I have little trouble looking truth in the eye and admitting it," he wrote. "Lies and deception are time-consuming, and time becomes essential."

In facing his fears and for the first time sitting still for them, he became clear-eyed, finding that they were not so terrifying as he might have expected. The certainty of death seemed freeing to him. Later he was to write of this time: "I was being taught how to deal with the inevitable. I was gradually coming into the final stage, acceptance . . . Patients become less focused on their illness, tests and treatment. They go back to living each day to the fullest . . . For the cancer patient 'doing everything' is reaching acceptance, or what Friedrich Nietzsche called Fati Amor—the love of fate, whatever that turns out to be."

In facing his cancer, I saw him letting go of anger and all of his other defenses and covers. I saw him, and I wondered if I had the courage to face my own fear.

CHAPTER FOURTEEN

O N A GREEN-TIPPED PENINSULA in Donegal, my father and I
ran, slowly now, climbing to the crest of the road. To the east,
we were flanked by dozens of shepherdless sheep dotting a vast expanse of green grass and gray rock. To the west, the land rose to the
precipice of the cliffs, which dropped sharply into the blue ocean dis-
tantly below. My mother followed us dutifully in the car as we
trudged uphill to the spot we had found the day before. A break in a
hedge revealed a pathway leading to flights of wooden stairs that descended to a horseshoe-shaped cove below. This would be our own
private inlet, serving up an offering of cold Atlantic surf for a morning swim.

We hobbled down those rickety steps, full of excitement at having
transported our ritual of run and swim to a place of such unfathomable splendor. As we jogged, then ran, to the waiting surf, my father let out the familiar "waaaaahoooo" at the frigid shock of the
water, and as we swam out into it, we looked up at the gray cliffs that
towered around us like castle walls. We rode the waves of the magnificent cove and emerged from the surf feeling the bite of the wind.

Quickly wrapping ourselves in towels, we turned and watched the September sun dapple the blue water with white light. But as we drank it all in, our serenity was broken by a midge, a nearly imperceptible small black fly. Hundreds of midges surrounded us in small black clouds, administering tiny little bites. We headed for the stairs at a run. "Everything God made has a crack," my father said, quoting Emerson between breaths.

Life, even at its best, would never be perfect, he seemed to say. The key was to accept it on its own terms. Now with his days clearly waning, my father savored life much as he would a cherrystone clam, slurping it down and devouring it whole, relishing its sweet passage. He was not the person he had been five years ago or even five months ago. His arms and legs had grown spindly and his energy was ebbing. But battered, bruised, or cracked, he seemed happy to take life on any terms at all.

The bittersweet reality of it all was becoming apparent to everyone. The cancer was beginning to take over. It was, at least, the beginning of the end, and it was the reason why we were in Ireland, the first of our family reunions in new places, family gatherings in anticipation of his death. Everyone knew that time was short. If anyone had grievances that still rankled, it would be difficult to air them now. As far as I'm aware, few, if any, were spoken.

He was the first to admit he had been lucky. To have been taken back by my mother and, at least on the surface, readily accepted by his children was a minor miracle that he didn't at all take for granted. Now, as his body deteriorated and his pace slowed, the focus was less on his past and more on how much longer he would be around. People wanted to be close to him, and he wanted to be close to his family. The sadness was that these feelings had come so late.

In his once-again undisputed role as head of the family, he had decreed that there should be large gatherings of all the Sheehans. Further, they should not be in Ocean Grove but in places we hadn't been before, where there would be explorations and a sense of specialness. The first of these reunions would be in Ireland, once a legacy to be fled, now a place he had reclaimed for his own. In recent years he had run the Dublin Marathon, been toasted in the Irish press, and befriended many Irish runners. Although not much of a drinker, he liked to tie one on now and again, and he loved drinking pints after a race. Both the Guinness and the music were part of his reclaimed ethnicity. An Irish friend told me he went to the Baggot Inn in Dublin with my father for a night of drinking and music. And to his amazement he saw my father climb on top of their table with a stout in hand. Holding his glass aloft, my father began to yell, "This is where we belong. This is where we belong."

There is a feeling I get in Ireland that this is in fact where we belong. How can we not feel that when we see ourselves in the freckled faces of the parochial-school kids and in the toothy grins of all the old people? My family had gathered together, that September of 1991, in a sprawling eighteenth-century manor house in County Cork named Castle Hyde. Jointly owned at the time by my brother-in-law Rick (a successful New York investment banker) and two of his partners, the castle had hosted a group of us the year before, but now we had returned with more Sheehans, and the parents in tow.

I split off from the group for a while and arranged to meet my parents a week later up in Sligo. When they joined me, the three of us went to Yeats's grave near Drumcliff Church and drove a rented car up to Donegal, braving the misted roads of Connemara and those windy cliffsides farther north. When we arrived, white-knuckled, at an empty bed-and-breakfast, we sat down in the dining room near a picture window through which we could look out at the foggy meads spotted with sheep and rams but with nary a soul in sight.

"Things are really hopping now," my father said, breaking into a laugh.

I felt a little guilty for having taken him away from the pubs and the family's laughter, but running and walking the moors of Donegal, we soon found ourselves swept up in the power of its beauty. Strangely at home in this place where none of us had ever been, we shared a silent recognition that we felt bound to it in some deep way.

When we left, the reporter in me proposed we head to Belfast to have a look around. My father would have none of it. "Look, I don't have much time left," he said. "I don't want to die in Belfast!" And so we headed to another Northern Irish town, called Rostraver, the home of an Irish friend I knew from Pittsburgh. Her father, an accordion player, took us in. Within an hour of our arrival he was playing for us in the local pub and had my father croaking along to "The Band Played Waltzing Matilda." ("Johnny Turk he was ready/ Oh he primed himself well. He rained us with bullets and he showered us with shell.") When the publican rose to give a recitation of a poem about two star-crossed lovers, one Protestant and one Catholic, my father seemed to brim with emotion and tears came streaming from his eyes. I watched his face crumple, reddened with Guinness, and I wondered: was he crying for those lovers—or for himself?

He cried often in those days, and watching him that night, I began to understand. It was as though the pent-up emotions of a lifetime could be denied no longer, and anything, even a song, could cause them to overflow. When I looked at him then, I saw a new man, someone free of rough edges, someone with a new openness and ease about him.

I wondered if people really could change, and change fundamentally, even in their seventies. And then it occurred to me that perhaps he was not so much a new man as the man he had always been. It was as if the real person, who had always been hidden—the one who was too wrapped up in anger and fear—had finally made his way to the surface. To my great relief and surprise, he was no longer the intrepid loner, guarded against human contact. He was opening himself up.

In the book he was writing, my father was invoking Thoreau, that kindred spirit of the Concord woods to whom he bore even a physical resemblance. As both he and Henry David were gaunt of face with long, thin noses, my father had long ago concluded that they were both ectomorphs—thus, outsiders from birth. During their lives, both had been timid and as a result had overcompensated—"attempting," in my father's words, "to make up for obvious defects by creating a new person."

Yet when Thoreau faced his own death, he too began to soften his solitary stance. When word got out, people sent him letters saying how much he had done for them. Greatly moved, Thoreau began inviting the townspeople, whom he'd been estranged from all his life, to come visit. Thoreau was so overcome by the kindness his illness engendered that he feared he would not die. "I should be ashamed to stay in the world after so much has been done for me," he wrote.

Thoreau, my father said, did not have a foxhole conversion, nor did he repudiate his philosophy. He merely found acceptance of his own mortality and his own limits. In one of his letters, the dying Thoreau wrote: "I suppose you know that I have not many months to live; but of course, I know nothing about it. I may add that I am enjoying my existence as much as ever, and regret nothing."

Similarly, my father had become an oddly social being. For years he had been guarded about his running, his private laboratory of ideas—and columns. It was only on occasion that he might ask you to accompany him. Mostly he preferred to run alone, keeping private company with himself and his precious thoughts. Now on trips home, I was invited to run with him—and shocked to see that we were joined by a dozen others as well, a group of retirees who had invited my father into their informal boardwalk running club.

Once a week he joined them, becoming one of a swarm of slow-moving bees, drifting down the boardwalk, talking and laughing as they went. Every mile or so, they would stop en masse to drink from a water fountain, a group effort that took at least five minutes. When I accompanied them one morning, I was amazed to see my father stopping and patiently waiting his turn, something that would have driven him to distraction in the past. And yet there he was, holding court in the middle, smiling his toothy grin, yapping away like a man who had been holed up for too long a time. About his newfound sociability he wrote: "It's as if I spent the last six months in Antarctica alone—like Admiral Byrd—and I can't wait to find out what's going on in the rest of the world."

In the summer of 1992 we returned to Takanassee, and there he unapologetically brought up the rear. Afterward, I joined his group for pizza and the usual postmortem. My father had humped along, completing the 3.1 miles in about thirty minutes, and was nonetheless happy with his effort. But as we sat with our slices, he said, "Andrew, tell them what you ran."

I looked up from my pizza slice and said, "Eighteen-twenty."

It was a more than respectable time, about six minutes a mile, but to my surprise the table gave me a round of cheers and applause. As I looked over at my father, I saw him smiling a smile of private satisfaction. I smiled, too, amused at this display of small excess, and at first I wondered if my father wasn't experiencing some kind of vicarious thrill. Then I realized that he was just happy to see me healthy and running well. I thought then how the old adjectives no longer applied. "Self-absorbed," "self-involved," "self-satisfied," "asocial," "antisocial," "aloof"—the words seemed to skate off him like autumn leaves over a well-polished limo. I remembered my mother telling me that no matter how great its apparent rewards, life had always disappointed him. Now it seemed that he got pleasure from even the smallest things—not the fame or prestige, but the things he had possessed all along. As he saw his days begin to have numbers, he saw that what really mattered to him were the people he loved.

One day a runner stepped off the boardwalk to use the water fountain on the front porch at the Ocean Grove house. He found my father sitting on a rocker, reading a book, and asked him about his writing, especially the recent columns on cancer. Now that my father was dying, the runner wanted to know, what in life was most important to him? The answer to that question spawned a column, and that particular column assumed a vaunted place of honor on the refrigerator doors of nearly all of my brothers and sisters:

" 'My family,' I said, without hesitation.

"In giving me cancer, fortune had smiled on me. Pain was a key to opening up a new and larger life. The interests of my past are still present, but finally seem in perspective. That is why I was able to answer when a stranger asked me to put my present life in one word—'family.' "

Individually, each of his sons and daughters seemed to be right with him, happy to have him back, happier still to accept his love. If there was any initial reticence, the time for recriminations had passed. There wasn't even a hint of discord. Certainly I no longer had any questions about his bedrock support for me as my life continued to change at a rapid clip. Back in Pittsburgh, I had a new job. Television. The Teamster drivers had gone out on strike, shutting down the city's two dailies and leaving Pittsburgh paperless. Fortuitously for me, the local CBS affiliate offered me a job as a TV reporter, initially covering the very strike that had put us out of work. Being new to television, I was a risk for the station, but the news director said she was willing to feature substance over style. Just how much substance over how little style, she may not have fully anticipated.

In my first year, the anchorwoman took to calling me Bambi whenever I did my proverbial deer-in-the-headlights act. This would happen every so often when, overwhelmed by this strange world of makeup, coiffed hair, and bright lights, I'd get stricken with fear and go blank on the air. I'd leave the station not so much craving a drink but wanting to crawl into a ditch and die. My father, who had spent a lifetime fighting stagefright, now advised: "Get into a flow state." Ever finding a lesson in sport, he told me that athletes rely on three things in competition: they find their confidence, they relax, and then they focus. My father advised me to do the same.

"Then when you talk to the camera pretend like you're talking to me," he said.

We were close now, closer than good friends, closer, I felt, than a father and son had a right to be. And yet there was still something unsettled between us, things still left to be said, walls still meant to be taken down. As his death approached, I suspected there would always be a gnawing sense of distance between us—a separation made in the past, still there, stubborn and unmovable. I didn't know whether to try to breach or just accept it. Yet something—the need to stay sober, perhaps—told me that the air had to be cleared.

∞

PEOPLE WHO QUIT DRUGS or alcohol sometimes find their first few months of sobriety surprisingly easy. Once the obsession with drinking finally lifts, you become unstuck, your world unnumbed, bursting with colors and smells. Emotions, senses, and impressions long dormant and left for dead are suddenly alive and kicking. There is a palpable excitement about life itself, about its possibilities. For a time at least, you seem to be floating through it all—"on a pink cloud," they say—happy to be alive, happy to take it all in. But like Hamlet worrying about what dreams would come, the person in early sobriety has also to worry about what new emotions will arise. As you are open, it seems, to a new light, you are just as vulnerable to your own darkness.

Until I began losing them, I had no idea how much I needed my illusions—the little lies you tell yourself to make life bearable. Chief among them for me was the illusion that I actually liked myself. Sure, I acknowledged some major defects and shortcomings, but in my final tally, I counted myself ahead and never beyond redemption. When hemmed in by guilt, I could generally fend it off, convincing myself I really wasn't a bad guy after all. Intuitively, I must have realized the necessity of holding on to that illusion for as long as possible, staying on the pinkish side of that cloud, avoiding the truths that I was not yet ready to take on. Then came the divorce lawyers, the angry friends, and the creditors; then various unfaceable incidents buried in memory unearthed themselves and came alive again. Soon, the pink cloud dissipated; the horrors of the past had to be faced. Real change had to be made.

Those in recovery will tell you that there are two major steps in getting sober. "Getting sober is simple," they say with tongue planted firmly in cheek. "First you have to quit drinking, and then you have to change everything about yourself." As always in AA, the joke is on you. Initially, the change involves breaking off ties with all the people who would like to see you drink again. Don't go to bars, the old-timers say, and avoid the old friends who try to convince you that you were the victim of circumstance—a run of bad luck and not alcohol addiction. Without those old friends and the old ways, you'll need new ways to occupy your time. Instead of sitting on a barstool, go to meetings; then find other things—fly fishing or something healthy like that. But in order to stay sober you must make even bigger changes. You must dig deeper, and then deeper still.

I, of course, wanted none of this. Once I had gotten sober, I had other things to do. After about eight months, I began drifting away from AA and attending meetings on a kind of as-needed basis. According to my former M.O., I chased women, and I moved quickly through several flings before falling hard. She was a beautiful and intelligent but volatile woman whom I had met in AA, and after a torrid few weeks together, she broke my heart. Walking out of my life as suddenly as she had entered it, she left me to face the sudden sting of rejection and loss. Here was that familiar pain, the pain of wanting someone unattainable and emotionally unavailable. In that pain there was also the realization that I had once again set myself up for heartache.

At three o'clock one morning, I found myself sober, awake, alone, and in pain, staring at my ceiling in the dark. But this time there could be no alcohol to dull the ache or transform it into that sweet melancholy I knew so well; there would be only hard, unvarnished reality. A few days before, my AA sponsor had taken me to breakfast and listened to me drone on about my heartbreak. He's a southern guy, and like most southerners, he listens long and speaks slowly and sparsely in response. He listened and listened, and after a time he looked up from his eggs and said, "I could be wrong about this, but it seems to me that you don't like yourself very much." He didn't say it to be unkind, and it wasn't an accusation. It was just what it was: a sad but true statement of fact. His words had passed through me like a stone falling through water, and I was defenseless against the truth of them. I knew that any effort to convince myself otherwise was really just so much dancing.

Now, depressed and alone in the middle of the night, I had run out of dance. The truth of my sponsor's statement returned to me, and I wondered: what does one do with that kind of knowledge? I had resisted AA, resisted the notion of giving up control and surrendering my will to God. I found myself praying to God to take away my pain. I prayed for peace of mind. As the minutes passed, I felt myself giving up all my resistance, letting go. A sense of peace seemed to descend on me. Mercifully, I fell asleep.

In the days after that dark night, I still felt that sense of peace, although it was tempered by ugly truths about myself. Unavoidable was the cold fact that I had betrayed my wife, and that I had inflicted upon her an unforgivable pain. Although tempted by the desire to rationalize, I began facing the fact that I could never make that right. And it didn't end with her. In a lesser way, I had done the same to dozens of people who had tried to get close to me and were burned for their efforts. I had squandered those friendships, scuttled my marriage, and ended up alone.

I felt shame. The shame I had been covering up for so long. The great hidden core of hot burning stuff that could flare up like lava at the slightest provocation. Shame it seems is something common to all alcoholics. For us, it is always there, close to the surface, ever threatening to sting. Alcohol had initially been an antidote to shame. In alcohol, we had all found our weapon, the great anesthetizer of shame. When alcohol quits working, however, we are enveloped by a shame greater than ever before.

They told me in AA that there could be no real growth in addiction. This is because when confronted with emotional pain, the addict immediately seeks escape through alcohol or drugs. Getting drunk or high is like taking a rain check on life. Since you've opted out, there can be no growth. They also told me that whatever your age when you become an addict, that's the emotional age at which you become stuck. By my accounting, that made me about twenty-one. In the interim fifteen years, alcohol had always held out the promise that all pain could be muted and transformed. Without alcohol I was helpless against the flood of shame and painful emotion. Now, however, the time had come to embrace that pain rather than evade it. Only then could I begin taking responsibility for my life. At long last, it seems, it had become time to grow up.

As part of learning to take responsibility, AA suggests that you take a "fearless moral inventory" of yourself, an unflinching look at the pain you've caused others. Once you begin to dwell on incidents long buried in your consciousness, they surface in wave after wave of mortifying shame. "How could I have done such a thing?" "How could I say something like that?" Unavoidable was the realization that I had been the worst of cowards, willing to sacrifice anything and anyone rather than face my addiction and my fears. For me, facing up to this was too painful, and I began looking for some outside help.

I began to see that there can be a great freedom in defeat. There is the freedom to try new things, the freedom to risk what could never be risked before. My inclination had always been to go it alone, self-reliance having always been the family way—and my own way. Now, people in AA were telling me that wasn't the right way, that it was important to learn how to ask for help. I returned to AA, and then I committed the cardinal sin against self-reliance. After years of resisting it, I entered therapy in earnest.

∞

MY BRIEF EXPERIENCES with therapists had always been the same. The same resistance, the same fear. I would sit down for the first session, and then, thinking better of it, I would angle for a way out before anything could happen.

"What is the problem?"

"What problem?" I would say.

"Why are you here?"

"I don't know," I would say. "Maybe I should leave."

It was always so terrifying, the prospect of opening up. For what protection would I have if I let myself be vulnerable, exposed? Where was the good in that? So I'd smell the scented candles, eye those life-affirming posters, and stonewall. This time, however, when I took my seat across from the unwavering stare of the therapist, I stayed, and I began to talk.

We began to work backward, this therapist and I, through the failed marriage and the failed relationships that had preceded it. Slowly and incrementally, I started to learn about myself, my patterns. How I had rejected those who tried to love me, viewing their love as necessarily suspect and counterfeit. How I had sought love only from those who I knew would never give it, each rejection reinforcing my core belief that I was flawed and unworthy. Digging deeper still, I discovered that I had always felt this way, from boyhood on. The pain I now felt over losing this woman was only the stirring of a very old wound.

When we unearthed these feelings, the therapist made me sit with them, made me experience their sting. It wasn't enough just to understand, intellectually. I had to feel the loss, and I had to grieve it. Even, most painfully, the sexual abuse by the pedophile priest, who had capitalized on my woundedness, taking my last ability to trust. No minor incident, I came to realize; the abuse had permanently fractured my sense of self, just as it had tied up all of my feelings of need with a taut rope of anger. To unloosen that rope, we continued to dig into the pain.

When possible, I would drive the Pennsylvania Turnpike to spend a week, or perhaps a long weekend, in New Jersey with my father. With time now short, we had never been closer, and yet therapy had complicated even that, reawakening long-forgotten feelings. I now carried a secret rage toward my father and felt vexed by it. Why should I feel anger toward him now that so much had changed? He was dying, after all—how could I dredge up these resentments about the past?

I was torn. Was it really necessary to speak to him about this? Wouldn't it be better, I thought, to deal with it by myself, at my own speed, after he was gone? Besides, I thought, hadn't I already said my piece at various times in the past? And yet, no matter what arguments I marshaled against doing so, I needed to talk to my father about these things. It wasn't about blame. To me, it was a need to understand. I decided that he needed to understand, too. I decided that, like it or not, he deserved my honesty.

It all came spilling out on one of those quiet, overcast afternoons that had left us wandering the house, together and alone at the same time. To me, the very air in the room felt pregnant and heavy, as if I could feel the weight of our past, some enormous presence grown out of big things unsaid, questions unasked and unanswered. We were sitting in the kitchen, drinking tea, and I began asking him about his own father. Did they talk much? Did his father force him to become a doctor? My father answered curtly, growing testy as if suspicious of my inquiries. His evasiveness started to anger me.

"Was he there for you or was he distant?" I asked.

"I don't remember him being distant or close," he said.

Becoming angrier by the moment, I blurted, "Yeah, well, you weren't there for me when I was growing up."

After I said this, there was silence. Once spoken, it was as if the words just continued to hang in the air. An uncomfortable mix of pain and fear washed over his face, and he seemed paralyzed, unable to respond. As awkward as it felt, I just continued.

Why had he been so distant when we were growing up? If he was tired of family life, why did he continue to have children? I rattled off my questions as if trying to get to the end of a long list.

"I don't have any answers for you," he said when at last I fell silent.

At that moment the phone rang. Fortuitously for him, it seemed, he had an excuse to get away from me. And when the call ended, he simply went into the other room, where I found him with his head buried in a book. I stood over him for a time without speaking, feeling awful about what I had just done. "Look, I'm sorry," I said. "I don't want to hurt you. I just had to get these things off my chest." I told him that this was not about blaming him or anyone else. Rather, I just needed to understand more about myself, about him.

He looked up and said, "It's not you. It's me." Then added, "I'm bad—I'm just really bad news."

"No," I said. "Listen, you've become a great father, a great friend to me. I'm only telling you this because I need to talk about it."

As I continued to stare down at him, I realized there was nothing else to say. When I turned to walk out of the room, I heard him say, "Thank you." Still, I feared that I had lost him, that I had pushed him too far. Perhaps the relationship between a father and a son was not meant for this kind of probing. Maybe our relationship had reached a degree of honesty that it could not sustain.

∞

EARLIER THAT WEEK, I had been reading *All the Pretty Horses,* by Cormac McCarthy, and I had quoted him a passage that particularly moved me, although its relevance to our relationship was lost on me at the time. It concerned the young cowboy John Grady Cole, and his profound love and knowledge of horses. Cole's estranged father, dying of cancer, had recently returned to visit, and as the two went out riding, the father watched his son ride out in front of him, watching in a kind of awe. McCarthy wrote:

> **The boy who rode on slightly before him sat on the horse not only as if he'd been born to it which he was but as if were he begot by malice or mischance into some queer land where horses never were he would have found them anyway. Would have known there was something missing in the world to be right or he right in it and would have set forth to wander wherever it was needed for as long as it took until he came upon one and he would have known that that was what he sought and it would have been.**

My father had long sworn off fiction, often declaring, unprovoked, that "man learns nothing from novels." On visits home, I always brought my own reading material. Though the house was full of my father's books, they consisted mainly of medical books and philosophical tracts from the likes of Kierkegaard, Heidegger, and Nietzsche. "Books, books everywhere," I would lament to myself, "and not a thing to read." But now he amazed me with his reaction to the passage I had just shared with him. "I've got to read that book," he said.

After our confrontation, we passed the rest of the week not talking much and never referring to what had transpired between us. But when I left, I put the book on the dining-room table, where he would see it. A few days after I got back to Pittsburgh, he called me in a strange state of excitement.

"What a fantastic book," he said.

"Yeah, it's a great book," I said.

"And, I realized, I'm the father in that book," he said.

He told me he saw himself in the fictional father, the father who had returned late and was dying; the father who wondered at the beauty of his son and could claim no influence; the father who felt he had little to offer his son so late in the game. "Look, I know I wasn't there when it counted," he said, his voice somber. "But now that I'm dying, the only way I can help you is by telling you what I know to be true."

In his subsequent talks and writing, he married that passage about John Grady Cole to his own thoughts. For him, it came to represent both his sorrow and his salvation. Although he considered himself a failure as a father, he felt his sons and daughters had learned from him, in spite of him. They had taken some germ of him, and they had become unique to themselves, leaving him only to stand back and wonder at them. After his years away, he had returned in time to see the youngest one, Michael, play in a college basketball game. Watching from the stands, my father saw Michael come charging down the court on a fast break. When Michael took off from the foul line, sailed above the defenders, and let the ball roll off his fingertips into the hoop, the sight left my father awestruck. Where had his son learned this? How had he achieved this kind of perfection?

After all those years away, my father wanted to know his family as deeply as possible, wanted to be reconciled with us, to have us somehow share in his dying.

∞

WHEN I RETURNED for a short visit a few weeks later, I realized for the first time that he was really dying. Suddenly I saw how shockingly thin his legs and arms had become, how his skin now draped his rib cage, how he was covered with scabs and lesions. His eyes were sunk into his head, and he had trouble walking, let alone running, even needing my help to get up the stairs for his afternoon nap. When we paused midway, he sighed: "The man who ran twenty-one Boston Marathons can't even make it up the stairs."

Strangely enough, my giving voice to my anger seemed to have brought us closer than ever. We talked now almost daily on the phone, and my weekend trips home became even more frequent. On those sun-drenched days in that spring of 1993, we sat together in the living room and talked while looking off at the ocean. I would make him a mixture of morphine and water into which he would dip a small sponge at the end of a Popsicle stick. He sucked on the sponge intermittently, then waved it casually in the air as he made this or that point and jumped from topic to topic.

All the while it seemed as though he was giving me something important to do. Something grown-up and something very real. He was offering me the opportunity to be with him in his dying. To feed him, to give him his meds, to sit with him, to read to him, to help him up the stairs to bed. Helping him was a great gift to me—but not one I could have accepted had I been drinking. I would have found a dark, comfortable bar to sit in and while away the bittersweet days of his passing. Losing my father would have been just another reason to drink, another excuse for lapsing into a maudlin stupor. Now that I was clear-eyed and sober, I felt a deep satisfaction in being there, in being this close.

"What is it you want from us?" I asked him one day, leaving unsaid the "now that you're dying" part.

"I can tell you that I don't want sentiment," he said.

He went on to talk about Tolstoy, who wrote about Russian

aristocrats crying at the performance in the opera house while their footmen stood freezing in the blizzard outside. That, my father said, was sentiment. Rather, he wanted us to go through this dying with him. "We should be like runners, running together in a race," he said. "It should be a shared experience." In his view, we were all in different stages of the race, but in time, we would all pass this way. Here was an opportunity for everyone to get a close-up of the death we would all someday experience for ourselves.

"We're all in the same boat," he told me with a little laugh. "You just think that you're not."

IN THE EARLY PART OF 1993, the television station sent me to Yugoslavia to cover local relief efforts for Bosnian refugees. I spent two weeks in Croatia interviewing scores of refugees in camps and in hospitals, their stories all becoming sickeningly familiar. They told me how the Serb soldiers entered their towns and rampaged their homes. How the women were raped and the men were rounded up and taken away, never to be seen again. Others told me how they had seen the men shot, shoved into ditches, and set on fire. Women showed me pictures of their husbands, hoping against hope that they were still alive and perhaps I had seen them. I saw beautiful children in the camps held by women with hard faces etched in pain. They told story after story into the eye of my video camera, and all the stories, all the days, seemed to blend into one another.

When I returned to Pittsburgh, I locked myself in an editing room and viewed twenty hours of tape, seeing their faces again, hearing the stories once more. I worked fourteen hours a day, time coding and fitting them into ten reports, and when they were finished and aired, I sat still. This was the first time I felt the impact of what I had seen and heard, and I was suddenly afraid to feel it. I couldn't reconcile the savagery with my own life. The horror of it crowded me, and it was as if I were holding a retaining wall against some pressing tide.

Then it was as though the retaining wall just split open, and I began to cry. I cried, and then I cried convulsively and could not stop. I no longer wanted to hold a wall between myself and the suffering of those men, women, and children. The more I cried, the more I saw that theirs was not just a pain felt by Bosnians or Cambodians or Somalians or some other faraway people. It was the pain of people no different from me. I saw that we were all as fragile and as brittle as fall leaves in a winter wind.

In my tears, the pain of my life merged with theirs. I cried for my father, and I cried for myself, all of us being carried along by the same inevitable tide of mortality. And as I felt the surging motion of that tide, I felt a sense of connection to everyone who suffered. I was undefended against the truth of mortality, and while that truth was no less horrible, it had suddenly become less fearsome. Life is ephemeral; we are all fragile. And yet somehow, that is as it should be. Our transience is the very source of that "terrible beauty" born of suffering that Yeats wrote of in his poem about the Irish rebels facing their death, and it became terribly beautiful to me, too.

The tears of the refugees, the kindness of the aid workers, their bravery in the face of an unstoppable barbarism—these were intensely beautiful sights that had moved me, and now it seemed had changed me as well. For suddenly in weakness, I felt empowered. In giving up control, I felt this connectedness. In being drawn to this pain, and in finally embracing it, I had found a blessed relief. I had gotten outside the bounds of my own self and free of my own self-involvement. After my tears, I felt washed out, depleted, and clean. For a time, at least, I wouldn't need all of those things I had used to keep pain at bay—alcohol, fame, prestige, money. I was traveling in a new world, and could see that it was possible to let go of those defenses—to open myself up to whatever life brought.

∞

IN EARLY APRIL there was a tribute to my father, a dinner for a few hundred friends to pay homage and say their last goodbyes. The idea seemed odd to some people, and my brother Peter objected strongly. "What is this?" he asked. "A living funeral?"

Initially, my father had the same reservations but soon he softened and granted his permission. Then, despite his professions of indifference, he hovered over the invite list and nagged my brother George about all the details. He began to look forward to it, and took to calling it "the last supper."

As the three hundred guests filed into a local banquet hall on that warm spring night, my father, in an unaccustomed tie with a knot the size of a small fist, greeted each of them at the door. Once each had sat down to dinner, a procession of speakers moved to the small stage, making remarks over the din of clanking plates and silverware. The various stages of my father's life were reviewed by friends, relatives, colleagues, and fellow runners. Throughout the evening, there were also readings of letters of tribute from people who could not be present. George Hirsch, the publisher of Runner's World, read a letter from one runner who described himself as a voice from the back of the pack. "As the 'guru' and 'philosopher king' of running, you have informed and motivated us to follow your teachings. You're an inspiration to us all." When Hirsch got to the signature, to everyone's great surprise it turned out to be "President Bill Clinton."

When my father finally took the stage, his face was red with tears.

Surveying the suddenly silent room with his baleful eyes, he began to speak in a low, hoarse voice.

"You think that once you become old, you become wise," he said. "You think it's automatic that when you get to your sixties and your seventies you'll be wise. But now I wake up in the morning and I feel like such a dolt. I don't know any more of the answers than I knew before."

My father looked down at my mother, then scanned the room, looking for his children I think. And he began to talk about John Grady Cole, the boy who loved horses, riding out in front of his dying father.

"When I look around and see Mary Jane and the family and the twelve children, it seems to me that everyone is a John Grady Cole," he said, "riding out in front of his father. They were born to do what they are doing. I think as parents that is what we have to do. We have to give our children the freedom, and the experience, and the education to come into that country where they were born to be."

He then spoke about a turn-of-the-century preacher named Philip Brooks. It was Brooks who said: "You at your best. That's the real you." It was a phrase that gave my father great meaning and comfort.

"I think that's a wonderful thing to remember, because you look back at all the things you've done, and you feel guilt and shame and everything. But that's not you. You can put that aside, and say, 'That's not me. I did those things. That's not me. It's me at my best. That's the real me.' And then you go out and try to be you at your best.

"And running did that for so many people. You went out and you started to run and it opened up so many areas in your life."

In saying this he stopped and, coming close to tears, shook his head.

"All the bad things I was doing besides the good things. But it all came together finally. I was so lucky to be able to come back to my family."

He began to cry, and he continued to stand up there alone, crying. From the back of the room, my brother John yelled, "You're the best, Dad." And it seemed never truer. He was at his best, and this was the real man. Up on stage, he looked almost vanquished, as he had after so many marathons, but he had done something so much greater than run twenty-six miles. His had been a search for truth, and when it came to him, he did not dodge it. He accepted the judgment, and he embraced it. There was no more time to mourn or to grieve over what he had done wrong. Now on this night, in this time, he truly was the best. The real George Sheehan.

I watched him totter off the stage into the waiting arms of my mother, then disappear into the crowd of people wanting to have their last moment with him. The evening had been a great booming success. Everyone had laughed and cried, and it seemed that most everyone left feeling at least slightly changed for having been there. The next day, as is our family custom, we did the postgame analysis. Who came? Who told what joke? Which speaker was the best? Who was the funniest? My father sat and relived it, too. Then there was a lull in the conversation as people searched their heads for details not remembered.

"The Clinton letter," my father said, breaking the silence. "That was the biggest surprise since *The Crying Game.*"

CHAPTER FIFTEEN

O NE DAY THAT SPRING, on impulse, he wandered into a local Quaker Church and found a scene out of *Friendly Persuasion*. Men and women faced one another in stony silence until, when moved, someone stood up and began speaking. My father sat and listened, allowing his mind to drift after a while.

He began thinking about a dying woman he had read about; she had lived in Minnesota, and she began crying one day when she saw the Canada geese flying overhead. They were flying south, and she knew that she would be dead before they returned north; she would never see the Canada geese again. My father sat for an hour or more, listening to speakers, and he thought about leaving, when suddenly he found himself standing up and speaking. He told everyone there about his cancer and his lifelong struggle with God. When he sat down again, he felt a mix of embarrassment and relief; perhaps a bit of catharsis as well. Whatever he felt, it was enough to bring him back the following week.

Soon, he was a regular, to the great displeasure of my mother. Her devotion to the Catholic Church made his attendance in a Quaker church seem as big an affront as his various affairs and abandonments.

"I won't stand for it," she told me. "I've put up with a lot, but I won't stand for this."

"What's the problem?" I said. "It's worshipful. Respectful. They believe in Christ."

"He already has a religion," she said.

"Which he hasn't practiced in thirty years," I said.

"Well, he's not going to blame that on anyone but himself," she said.

To assuage my mother, my father agreed not to return to the Quaker services. But one day I got a call in Pittsburgh from my sister Sarah.

"Dad's gone," my sister said.

"Oh my God," I said. "Where?"

"He's gone out to the Quaker church," Sarah explained. "He left just after Mom went out the door. When she comes back, she'll go berserk."

It struck me as funny, and I laughed when Sarah asked me what she should do. "Don't do anything," I said. "He's seventy-three years old. He can make his own decisions."

∞

QUIETLY AND ON HIS OWN, my father had begun his final preparations for death, a death no longer in hiding. Try as he might to conceal it from others, the imminence of death was in full view. His legs and wrists had withered pencil thin; his skin was white and translucent; his face, once gaunt, was puffed up with cortisone. At home, he was confined to a chair. Ever the athlete, he had gotten a pedaling machine and placed it at his feet, and intermittently, throughout the day, he would slowly turn the pedals. Often, however, he would fall off to sleep as he pedaled. Early each evening, one of us would help him trudge up the stairs to his bedroom.

Most of all, it was the pain that told him his time was coming. The pain came in waves, and he would grimace when it shot through him like a bolt of electricity. He had suffered the pain of sixty marathons, but this was something altogether different. A self-described chicken, he had a deep aversion to any pain that was not self-inflicted. Even a cut finger could drain his face of color, leaving him alabaster white. He had resolved to minimize the physical discomfort of his cancer, and happily, when the real pain came, he was ready for it—thanks to the offerings of Western medicine, the target of so many of his attacks over the years.

"You should have no pain," his doctor told him. And my father proffered this advice to all cancer patients.

His pain-abatement regimen consisted of morphine, morphine drips, and a variety of local anesthetics; and while occasionally his meds made him groggy, for the most part his mind stayed clear. Still, the pain was always there, lying in wait for him like a purring lion that had been soothed and sated, but only temporarily. It was a constant reminder that the time was near. Which made him wonder what would happen on the other side of death, which in turn made him wonder about God. He believed in God, but it was never clear what God meant to him.

What did he really know of life or of death? What did he know about his place in the universe? He was ready to start at the beginning, open to all suggestions, ready to consider all theories, and looking for insight from the usual multitude of sources.

He came across a story of a woman who seemed to have found the rapture at the moment of her death. Just before her eyes closed forever,

they widened one last time and she spoke the words: "How beautiful."
Now my father professed to be looking forward to that moment. By
way of preparation, he listened to Willie Nelson singing Paul Simon's
"Graceland," over and over again on the stereo, and it became his
theme song for dying. He would hobble around the house, singing
quietly to himself, "I'm going to Graceland, Graceland . . ."

One day while he was sleeping, my mother had a local Irish priest
come to call. My father awoke to the priest's kind blue eyes and soft
brogue, and they began talking. Launching into his usual routine of
quoting philosophers and theologians on all sides of every issue, he
was soon interrupted by Father Brady. "I'm not here to help you with
your theological problems, George," he said. "I'm here to help you
with your relationship with God." They talked the afternoon, and in
the end, my father, long the lapsed Catholic, allowed Brady to hear
his confession and to anoint him in the Sacrament of the Sick. Afterward, my father proclaimed himself a Christian and a Catholic once
again. After decades of struggle, his resistance had crumbled.

When my father told me the story, I was highly skeptical, and I
couldn't help but aim a barb or two in his direction.

"You've accepted Jesus Christ as your personal savior?" I asked, incredulously.

"I have," he said.

"You believe in Heaven and an afterlife?"

"I do," he said firmly.

"I'll bet you're glad about that," I said.

"You bet I am," he said, laughing.

∞

HE WOULD NEED GOD, and he would need faith, as he was now on a
kind of roller-coaster ride with the cancer. Sometimes he appeared

close to the end, confined to bed, pale and drawn. Then, just as everyone would begin preparing themselves for his death, he would get a blood transfusion and suddenly rebound with a fresh surge of energy. After one such surge in June, we had another reunion, the second of our gatherings in the Hamptons. We felt sure this would be the last reunion. But whether reconciled with his God or not, he wasn't finding it easy to let go. As much as anything, these reunions were a way of saying goodbye, taking his leave of all that he had loved. And one day, when he and I went off alone for a drive across the island to the beach at Sagaponack, I saw how strongly life still tugged at him. He had been sitting on the sand, watching me swim in the surf. When I returned, we sat together, talking and staring at the ocean.

"I thought I was ready to go, Andrew," he said, "but now I don't want to leave."

The words hit me in the throat, making it impossible for me to speak. Outside of the cancer, only the sweetness of life remained. There was now a sweetness in everything that came into view: the ocean, the wind, and the sky. And sitting beside him, I couldn't help but see all these things through his eyes. I realized that it's something of which we are only dimly aware most of the time, this preciousness of life. Being with my dying father and feeling it all slipping away, however, I had become acutely conscious of it. And yet the more I tried to savor it, the more it broke my heart. We sat quietly, taking in the inevitability of his passing, as we continued to stare at the breaking waves.

He would survive the summer, and that September we would all be together one last time at the beach house in Rehoboth. There, under the cool September sun, we played it all out again: the runs, the days on the beach, the hard-shell crabs and steamers, and the stories.

This time, though he made the occasional effort to orchestrate the event, he mostly just looked on from the sidelines as we tried to put on our very best show. Then there was that day he decided to go for his last swim. I was taking a postrun dip and was treading water off shore when I saw him walking toward me, flanked by all the others, across the wide strand of beach.

He was nothing more than a reed now, and I was amazed at his fragility as I helped John and Tim escort him into the water, stepping carefully: first, through the white foam, and then into the breaking waves, whose motion he had always loved. After a brief, almost ritual submersion, he signaled that he was ready for dry land again. We walked him out onto the beach into the clicking cameras of my sisters. It was clear that this was a great victory—not just for him but for all of us. We had done our best and come together at the end, having made our peace with the past.

He had only a couple of months more. He passed his last weeks lying in a hospital bed in the middle of the living room at Ocean Grove. On the wall beside him my sister Monica, who attended to him daily, had taped a poster of a painting by Degas of the horses and jockeys at Longchamps. He wanted it there, for he was moved by its beauty as a painting, and also by the image of the horses themselves, which seemed to have new meaning for him after reading the Cormac McCarthy novel.

In the weeks before he died, he would adjust the head end of the bed upward to allow him to half lie, half sit, looking out at the panorama of ocean and shoreline. The stereo beside him played the incessant "Graceland," and he sang along in his flat, toneless manner, seeming quite the eager passenger on that journey. On most days, the entire room was awash in sunlight, filled with the blue of ocean and sky. It was a beautiful place to die.

He tried to make a party of it. Far from catatonic, he seemed more social director than dying patient, receiving visitors and, of course, carrying on simultaneous conversations with one or more of the children who surrounded him each day. The cordless phone was forever cradled between his shoulder and chin, as he spoke with friends across the country and took calls from other cancer patients, telling them all he had learned about potential cures and, if they were willing to hear, of his own spiritual changes. One day, he responded abruptly to the person on the other end.

"What are my plans?" my father repeated incredulously. "My plans are to expire anytime now."

When he got off the phone, he said, "How about that guy?" And he gave a great laugh.

Two weeks after Rehoboth, he wrote me a short note. His condition had worsened suddenly, and he wanted to let me know.

> *Dear Andrew,*
>
> *I wanted to make it until Christmas, but it now appears that this crab has gotten the best of me. Thank you for all of your love and your friendship. If there's anything you need let me know. You know I would do anything for you.*
>
> > *Love,*
> > *Dad.*

As I read the letter again, my eyes welled with tears and turned his words into a watery blur. Getting up to leave the office, I walked out into downtown Pittsburgh and found a bench. There, I sat, watching the passing people and cars, thinking about the world without him.

I flew home that weekend, and found him out of bed and sitting in his wingback chair in the living room. As I approached from behind and he heard my voice, he waved his bony hand aloft and said, "Yippie." His body was vanquished, his chest shrunken, his arms bereft of muscle, but the voice that came from his mouth was still deep and resonant. And then there were his eyes, his terrific eyes, which were what I tended to focus on. Blue-gray and searching like those of a bird: searching the room, searching your face, and glancing ever and again at the ocean.

When we settled in for our talk, for some reason we began talking about birds, and suddenly he said, "Oh, I love to see a hawk." His eyes brightened as if excited by the thought, and his voice carried that excitement. "Sometimes when I'm driving on the parkway, I see them high up and circling, and I say to myself, 'Things aren't so bad. At least we still have hawks.' "

It struck me then that we had always been alike, he and I. For years, while driving the Garden State, I too would crane my neck up close to the windshield to see those hawks, and I'd feel the same surge, the same thrill. I'd wonder how they survived New Jersey and the refinery smog nearby, and then I'd feel the same relief: things must not be so bad after all. We still have hawks.

It struck me as well as I looked at his sharp nose and searching eyes that he had always been a hawk to me. He had been that hawk, "solitary and alone" as Thoreau had written, making everyone else feel lonely. Only now he was a hawk transformed: free of anger, free of pettiness and worry. There were no sharp talons, no rough edges. He was free like the hawk: free of all that would make him seem less than free. Even as his body had deteriorated, it only allowed him to fly higher, to escape the earth below. I felt as if our spirits were entwined, and that in this brief time we were free to fly together.

That was late October, and I went back to Pittsburgh, but within the week I got the call from my mother.

"He keeps asking for you," she said.

"Is he near?" I asked.

"He may be," she said, "but he seems to want to tell you something."

"You have any idea what that might be?" I asked.

"He's worried about you," she said.

This surprised and somewhat shocked me, for I no longer thought of myself as a cause for concern. Then, it felt kind of nice to be worried about. And when the weekend came, I jumped in the car and drove the seven hours. Again, I found him on the chair, but this time unable to talk during flashes of pain. "Here it comes again," he would say, and then grimace in silence for two or three minutes. "Woo," he would say after it subsided. I fed him the mixture of water and morphine, with the little sponge at the end of a stick, and we talked between the crests of pain. I asked him about my mother's phone call.

"Mom says you're worried about me," I said.

"She did?" he said. And then he laughed, saying, "Of course she did."

"What are you worried about?"

"I'm worried that you're not enjoying your life. You seem worried. You seem like you feel out of place."

True enough, but he seemed an odd messenger to deliver those thoughts.

"That sounds like a pretty apt description of yourself most of your life," I said.

"Certainly," he said.

"When did you figure things out?" I asked.

"I think about three weeks ago," he said.

I told him that I had always felt there was something that would keep me separate from the world. It was the Irish in me, or maybe it was the George Sheehan in me, but whatever it was I figured I was likely to be saddled with it for the rest of my life. I was working at it, I told him, but I didn't know if it would ever get any easier. "I'd be happy for any suggestions," I said.

"I don't really have any suggestions," he said. "I just want you to know that it will work out for you, and that I love you."

With that he took a nap.

∞

ONE DAY AT REHOBOTH, we sat together working on his last book, *Going the Distance*. He told me he wanted to end it with his visit from Father Brady, the day he felt he had reached reconciliation with God. I gave him a gentle nudge.

"Is that what this is?" I asked teasingly. "A religious book?"

"What's wrong with that?" he wanted to know.

I paused, surprised by his seriousness.

"Nothing," I said. "Nothing at all."

Why would I argue with that? As I looked at my father, I saw that his had been a search for God all along—the God he hadn't found in church, the God he was looking for in his running and writing. His searching had sent him down all the usual dead ends, until he got completely lost. Then he got his cancer, and the way he saw it, in giving him cancer God had smiled on him.

I believe in God. I don't believe that God micro-manages the world, but He seems to have constructed it in such a way that you just keep running into the same walls until you get the message. Just as I needed alcoholism, divorce, and isolation to make some changes, my father needed to lose his wife and family. He needed to get cancer before he could see any light at all. Cancer had humbled him, and in his newfound humility he saw that he was only a very small part of a very big universe. Rather than disappointing, this knowledge was freeing. In finding his place and in finding his God, he could finally let go.

∞

THE NIGHT BEFORE HE DIED, he lapsed into a comalike state, breathing hard, snoring breaths. The following morning, a cold bright November day just four days short of his seventy-fifth birthday, a group of us sat beside him as his breathing became louder and more labored. His eyes were shut tight, but then he stirred and opened them. For a second, he seemed to see us. Then he closed them, and just in that instant his spirit seemed to leave his body. An instant later, he was still and motionless. As all the others crowded around him, I stepped away.

On the stereo, Willie Nelson was singing about infidelity. It was a John Hyatt song called "The Most Unoriginal Sin." I had heard the song a hundred times in the past few weeks, but now as I listened it occurred to me that the song seemed to be about my father, and about me as well. We were both infidels brought down by our own foibles. Infidels saved, in the end, by the truth.

My mother was out buying groceries when he died, and when she came in the door and saw our faces, she knew immediately what had happened. She rushed up the stairs and pulled his torso into her chest. "I wasn't here, but wasn't that our way," she said. "We were always so busy. We never had any time." Then she held his dead torso against her own. "Thank you, for a wonderful life," she said.

We all thought she would live until ninety. But after his death, she told us she'd be gone in three years. She died less than four years later, of cancer as well. It was not as though she was consumed in grief; she appeared to enjoy her time alone. But she seemed to feel she had completed things, that after she'd restored her marriage and her family, there was nothing pressing for her to do.

What had she seen in him? I asked her, close to her death.

"After all this time, you have to ask?" she said, and changed the topic.

In the last years of his life, my father wore a wedding ring, something he had never done before. "Love," he had told me in a letter, "is an act of will." It sounded cold and reductive at the time, but in time I heard it differently. He was saying that it was useless to seek perfection in someone else. To love someone is to see all the faults and love anyway. In the end, this is the way to accept yourself.

In their odd way of being together, my parents carried a deep knowledge of each other, gleaned over the course of a lifetime. It was a familiarity that sometimes skirted the line of contempt, but it gradually evolved into something much warmer in their last years together. The same qualities they had once found so annoying in each other came to seem comfortably familiar, even endearing. If it wasn't intimacy, it was surely something very close.

One weekend before he died, I brought home the woman who would later become my second wife. It had been a stormy trip, and though she was beautiful, intelligent, and kind, we had trouble. I was crazy about her, but she was also a good deal younger than I, and that was something that frightened me. When I told my father, he scoffed. "Andrew, expand the circle," he said. "Expand the circle." It was his way of saying that I should be more generous, more inclusive, and that perhaps I should take a chance. Eventually, I would. It's funny, but to this day, my love for her has rarely needed to be an act of will.

He would die before we were married, and my mother would be dead before the birth of our first son. I sometimes strain to see my father's face or my mother's face in his face. I rarely do, but when he smiles, his face is the light of the world to me. Recently, I took him to Ocean Grove, and we walked by the old house, which is owned by someone else now. As I looked from the boardwalk, it was as though they were both still in there, writing and cooking and moving through the rooms. It was just that my son and I weren't allowed to enter. I couldn't show them the way he laughs or how he squints and points his crooked little finger at the sea gulls overhead. Now, a second son has arrived, and I wonder what kind of father I am making out of all I have gained and lost.

After my father died, it surprised me how empty I felt. I had expected the sweetness of his dying to stay with me after he was gone. People told me I had to grieve, but I felt I didn't have a right. I thought, He was seventy-four years old, and I am a grown man. What do I expect? After about six months, I let myself feel my sorrow. The walls caved in again, and I sobbed for weeks on end.

Now, years later, it is as though he lives inside me. I couldn't lose him if I wished. I run the trails in Schenley Park, and on hot days I sometimes make a hard push up a final hill that climbs on for half a mile. I hear myself groan, and it is his groan—an elephant's groan— emanating from my chest and filling the air. There is a hawk that lives there in the woods of the park, and often when I'm running, I see him perched on a branch or flying over the treetops. He's a red-tailed hawk, and when I see him, he interrupts my thoughts and I wonder if he's a sign from my father, trying to tell me something. I find myself running faster along the trails, chasing after him as he flies overhead, fixing him in my sights, trying to get a better view. I don't believe—not really—that hawks carry the spirit of the dead or that this particular red-tailed hawk carries a message. I chase the hawk anyway, and I know that my father is with me as I struggle to be the person I am.

ACKNOWLEDGMENTS

I am humbled by appreciation for those who have helped me with this. Though I had always dreamed of writing a book, laziness, drinking, and newspaper work always seemed to get in the way. My kitchen cabinet—Peter Leo, Wil Haygood, and Michael Newman—never let me forget that dream. Neither did John Seidman nor my sister-in-law Margaret Sheehan.

I shall always owe an unpayable debt of gratitude to other friends who have stayed by me all these years. Craig Smith, Nick Haddad, Max Bergholz, Lewis Nordan, and Sue Van Doeren sat with me in dark places while I sought the light. Mary Robb Jackson, Doug Bradley, Lynne Squilla, Bill Steigerwald, Bill Moushey, and Kenny Sims have always been there for me.

Special thanks to Julie Albright, friend, elegant writer, and terrific editor, who shaped the mud of my first draft into something that could reasonably be called a manuscript. To Joe Henderson, my father's great friend and editor, who became my friend and helped me fill in the black holes. And to Peter Quinn, whose initial approval meant everything to me. He never stopped working to get this book into print, and without him, I feel it never would have.

To Mike D'Orso, whose infectious spirit propelled me onward and whose belief in me landed the manuscript on the lap of my agent, David Black. To David, for his unwavering faith in this book and his untiring efforts to get it published. He is the best of agents, a friend and warrior.

My original editor at Delacorte, Tom Spain, had a vision for this book and challenged me not to hide within its pages. Then, with a tender hand and consummate skill, Beth Rashbaum turned a woolly sheep into a sleek greyhound. She is a remarkable editor, who with care, prodding, and good cheer made sure this book realized its potential. Thanks also to Andie Nicolay for all of her help.

I'd also like to thank my boss, Gary Cozen at KDKA-TV in Pittsburgh, for his belief in me, his support of this project, and his appreciation of my need to tell the truth in this book. Thanks to him, I was able to take some time off and get this finished. Thanks also to George Hirsch and Amby Burfoot at *Runner's World* for all of their help and encouragement.

That my family is properly recognized is my chief concern. My father's brothers and sisters, Ann Murphy, Skip Sheehan, and Mike Sheehan, were immensely generous and helpful with their remembrances and have always made me feel part of an unbroken chain constituted of humor and love.

But a special note about my own siblings. The Sheehan family is not a monolithic block. Rather, it is a loose consortium of twelve rabidly individualist members, for whom no one can speak with impunity. So in writing this book, I did not hazard to tell their truth—only my own.

To George, Mary Jane, Tim, Ann, Nora, Sarah, Peter, John, Stephen, Monica, and Michael, thank you for a lifetime of warmth, laughter, and love. I know a lot of that warmth, love, and laughter got short shrift in this book, and to those of you who find parts of my account painful, my deepest apologies. Believe me when I tell you that I know I am profoundly blessed to have been born to our two parents and to have you beside me in this life.

In my thanks, I must single out two of my sisters, Nora and Ann. They are the patron saints of lost brothers and deserve special praise for their close involvement with the book. Their sensitivity, insight, and empathy are unmatched in the western world. Nora's beautiful cover graces the front of this book, and I have never received so perfect or so great a gift.

Finally, words fail to describe the love and gratitude I feel toward my beautiful wife, Abigail, without whom my life itself would not be possible. Her arrival in my world will always be an inexplicable bless-ing, undeserved, unearned, but with me every day. She is my best friend, the center of my universe, and the mother of our two beautiful boys.

Eamon and Emmet, when you are old enough to read these words, know that you have brought joy to my life I had never before imag-ined and that my love for you both is profound. Wherever life takes you, know that your daddy will always be with you.

Pittsburgh, January 21, 2001

AUTHOR'S NOTE

Alcoholics Anonymous is a fellowship of men and women whose only mission is to get and stay sober and to help other people do the same thing. In trying to achieve this end, they do not promote or "sell" AA to anyone. Their "public relations policy is based on attraction not promotion." In identifying myself as a member of AA, I am breaking a tradition of anonymity. I am doing so because I feel it integral to the telling of this story. If breaking anonymity in this fashion offends some people, I apologize. I owe my sobriety and my life to the people in AA, and I want to stress that I am merely a member, and I do not speak for the fellowship.